Praise for *The Career Within You*

"An eminently practical application of the Enneagram's insights, punctuated with many real-life examples. This book is an excellent guide through times of change. It will help you fine-tune your career goals, improve a job-search strategy, and show you how to always play to your strengths."

—Thomas Condon, Enneagram teacher and author of
The Enneagram Movie & Video Guide

"A groundbreaking work. For each Enneagram style you will find thoughtful and clear descriptions, how each style relates to the spectrum of career choices, and a powerful method to determine the path that best fits you. You will discover what career best fits for your style and in the process a more fulfilling life."

—David Daniels, MD, clinical professor of psychiatry and
behavioral science at Stanford Medical School, and author
of *The Essential Enneagram*

"What a tragedy it is to possess such natural gifts and to hide them from ourselves and the world. Wagele and Stabb are great detectives who will help you understand your perfect habitat for all you can bring to the workplace."

—Chip Conley, founder and CEO of Joie de Vivre Hospitality
and author of *Peak: How Great Companies Get Their Mojo
from Maslow*

"Take your time in reading this book. Be brutally honest with yourself. Why? Because it will free you! It will free you to become the person you know you really want to be. The book is of immense help in understanding yourself and your colleagues. It will empower you to take those steps that will result in new and even joyful professional satisfaction."

—Gil Garcetti, former Los Angeles County district
attorney, consulting producer of *The Closer*, author,
and photographer

"This book is full of valuable information on developing one's career. A great strength of the book is its entertaining style—I loved the charts, cartoons, exercises, etc., which add a light touch to the serious material covered in the book."

—Subrata K. Sen, Joseph F. Cullman Professor of
Organization, Management, and Marketing at Yale School
of Management

"Will help you recognize who you are in the working world, and the kind of job you'll thrive at and how to find it."

—Jonathan Feinstein, John G. Searle Professor of Economics
and Management at Yale School of Management

The Career Within You

How to Find the Perfect Job
for Your Personality

Elizabeth Wagele
Ingrid Stabb

HarperOne
An Imprint of HarperCollinsPublishers

HarperOne

THE CAREER WITHIN YOU: *How to Find the Perfect Job for Your Personality*. Copyright © 2010 by Elizabeth Wagele and Ingrid Stabb.

HarperCollins books may be purchased for educational, business, or sales promotional use. For information please write: Special Markets Department, HarperCollins Publishers, 10 East 53rd Street, New York, NY 10022.

HarperCollins Web site: http://www.harpercollins.com

HarperCollins®, 📖®, and HarperOne™ are trademarks of HarperCollins Publishers

FIRST EDITION

Library of Congress Cataloging-in-Publication Data

Wagele, Elizabeth.
    The career within you : how to find the perfect job for your personality / by Elizabeth Wagele, Ingrid Stabb.
        p.   cm.
    ISBN 978–0–06–171861–8
        1. Personality and occupation.   2. Vocational guidance.
    3. Enneagram.   I. Stabb, Ingrid.   II. Title.
    BF698.9.O3W34   2010
    155.2'6—dc22   2009026324

        10   11   12   13   14   RRD(H)   10 9 8 7 6 5 4 3 2 1

This book is dedicated to Ingrid's grandmothers,

Eivor and Jenny, and to Elizabeth's grandchildren, Annika,

Chase, Jalani, Justin, Katya, Lidia, Savannah, and Tyler

Contents

CONTENTS

Introduction

WHERE ARE YOU IN YOUR CAREER TODAY? Perhaps you're just starting out—anticipating the end of your education and brimming with hope for your future. Maybe you're unhappy with your career. You've been on a treadmill for a few decades and contemplating stepping off, but to where? Or you recently lost your job and want to get back on track. But which track? You have important decisions to make, and you want to honor your passions, your financial needs, and your sense of belonging when you make them.

Wherever you are at this point, you have a feeling there is an authentic *career within you*. Watch it unfold as you learn about the nine career types, discover which one fits you, and then match yourself to a career that is right for your particular combination of traits, gifts, and wishes. Then, this book will help you determine how to best fit into today's job marketplace.

The first step is to ask some questions that have fascinating answers. Who are you? What are your greatest strengths? What do *you* need in a career (which may be different from what an employer is looking for from you)? This book will help you answer these questions and teach you how to avoid common career traps and obstacles.

Why do we choose the work we do? Some of us try to follow in our family's footsteps, only to find out later that our temperament is more suited for a different line of work. Or a favorite teacher may encourage us to pursue a talent we have, but deep down we cherish another set of gifts even more. People who care about us mean well when they give us career advice, but because it is based upon their own experiences and standards it can miss the mark. When we are young, getting approval from others—or the opposite, staking out our own separate territory—may be important to us. But as we get older many of us are more interested in choosing a career that truly pleases us than in winning either approval or raised eyebrows. After you read this book you will be able to express your unique strengths, weaknesses, needs, and desires more clearly. Knowing who you are relative to others will put you in a strong position for planning your next career moves or landing a job. Friends and family can then support you with the assistance you request.

Growing up, Cherie received much praise for her intellect. When she graduated from college with a BS in computer science, she was recruited into a rotational program in a reputable software company with a good paycheck. After working there six months, she attended a workshop where she discovered the nine career types. She determined that hers was the Romantic, the person who loves authenticity and self-expression above all. Over the next few days she had trouble concentrating at work. She thought about the part of herself that was artistically creative and longed for a way to express herself in her work. At the end of the week she called her best friend to tell her she was starting to feel depressed. Her role within information technology seemed to lack meaning, and she needed to talk about it. That Friday she couldn't make herself go to work. Instead she made the chocolates that had become her passion to create and that she loved to give to everyone on birthdays and holidays. This cheered her up and brought her back to a sense of feeling alive.

In the career workshop she had learned that Romantics can be fearless in pursuing their hearts' desires. Among their greatest strengths are their aesthetic sense and their imagination. Cherie realized she wasn't expressing herself sufficiently. While she did use creativity as a software developer, she couldn't make use of her excellent aesthetic sense in the way she would have liked. Cherie felt most happy when she was creating new chocolates. On weekends she invented imaginatively shaped candies and new recipes, tried them out on friends, and did research about how to start a small business. Eventually Cherie started selling her chocolates at the local farmers market on weekends. Business boomed from there to specialty grocers. Then she sold her confections online, using her Web development abilities to further her marketing. Since then Cherie has quit her job. Now she is so successful she makes more money making chocolates to express her creativity.

Sound career advice for Cherie might be completely different from appropriate advice for *you*. Cherie is a Romantic, but what are some other choices? What career type are you?

There are many ways to describe your career strengths, weaknesses, and interests. Materials abound that can be applied to aid sound career decision making, including popular typing systems such as the Myers-Briggs Type Indicator™ (MBTI) and the Strengths Finder™. However, the typing system called the Enneagram ("Any-a-gram") is most powerful for understanding yourself because it goes a step further and examines your core values. Other systems stop short by only describing traits and not analyzing the motivation for those traits.

You will readily identify the nine kinds of people as described by the Enneagram in people you know and in yourself. Beyond that, you will learn why you and your co-workers are motivated to do what you do. So,

"At last—a career that fits my style!"

for example, if you value making the world a happier, fun-filled place, you may have a joyous temperament like the Adventurer career type. If reducing risks is your focal point, you will seek answers to all of your safety questions in order to feel sure you're okay. This career type, the Questioner, wants to have fewer unknowns to fear.

You will get to know each of the nine different career types' sets of strengths, needs, and weaknesses. But first, here's a list of what drives them. Which of these is most important for you?

1. **The Perfectionist** is motivated to make improvements.

2. **The Helper** is motivated to meet other people's needs.

3. **The Achiever** is motivated to attain a successful image.

4. **The Romantic** is motivated to express individuality.

5. **The Observer** is motivated to acquire knowledge.

6. **The Questioner** is motivated to reduce risk.

7. **The Adventurer** is motivated to explore possibilities.

8. **The Asserter** is motivated to set clear boundaries.

9. **The Peace Seeker** is motivated to maintain inner calm.

To find the type that describes you, check off the phrases below that you most relate to, or download the free quiz at *www.careerwithinyou.com*.

1. **The Perfectionist**

☐ Doing the right thing is important to me.

☐ I have a strong inner critic that constantly tells me I could have done something better.

☐ I'm usually a stickler about following rules.

☐ I want to be seen as highly ethical.

☐ If someone makes an error, it is important to me that they try to improve next time.

2. **The Helper**

☐ I am more aware of others' needs than my own.

☐ I tend to overwork—giving my time for others, doing errands for people, and offering helpful advice.

☐ I am so perceptive about human interactions that people come to depend on me to solve their interpersonal problems.

☐ I am most proud of the times I have been an asset to someone else's project.

☐ Relationships are of utmost importance to me, and I frequently show people how much I appreciate them.

3. **The Achiever**

☐ I thrive on competition, especially winning.

☐ It is important for me to convey a successful image.

☐ I seek out mentors for myself and make a point to also mentor others.

☐ I don't consider failure an option.

☐ I'd rather be efficient and go for maximum productivity than to go for perfection.

4. **The Romantic**

☐ Expressing myself in a creative way is important to me.

☐ I would rather be special or different than ordinary.

☐ I often feel like I am on the outside looking in.

☐ I am often aware that something in my life is missing.

☐ I like emotional intensity, whether happy or sad.

5. **The Observer**

☐ I like to focus in depth on my interests.

☐ I don't like to be intruded upon when I'm concentrating.

☐ I am constantly on a quest for knowledge.

☐ I don't like it when people are emotionally overbearing.

☐ Privacy and quiet are important to me.

6. **The Questioner**

☐ I often ask questions to try to achieve more certainty in a situation.

☐ I want to know I can trust people in authority.

☐ I often check out the risk level of situations.

☐ I think through worst-case scenarios to prepare myself for whatever may happen.

☐ Loyalty is one of my best assets and something I value immensely in others.

7. The Adventurer

☐ I like to plan exciting possibilities.

☐ I'm good at multitasking and combining diverse skills.

☐ It's important to have fun in whatever I do.

☐ I need variety and constant learning so I don't get bored.

☐ I'm a connector of a large network of people.

8. The Asserter

☐ I am self-reliant and strong.

☐ Others regard me as confident.

☐ People look to me to take charge.

☐ I stand up for truth and justice.

☐ In conflicts I don't back down.

9. The Peace Seeker

☐ I am good at understanding different people's points of view.

☐ I can often reduce conflict in a group.

☐ I like the comfort of routines.

☐ I like to feel connected to others.

☐ People tell me I have a calming effect on them.

A boss who understands that efficiency depends upon having a work team with a wide variety of skills will never hire individuals who are all experts at the same thing.

Once you're aware of your career type, you can use this information to make good decisions in all aspects of your career. You'll get a clearer picture of your *strengths* so you can make career moves that will put them to their best use. You'll get in touch with your *needs* so that you can seek out environments and roles in which you'll feel most happy. And you'll come to better understand your *weaknesses* so you can try to avoid some pitfalls along the way.

Wagele-Stabb Career Finder

At the end of the chapters about each career type you'll find a Wagele-Stabb Career Finder. After you know your career type, this instrument will lead you to suitable careers by asking you to match up your two or three favorite strengths to possible jobs that also call for that combination of strengths. Here's how individuals who used the Career Finder in workshops have already profited from it:

- After studying literature in college, Lindsay wasn't sure what career to pursue. When she used the Career Finder she was excited to find out that her strengths matched well with becoming a book editor. She pursued an editing internship and now plans to enter this field full-time.

- Jesse had dreamed of being an inventor and thought she had a strong aptitude for it but had forgotten this over the years while trying to build her career as a business analyst. The Career Finder reminded her where her strengths lay. She is now researching how to move out of business analysis and create opportunities to become the inventor she would like to be.

- Jack, a former real-estate agent with a hobby of writing fiction, found that his skills were well matched to journalism. Now he's submitting freelance writing to periodicals with much success.

- Sarah's eyes were opened to the fact that she was well equipped to become an advertising agency consultant. As an online marketing director, she found the prospect of more variety and challenge from serving multiple agency clients especially appealing.

- A retired schoolteacher used the Career Finder and realized he would have liked to be a nurse. This inspired him to do volunteer work at the local assisted-care facility.

Just as important as knowing your strengths is understanding your needs. Cherie came to realize over time that to be happy as a Romantic she needed a higher degree of self-expression in her work—creating unique chocolates instead of lines of code. In this book you'll learn more about your needs particular to your career type. Then in chapter 10 you'll complete written exercises to get clear about what you require from a job in terms of salary, work hours, career advancement, and so on, specific to your career type.

Every career type comes with a set of weaknesses to watch out for too—what we call the "other side" of your type. By reading about weaknesses in others who share your type, you can avoid mistakes. Albert, a Perfectionist, had a stellar career as a biological research scientist and academician. He placed a high value on doing everything right and paying attention to detail. If you're the Perfectionist career type, being focused on the quality of your output to the point of overkill can limit your career. Albert's compulsion to have all the answers was so strong that he would often spend ten hours preparing for a one-hour lecture to be sure not to make any mistakes. He wasn't willing to accept that good enough was good enough. The university wanted him to bring grant money into the institution more than it wanted perfect lectures, and Albert often didn't have enough time left over to apply for them. Albert also put out too few publications to please the university, again because of his overdone flawlessness.

In addition to affirming Perfectionists for their strengths, such as attention to detail and high ideals, this book advises Perfectionists to free themselves up a little from their traditional sense of responsibility and their need to please. Albert worked so hard to meet the university's expectations that his natural curiosity suffered. Toward the end of his career he realized what he loved most about working in the lab was actually inventing the gadgets to facilitate the experiments. If he had known himself better, he might have realized he wasn't quite as interested as he had thought in lecturing and in the publish-or-perish routine. Looking back, he would have been even happier setting aside more time for his inventions. People like Albert and others interviewed for this book can be resources for you through their examples.

Once you've identified your career type, including your particular strengths, needs, and weaknesses, you'll put it all together. Chapter 10 helps you create your own personal priority list of what you need most in a job. And chapter 11 guides you through the job-hunting process. You'll learn how to highlight your strengths in your résumé and interviews as well as how to land a job and negotiate good terms for yourself.

Are you ready to learn more about the career within you? Let's get started.

CHAPTER ONE

The Perfectionist

Making Improvements

I F YOU ARE the first career type, you are interested in doing what is right. You are clean, neat, fair, idealistic, physically fit, health conscious, or a combination of these. You like to *make improvements,* to be *conscientious,* and to *work hard.* Perfectionists shine in roles such as auditor, dentist, fighter pilot, and chef, where they must pay attention to *details.* Down-to-earth jobs where they can be *orderly* include being nurses, mechanics, and personal organizers. Particularly *idealistic* Perfectionists may be found as reformers, political columnists, heads of charitable organizations, teachers, and ministers, where they bring *principles*—an interest in *morality* or *belief systems*—to the workplace.

As a Perfectionist, you try to be good. You can forge ahead on a project, do well in school, and are likely to have been teacher's pet. Putting a high premium on education, you will continue to learn through life, picking up traditional cues from your surroundings and polishing your values of fairness, cooperation, and self-sufficiency.

Measuring yourself *often* against others' performances and your past performances can lead to dissatisfaction, but you try to maintain a pleasant demeanor even if you fall short of your ideal. Having good manners is just one of the areas in which you hold yourself to high standards. Speaking correctly is another.

Getting to Know Yourself

As an idealistic Perfectionist, you have a philanthropic nature. Wanting to make a difference in individual lives and in the direction society is going, you are the classic teachers, preachers, or reformers, leading the fight against alcohol abuse, for or against gun control or abortion, or seeking the mandatory use of seat belts. Examine yourself to see if you prefer reforming existing social institutions or teaching individual students how to be the best they can be. Perhaps there's a specific cause you feel passionate about and to which you would like to devote your career.

Getting to know herself, Tina realized she wishes to work in a company that fits her ethics. "In the past I worked in corporate finance, but to be true to myself I'd like to switch to working for an NGO [nongovernmental organization] or socially responsible company."

Perfectionists usually say, "The person I criticize the most is myself." So a good rule (Perfectionists love rules!) is to try to give yourself a break by appreciating the positive things you do. And choose a career that is not overly stressful.

Looking at it a different way, Karen benefited tremendously from understanding the compulsive side of her career type. She had wanted everything to be the best it could be—from little things to the whole world. With a mind-set to be empathic, fair, and good, she didn't realize that in always seeking excellence, she risked becoming a workaholic. She was so sure she stood for everything positive that it was difficult for her to acknowledge that wanting improvements so avidly also had some negative consequences. When she did, though, she experienced a feeling of liberation in knowing that it was okay not to strive so hard all the time.

You may lean toward the style of one of the career types next to yours, called your wings. The Helper (the second one) and the Peace Seeker (the ninth one) may especially influence your work style. Perfectionists with a more developed Helper wing tend to be more interested in working with and caring for people; Perfectionists with a more developed Peace Seeker wing tend to make use of more objectivity in their work.

Strengths Perfectionists Bring to the Workplace

As a Perfectionist, you are highly valued by bosses, co-workers, and clients for your *dependability, ability to organize, attention to detail,* and *ethics.* You are looked up to as the person setting the work standards for everyone else.

CALL MR. SCRUTIN-EYES, the enemy of uncrossed t's and undotted i's everywhere...

FOR ALL YOUR PROOFREADING NEEDS

Ability to Organize

You are one of the most structured people on the team due to your project plans, timelines, schedules, matrices, and notes. Under your leadership, meetings move along in an orderly fashion and key objectives are covered. Your workspace is usually clean. Bosses wish all their employees would show up for work on time, as you probably do.

Some say Perfectionists are the most helpful of all career types because they zero in on weaknesses and teach others how to improve. They often have the skill of imposing structure on a chaotic situation—and cannot rest until they have helped others organize their work and restored order and predictability. It bothers them when co-workers aren't as organized as they are.

Attention to Detail

Because you have an eye for error, you see things other people gloss over. Others might follow the 80–20 rule, skipping over that extra 20 percent of work. They might get the job done, but they do not achieve the elegance of your signature flair or impeccable attention to detail. They might not digest information at the level that you do.

Many skip over the little things because details are not fun to deal with. Perfectionists, however, champion details because, after all, who else will watch out for them? Perfectionists understand that the world doesn't really work without details.

The neatness of Jonah's cupboards draws many comments from visitors. While he says this attention embarrasses him, neatness is a huge asset at work and has resulted in promotions. With an up-to-date filing system like Jonah has, you might find your boss giving you a large bonus to make sure she doesn't lose you.

Conscientiousness

As a Perfectionist, you quickly assume responsibility in a new job and become the go-to person who can answer questions pertaining to the office or your project. You take charge, create predictability, and try to treat everyone according to the same standards. When you get frustrated with someone, you take an objective view, accept your share of the responsibility, and apologize if you have done anything wrong.

While many of us look for the easy way to get things done, Perfectionists put a high value on following through methodically on an assignment. When Philip does a good job, he feels excitement in his body. "As a child, I was never interested in anything easy. I'd only take subjects in school that were difficult for me. Doing what needs to be done is more enjoyable than what others call playing."

Augustus started out as a teller in a bank in a small town in the country. He was friendly, courteous to the customers, and always did more than asked or expected to do. In two years he was promoted to a larger bank in a bigger town. He was quickly made manager with more varied duties to perform, and by taking courses he learned even more about banking. Before he knew it, he was asked to move to San Francisco to be a vice president of the Bank of America. Of course, Augustus was intelligent and paid attention to what was going on, but his conscientiousness more than anything got people's attention during his career. The higher-ups could count on him to do a thorough job, and he was as honest as the day was long.

Famous Perfectionists

Mahatma Gandhi (1869–1948), a political and spiritual leader, was an attorney who later organized boycotts and took part in non-violent civil disobedience to advance the status of India's untouchables, to free India from the British, and to grow native industries. He was relentless in striving to do the right thing, whether leading nonviolent demonstrations or sewing his own cotton clothes. He gave up all possessions and lived a spiritual life of fasting, meditation, and prayer.

Hillary Rodham Clinton (born 1947) has a long history of reform, including taking on cases of child abuse, providing free advice for the poor, and helping to upgrade testing standards of new teachers. As First Lady, Clinton led the Task Force on National Health Care Reform and helped increase research funding for prostate cancer and childhood asthma. As a senator from New York, she argued against practices that abused women around the world. She ran to be the first woman nominated as presidential candidate by a major political party and became secretary of state under President Barack Obama.

Mary Baker Eddy (1821–1910) was a controversial religious leader, author, and lecturer who believed she was on a mission from God. She suffered from many illnesses and founded the Christian Science Church. She thought you could heal the body through a strong enough belief in God—and there would be no need for doctors. The power of striving could overcome physical limitations.

More examples of famous Perfectionists: Johann Sebastian Bach, Charles Dickens, Ralph Nader, Colin Powell, and Margaret Thatcher.

(Please note: Figuring out the career type of famous people is guesswork. Some project public personas that are different from how they behave in private life.)

Courteousness

Most Perfectionists are well mannered, tend to have refined speech, and are a model for treating people with decorum. They go out of their way to make people's jobs easier—even if it's not in their job function. Ministers who are Perfectionists combine the love of principles with offering help and comfort to others and improving their knowledge. They enjoy the position of leadership and keeping their church well organized with all of the parts running smoothly.

A family of Perfectionists

Strong Ideals

Many of you have straight posture, which symbolizes your uprightness within. You take life seriously and hold yourself, the organization, and society to high ideals. Corruption is your enemy; you would never pretend to be working when you're not—as some others do. You inspire others to make ethical choices in their work and personal lives, encouraging them to be truthful, to recycle, or to volunteer for a charity.

Hari brings equality and fairness to the college where he teaches, which he chose for its diversity of students. Being fair to him means trusting his own judgment to make the right decisions about his students' work. When he grades their papers, he always tries to make the right call and not show arrogance or self-righteousness, keeping in mind that the students are much less experienced in the subject than he is. "Teaching is a higher calling," he says. "I can't understand it when people talk about 'poor teachers.' Having the relationships I have with my students—enriching their lives with great literature—is worth much more than a high salary would be."

Being a judge or a prosecuting attorney is a good way for Perfectionists to protect and improve society. Another area of law might pay higher salaries, but for Perfectionists it may be more important to go to work every day believing they are making a difference.

What a Perfectionist Needs on the Job

One wants to improve the Universe.

—John Hope Franklin, historian and civil rights activist

Here are key things Perfectionists report they require to feel satisfied in their day-to-day work.

Fairness

If an organization is continually compromising fairness, a Perfectionist won't be happy working there long term. Despite her successes in marketing, Alice was unhappy with two prestigious companies she worked for. One company had a high-stakes political environment, rewarding the more Machiavellian managers and ignoring some of the managers who were doing the best work. The other firm continually hired new managers from the outside rather than promoting loyal, high-performing employees from within. These practices were in conflict with Alice's values.

Sean was unhappy about being underpaid. Even though he was a prized employee who, according to his boss, would have received a large raise if he had asked for it, Sean left the company because it didn't do the right thing and offer him a raise. The situation could have been resolved quickly, but Sean quit instead as a way to protest a policy that he felt treated the employees unfairly.

Respect

Perfectionists often compete to earn the respect of teachers and peers. Even if they abhor a subject, they may work incredibly hard to prove they can keep up with the smart kids in school. Sometimes they persevere to what might seem an almost punishing degree.

Jake manages the information security program for a credit card processing company; his security team doesn't get the respect it deserves. Though his department maintains 99.99 percent reliability, co-workers notice his department only on the rare occasion when something breaks. On the other hand, the salespeople at his company are treated like heroes when they blow their sales quotas out of the water. "Now that I've been promoted to the director of security, I'm developing metrics to better showcase the excellent work *we* do. I am determined to build up the esprit de corps of my team and respect from the rest of our company."

To Get Things Right

The ideal work situation for a Perfectionist is to be surrounded by a team of other Perfectionists, where each can count on the others to strive for the same high standards.

Perfectionists can be such sticklers that they take forever to get something done, like composing a paper in school. They may agonize over every word, telling themselves, "Leave no room for error." Later, in a work situa-

tion, they may have to change this attitude or they won't earn their salary! Being Perfectionists, they'll somehow manage to accomplish this change too, and let themselves be content stopping at *good enough is good enough*.

The man talking to the chicken, above, represents the critical voice in the Perfectionist's own mind, which almost never stops: "Did you do it right? Did you make any mistakes? Couldn't you have tried harder?" And now this . . .

To Release Stress: "Trapdoor" Phenomenon

Though there are many ways Perfectionists relieve stress, the extent to which they enjoy *going away on vacation* is particularly notable. Being away from the tasks that are always staring them in the face enables them to relax, shed their stress, and forget about all the voices in their heads telling them to do this or that. Some get away from themselves by incorporating a "trapdoor" into their daily lives—relieving tension by doing something on a regular basis that doesn't fit their usual self-image.

A 1
MASSAGES

Given only after a thorough shower with lots of soap.

Showers and towels graciously provided.

Perfectionists need to relieve stress.

There have been movies based on this phenomenon, where a conventional or upstanding member of the community by day goes to the dark or seamy side of life by night. One example of this is *Crimes of Passion* (1984), a Ken Russell movie starring Anthony Perkins as an itinerant preacher and Kathleen Turner as a woman who alternates between being a proper fashion designer and a sleazy hooker.

Working Hard and Making Sure Others Do Too

Jake appreciates people who admit their mistakes and live up to their commitments. "The person at work who has no credibility in my eyes," he says, "is someone who keeps creating problems but will never admit his own fault. When four hundred things break, he always blames it on the last guy who left the company, saying, 'But that guy is gone, so it's all better now.' It's so much better when someone gives us a list of the things that need fixing and helps us drill down to the source of what happened. I'd rather know what actually caused the outage. How do we fix it? How do we make sure it doesn't happen again?"

Samantha agrees: "It bothers me when someone we depend on has a poor work ethic—just being selfish or lazy—especially when the others pulling the weight on the team are good, honest, and hardworking."

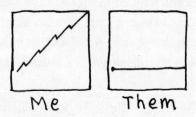

Me   Them

"It's *death* when the people you're working with are not improving."

The Other Side of Being a Perfectionist

Trying hard is exhausting. You feel you deserve credit for working so hard to sort through what you think is possible and choosing the thing you think will do the most good. Here are some areas Perfectionists typically struggle with. As you manage your own career, keep these themes in mind:

IT CAN BE HARD:

✓ to be self-critical.

✓ to have such a crowded schedule.

✓ to have such high standards I can't meet them.

✓ to be seen as judgmental.

I WORK ON:

✓ scheduling in time for restful and recreational activities.

✓ realizing the world won't end if I make a mistake here and there.

✓ acknowledging there are many ways to do things besides my way.

Being Critical of Others

Perfectionists often look for what's wrong instead of stopping long enough to enjoy what's right. Birgitta, the dog show judge, says she used to think she could eliminate her emotions from decisions better than most judges do. She was so objective that she believed she would be the best. The trouble was, she admits, that instead of limiting her decisions to dog owners' actions, she also judged their *lives,* a habit formed from years of criticizing herself. She eventually tried to not make everyone else's business *her* business.

Similarly, Anders kept a running list of what was wrong within himself when he started his career and extended it to include his workmates: "I would keep track of when people came to work, when they said something that was only half true, and when they did something that was half baked. But these days I try not to do this; I don't think my co-workers would take so kindly to my judging them."

Guilt

The Perfectionist category is a fertile breeding ground for guilt. Try as they might, Perfectionists never live up to their own expectations: "It may sound strange coming from someone who is such a goody-goody, but I tend to feel like a criminal half the time. Teaching is second only to motherhood as a place where guilt can easily develop. You try your hardest, but in the end the students have to learn the material themselves. You can't force them to have enthusiasm or to absorb all the wonderful knowledge you're exposing them to."

Being Overly Self-Critical

Jason is a retired head librarian in the New York City library system. Over fifty years ago in college a friend corrected him for pronouncing the Irish poet and playwright William Butler Yeats's name "Yeets" instead of "Yates." He still feels humiliated when he recalls the incident. Some Perfectionists are so critical of others' pronunciation and grammar that they assume others are always looking for flaws in theirs also.

It's great for her employer: Ei-Ling feels as though she has taken an oath to not be overly emotional or to do anything inappropriate. "What a taskmaster I am!" she says. "If only I were half as hard on myself as I am. My mantra as a recovering perfection-ist is 'I don't have to be perfect.'"

Being Overly Nice

Most Perfectionists have a "good girl" or "good boy" image of them-selves. Karen was always going to spend more time helping her aging mother and be a better friend and an ideal employee. On the job she had to learn to enforce boundaries or she'd be doing the work of three employees instead of one. Finally she realized that she was being unfair to the other employees by showing them up and giving the employer unrealistic ideas of what an employee should be expected to do.

Tina is working hard on trying to be less "pathologically polite." She's trying to put balance back into her life by not staying late at work and by saying no to extra projects.

Self-Sabotage

Ironically, Perfectionists are sometimes unable to delegate work, which keeps them from advancing and gives co-workers the message they aren't

The Ultimate Self-Sabotage

World-renowned chef Bernard Loiseau (the inspiration for Gustave in the movie *Ratatouille*) was celebrated for his traditional French cuisine at La Côte d'Or restaurant. In the late 1990s, however, a new form of Asian-inspired fusion cuisine swept France, pleasing trend-driven foodies. When Loiseau committed suicide in 2003, shooting himself in the mouth with his hunting rifle, the media attributed his depression to the success of the newer trends and the fact that the *Gault Millau* guide had recently downgraded his restaurant. There were also rumors that Michelin was planning to remove one of La Côte d'Or's three stars. This was not true, however. Loiseau's restaurant remained a three-star restaurant, and he had committed suicide—*the ultimate self-sabotage*—needlessly.

trusted—which is true. When the Perfectionists do get ahead, they may become micromanagers, which employees also don't like.

Resentment

Perfectionists usually fight feeling strong emotions because they fear they could lose control. One emotion they readily admit, however, is resentment for not receiving recognition for a job well done or resentment toward those who haven't put out enough effort.

The only time Jake's credit card company rewarded him properly was under dire circumstances—when it was trying to purchase another company while an audit was going on. The company was so cautious that the project dragged on eight or nine months when it should have taken two or three weeks. "They had me working fifteen-hour days for months. Once it was all over, they finally recognized me and made me Employee of the Quarter. I would never want any part of that frustrating experience again!"

Worrying

When Anders tries to cut down on worrying, he reminds himself that there is a class of things you can't control, one of which is the past. This should free him up for all those healthful nature hikes he's wanted to take. Deana has learned how to stop worrying out loud, though it has taken her almost a lifetime and she has occasional relapses. She has made some progress by confining most of her worrying to nighttime. At least it's not twenty-four hours a day, as it once was.

CHANGING JOBS

"I'm a wreck! I'm not worried about making money or being a success. I'm worried about doing it RIGHT!"

At the End of the Workweek . . .

If you are a Perfectionist who is good at following through on details, you will be sought after by those who know how efficient and responsible you are. Be careful in your career, however, if you don't want to get stuck performing details at lower levels. Hold back a bit on the details, and show them the other strengths you have that will enable you to advance.

MY LIST FOR SATURDAY
1. wake up
2. make bed
3. vacuum
4. breakfast
5. brush teeth
6. Safeway- bargain on
   paper products. Receipt.
7. Bargains Galore for toiletries-
   save receipts. File.
8. Farmers market- organic.
9. Gas station
10. Lunch
11. brush teeth
12. nap for health 5 min.
13. run for health 5 min.
14. vitamin store + diet book-
   receipt
15. buy self- help book
16. read self- help book 5 min.
17. practice violin
18. dinner
19. recycle
20. brush teeth + floss
21. go over list
22. bed

The Wagele-Stabb Career Finder for Perfectionists

Here are a few of the many possible avenues for you to apply your talents in making improvements. Determining the results involves three easy steps: evaluating your strengths, selecting your dream careers from a table, and considering some practical concerns. The results are worth it! Follow the instructions below to identify your top strengths. You will then be asked to match them to career paths and to observe yourself, watching for which of them spark your greatest enthusiasm.

Try it once and see how easy it is. This test is engineered to coax your career preferences from the truest part of yourself. If you are uncertain about an answer, we suggest you stay with your first choice. Don't worry if you experience a little confusion; a certain amount frees you up to be all the more uninhibited in your choice. The key in steps 1 and 2 is *speed*.

Instructions for Using Career Tables

Step 1: My Strengths

First, read these five definitions. Rate them as they pertain to you and order your preferences in the box at the end.

Note: Any career type is capable of doing any job. The list of suggestions in the career table is not exhaustive, so we invite you to further investigate careers according to how well they use these five strengths.

Courteousness

To what degree do you strive to remain dignified and gracious when relating to others, including as a good team player, as a good listener, and when communicating?

LO 1 2 3 4 5 HI

Logical Thinking

How skilled are you in determining facts in a methodical fashion?   LO 1 2 3 4 5 HI

Making Improvements

To what degree do you raise the standards of your individual work, move the group project ahead, and/or make the world a better place?   LO 1 2 3 4 5 HI

Meticulousness

Rate your ability to do precise, thorough, detail-oriented work.

LO 1 2 3 4 5 HI

Responsibility

How much accountability are you willing to accept?   LO 1 2 3 4 5 HI

Now rank your strengths in importance from A to E, with A being your strongest trait, and write them in below, as in the example.

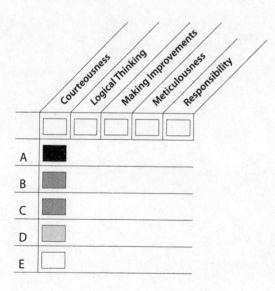

EXAMPLE

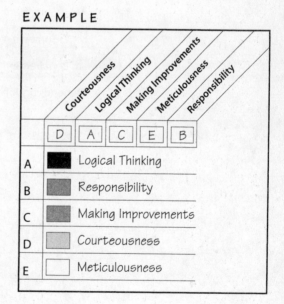

Step 2: My Favorite Career

Check the Career Tables below, starting with the ones that have the darkest-colored boxes (highest ratings) under your main strength. If you feel a special spark of excitement when you see one of the careers, write that one down. List up to four careers that most interest you:

Career _____

Career _____

Career _____

Career _____

Key: This chart shows the level at which each of the five strengths is used in each field (from the point of view of others who have held these jobs):

Exceptional	■
Significant	■
Somewhat	■
Minimum Requirement	☐
Depends on Job	⊞

Business

	Courteousness	Logical Thinking	Making Improvements	Meticulousness	Responsibility
Accountant (independent CPA with private customers)	░	■	□	■	■
Accounting staff (corporate accounting, budget analyst, etc.) # ®	□	■	□	■	■
Actuary ↑	□	■	▨	■	■
Administrative assistant (entry level) # ®	▨	▨	□	■	▨
Administrative executive secretary # ®	▨	▨	▨	■	▨
Advertising specialist	▨	░	▨	□	░
Auditor (e.g., CPA in large accounting firm conducting audits of other companies) #	□	▨	▨	■	■
Bookkeeper #	░	░	□	■	▨
Brand manager	□	▨	▨	░	■
Business analyst (e.g., software implementation) $ # ®	□	▨	░	▨	▨
Buyer (wholesale, retail)	□	▨	▨	░	■
CEO	■	■	■	⦂⦂	■
Compliance officer (e.g., brokerage, health care) $	▨	░	░	■	▨
Customer support rep # ®	■	░	░	□	▨
Entrepreneur	░	■	■	⦂⦂	■
Finance & accounting executive $ ®	▨	■	▨	■	■
Finance staff (corporate) # ®	□	▨	▨	■	░
Financial advisor ↑	▨	▨	▨	■	■
Financial analyst (equity research) ↑	■	■	░	■	▨
Human resources manager	■	■	░	▨	▨
Investment banker/venture capitalist $	□	■	■	▨	■

Business (continued)

	Courteousness	Logical Thinking	Making Improvements	Meticulousness	Responsibility
Management analyst ↑ $ # ®	light	black	light	medium	medium
Management consultant $	black	black	black	light	medium
Marketing manager $	light	medium	medium	light	medium
Product manager $ ®	light	medium	medium	light	black
Project manager $ ®	light	light	light	light	medium
Retail banker (teller, representative, etc.) #	black	light	light	black	medium
Sales executive $ ®	black	light	light	white	black
Sales representative/business development manager # ®	black	light	light	white	medium
Small business owner	medium	dotted	light	dotted	black
Tax preparer	light	light	light	black	black

Construction & Manufacturing

	Courteousness	Logical Thinking	Making Improvements	Meticulousness	Responsibility
Carpenter (finish woodworker)	white	light	medium	black	light
Carpenter (general construction) #	white	dotted	light	medium	light
Elevator installer and repairer	white	light	light	medium	black
First-line supervisor of operations #	light	light	light	black	medium
General contractor	medium	medium	medium	light	black
Plant manager	light	medium	medium	light	black

Education

	Courteousness	Logical Thinking	Making Improvements	Meticulousness	Responsibility
Educational researcher	light	black	black	medium	medium
English-as-a-second-language teacher	black	light	black	light	light
Principal	black	medium	black	light	black

Education (continued)

	Courteousness	Logical Thinking	Making Improvements	Meticulousness	Responsibility
Professor	medium	dark	dark	dotted	medium
Speech language pathologist ®	dark	medium	dark	medium	medium
Teacher (K–12 #) ®; (postsecondary) ↑	dark	dotted	dark	dotted	medium

Government & Nonprofit

	Courteousness	Logical Thinking	Making Improvements	Meticulousness	Responsibility
Administrative services manager	medium	medium	medium	medium	medium
Building inspector ↑	light	medium	medium	medium	medium
City planner	medium	medium	dark	medium	medium
Civil service office worker	light	light	medium	medium	medium
Consumer rights advocate	white	medium	dark	white	medium
Corporate responsibility consultant	medium	medium	dark	white	medium
Court reporter ↑	medium	medium	white	dark	medium
Environmental watch ecologist	white	dark	dark	white	medium
Executive director (nonprofit)	medium	medium	dark	white	dark
Forensic science technician ↑	white	medium	medium	dark	dark
Government contracts administrator ®	white	medium	medium	medium	medium
Politician (city council member, governor, mayor, representative, senator)	dark	dark	dark	medium	dark
Program manager (nonprofit and govt.)	medium	medium	dark	medium	dark
Social justice worker (at a nonprofit)	medium	medium	dark	white	medium
Treasurer or comptroller $	medium	dark	medium	dark	dark
Treasury or office of the comptroller staff	medium	medium	medium	dark	dark

Health Care

	Courteousness	Logical Thinking	Making Improvements	Meticulousness	Responsibility
Clinical laboratory technician	▒	▒	□	■	■
Counselor/social worker ↑ # ®	■	▒	■	□	■
Dental hygienist ↑ ®	■	□	■	■	░
Dentist $	■	▓	■	■	■
Doctor (especially anesthesia, cardiology, emergency, endocrinology, hematology, medical faculty, plastic surgery, public health, radiology, surgery) $	■	■	▒	■	■
Nurse ↑ # ®	■	■	■	■	■
Pharmacist $ ®	▒	■	▒	■	■
Pharmacy technician ↑	■	▒	□	■	░
Physical therapist ↑ ®	■	▒	▒	▒	░
Psychiatrist/psychologist ↑ $	■	■	■	□	■
U.S. Public Health Service officer	▒	▒	■	□	▒

Information Technology

	Courteousness	Logical Thinking	Making Improvements	Meticulousness	Responsibility
Computer systems analyst ↑ $ ®	▒	■	▒	▒	▒
Database administrator ↑ $ ®	□	▒	▒	▒	■
Desktop support/help desk rep	■	▒	▒	▒	░
Information systems manager ↑ $	▒	▒	▒	▒	■
Information technology support engineer	▒	▒	▒	▒	▒
Network/systems administrator ↑ $ ®	░	▒	▒	■	░
Software developer ↑ $ ®	▒	▒	▒	■	░

Information Technology (continued)

	Courteousness	Logical Thinking	Making Improvements	Meticulousness	Responsibility
Technology executive $ ®	medium	light	light	black	black
Testing/quality assurance specialist ®	white	medium	light	black	black

Literature, Arts & Entertainment

	Courteousness	Logical Thinking	Making Improvements	Meticulousness	Responsibility
Actor	white	light	black	dark	light
Artist (painter, photographer, sculptor, etc.)	white	light	black	medium	light
Commercial artist (graphic designer, product designer, etc.)	white	light	medium	black	medium
Copywriter (ads, brochures, Web sites)	medium	medium	medium	medium	medium
Critic (books, movies, music)	white	black	medium	medium	medium
Editor (copy, books, newspaper)	light	black	black	medium	medium
Journalist (advice columns, such as Miss Manners, Ann Landers, Dear Abby)	black	medium	medium	medium	medium
Journalist (hard news)	black	black	medium	black	medium
Journalist (human interest)	black	medium	medium	medium	medium
Managing editor $	medium	medium	medium	black	black
Media production specialist	medium	medium	black	black	medium
Musician (composer, conductor, vocalist, instrumentalist)	white	medium	black	black	dotted
Photographer (professional: ads, events, photojournalism, portraits, weddings)	light	medium	light	black	light
Recording, light, or sound engineering technician	white	medium	black	black	medium
Technical writer ↑	white	black	medium	black	white
Writer (lyrics, nonfiction, novels, poems, scripts)	white	dotted	black	dotted	light

Math, Engineering & Science in Industry

	Courteousness	Logical Thinking	Making Improvements	Meticulousness	Responsibility
Mathematician	□	█	░	█	▒
Engineer					
Aerospace engineer $	░	█	▒	█	░
Biomedical engineer ↑ $	░	█	▒	█	░
Civil engineer ↑	░	█	█	█	░
Computer hardware engineer $	░	▓	▒	█	░
Electrical engineer $ ®	▒	█	░	█	░
Environmental engineer ↑ ®	░	█	▒	█	░
Industrial engineer ↑	░	█	█	█	░
Mechanical engineer ®	░	█	▒	█	░
Nuclear engineer $	░	█	▒	█	▒
Petroleum engineer $	░	█	▒	█	░
Product safety engineer	░	█	▒	█	█
Scientist					
Biologist	▒	█	▒	█	▒
Chemist	░	█	▒	█	▒
Ecologist	░	█	█	█	░
Environmental scientist ↑ ®	▒	█	▒	█	░
Epidemiologist (public health)	░	█	▒	█	█
Manager of research dept. (e.g., mentor young scientists and do PR for funding) $	█	█	▒	█	█
Materials scientist & engineer (e.g., nanotechnology)	▒	█	▒	█	█

Math, Engineering & Science in Industry (continued)

	Courteousness	Logical Thinking	Making Improvements	Meticulousness	Responsibility
Physicist $	□	■	▨	■	░
Social scientist	⋮⋮	■	▨	▨	■

Service Industry

	Courteousness	Logical Thinking	Making Improvements	Meticulousness	Responsibility
Butler	■	□	▨	▨	▨
Chef	□	▨	▨	▨	▨
Child-care worker or nanny #	■	░	▨	▨	■
Personal organizer	■	░	■	▨	▨
Restaurant, banquet, or bakery staff #	■	□	▨	▨	▨
Skin care specialist ↑	■	□	▨	░	□
Store or restaurant manager #	■	▨	▨	▨	■
Trainer (athletic, fitness, personal) ↑	■	░	■	▨	▨

Spiritual Field

	Courteousness	Logical Thinking	Making Improvements	Meticulousness	Responsibility
Funeral home director	■	░	▨	░	▨
Meditation or yoga teacher	▨	░	□	□	▨
Monk, nun, yogi	▨	□	⋮⋮	□	⋮⋮
Religious leader (chaplain, imam, pastor, priest, rabbi, etc.) ®	■	▨	■	□	▨

Uniformed Professions

	Courteousness	Logical Thinking	Making Improvements	Meticulousness	Responsibility
Administrative noncommissioned officer (e.g., secret publications custodian)	□	▨	□	▨	■
Astronaut	▨	■	░	■	▨
Commanding officer (especially marines)	□	▨	░	□	■

Uniformed Professions (continued)

	Courteousness	Logical Thinking	Making Improvements	Meticulousness	Responsibility
Embassy protocol officer	medium	white	white	white	light
Flight attendant	black	white	white	medium	medium
Inspector general staff	medium	medium	black	white	light
Naval submarine officer	light	black	medium	black	black
Nuclear reactor operator	white	light	light	black	medium
Pilot (airline, co-pilot, flight engineer) $	dotted	black	white	black	black
Pilot (highway patrol) ↑	white	medium	white	black	black
Police officer	medium	medium	black	black	medium
Precision welder (armed services)	white	white	medium	black	medium
Service support clerk (e.g., disbursing clerk)	light	white	white	black	medium
Transportation inspector	medium	medium	light	black	black

Other Fields

	Courteousness	Logical Thinking	Making Improvements	Meticulousness	Responsibility
Air traffic controller $	white	black	medium	black	black
Athlete	light	dotted	black	black	dotted
Athletic coach	medium	medium	black	black	black
Coach (career, executive, life)	black	medium	black	white	light
Environmental science & protection technician ↑ ®	light	medium	black	medium	black
Inventor	white	dotted	black	dotted	dotted
Judge $	white	black	medium	black	black
Lawyer (especially prosecutor) $	medium	black	black	black	black
Librarian	medium	medium	medium	medium	black
Maintenance & repair worker # ®	light	white	black	black	medium

Other Fields (continued)	Courteousness	Logical Thinking	Making Improvements	Meticulousness	Responsibility
Mechanic (airplane, car, motorboat, ocean liner)	▧	▦	■	■	■
Paralegal ↑	☐	▦	☐	■	▦
Stay-at-home parent	■	▦	▦	▧	■
Surveyor ↑	☐	■	▧	■	▦

Step 3: Practical Considerations

After you've gone through the tables, note whether your favorite career fields match your needs for pay and security by checking for the following symbols in the Career Tables:

↑ = **Predicted Future Growth Area for Jobs**

$ = **High Pay**

= **Large Number of Present Openings**

® = **Recession-proof**

For more career ideas for the Perfectionist,
see the recommended lists for the Helper
and the Peace Seeker.

CHAPTER TWO

The Helper

Meeting Needs

I F YOU ARE the second career type, you understand *feelings*, know how to *please*, and like to *assist* your boss and others. You take *pride* in being needed and in being instrumental to the success of the group. *Relationships* are of utmost importance to you. Since many careers for Helpers require *assessing needs* of others, popular roles are as psychologists, caregivers, teachers, human resource directors, receptionists, medical practitioners, and chiefs of staff. Helpers can be found in just about any profession, including law, finance, accounting, science, journalism, and the arts, especially in roles that require interacting with *people.* However, some successful Helpers spend long hours alone, such as Danielle Steel, who writes bestselling novels about love relationships.

Personal *warmth* and going *above and beyond* what is required stand out about both male and female Helpers. While most are extraverted and have strong people skills, introverted Helpers feel more comfortable contributing behind the scenes.

My True Love Makes the World Go Round

Getting to Know Yourself

If you are a Helper, you are good at reading people—to the extent of knowing what others need before they do. This skill helps you get where you want to go, whether by being kind, altruistic, dignified, cordially welcoming, affectionate, or seductive.

You may lean toward the style of one of the types next to yours (called your wings). If you are a Helper who is more influenced by the Perfectionist career type, you may be more objective than some Helpers. If the Achiever wing influences you, you may be quite image conscious and unusually ambitious for a Helper career type.

Strengths Helpers Bring to the Workplace

The careers of Helpers are characterized by a *personal touch* and *genuine feeling.* Compare your own strengths to the typical strengths of this career type.

Helpers excel at personal warmth.

Caring

In the workplace you are known as someone who "gets it," not just intellectually but on an emotional level. You listen carefully and then respond cordially. For example, psychotherapist Peter cares for his clients—many of whom have suffered traumas—by creating a safe place to talk. Giving, to him, means acknowledging his clients' experiences and showing them they are valid and important. He gives them unconditional positive regard, which they ultimately learn to provide for themselves.

Whenever her co-worker is having a bad day, the attendance officer at the junior high school leaves little

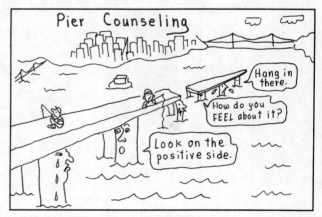

notes on her desk, such as, "You're doing a good job," "Tomorrow will be a better day," or "Hang in there!" She loves to see the surprise and pleasure on her co-worker's face when she returns from lunch.

Creating a Feel-Good Atmosphere

You pay attention to the physical and emotional ambience of the work-place. And even after work, at happy hour, you make sure everyone feels included. Every summer you might invite the entire department to a bar-becue at your home. You may even install a pool and hot tub for your visi-tors so they'll feel special—as though they are visiting a spa.

Vicki places a fresh flower arrangement—usually orchids—at every styl-ist's station in her hair salon. She greets her clients cheerfully dressed and with her hair in zippy new styles. Her pleasant voice invites conversation: "I love stories, and everyone has a tale to tell." With this welcoming attitude, she is drawing people toward her and fulfilling her strong desire to make the world a better place for the people she comes in contact with.

Some devote themselves to helping on a corporate level, for example, by forming a consulting practice for work environments that promote

employee well-being. Darlene has business analysis skills, which helps her show clients how to improve their company's bottom line in terms of lower health insurance rates and higher productivity. She also helps employers by providing stress-relief programs like massages, a running club, and a public speaking club and by encouraging flexibility to work from home.

Creativity Centered on Relationships

Connecting to the stream of life through relationships brings out the compassionate artist in you: singing to your child, learning a craft, life drawing, or depicting the meaning of a special occasion for someone by writing poetry. Perhaps you become an actor or a violinist. Great song-writers inspired by their lovers may be Helpers as well.

Dori is an artist and an art therapist. The strength of her artwork lies in its independence and individuality. It's not "fash-ionable" but flows naturally out of her soul. Her paintings are exciting! "I have a strong need to be creative—not in order to be admired, but rather to get into a state of complete self-motivation," she says. "This is what authentic creativity means to me." Dori is so relationship oriented she almost always shows a human or animal in her paintings, even now that she has begun to break away from realism.

Going the Extra Mile

You give your time and energy to others, anticipating extra touches needed for a job well done. Tom, a school principal, does more than is asked of him: replacing boilers, buying colored paper with his own money, cleaning up the garden, talking with a teacher who needs help with a child, and sitting in on eighty parent-teacher conferences a year. Because his school lies in a dangerous area of the city, teachers supervise recesses and class breaks, so he makes sure to do that too. Helpers can be heroes when animals or fellow humans are in danger. You can find them on ski patrols, in the civil air patrol looking for the lost pilot, and in the coast guard looking for lost crafts.

Helpers are less interested in being the star than in being seen as helpful. In graduate school, even when he had demanding lab experiment deadlines, Cody would always stop his work to help another student with printing his photographs. As finance director for the Gap, Laura sometimes works as many as eighty hours per week. Nonetheless, she was able

Famous Helpers

Desmond Tutu (born 1931) is a cleric and human rights activist who rose to worldwide fame as an opponent of apartheid and was awarded the Nobel Peace Prize. Tutu was once a teacher and the first black Anglican archbishop of Cape Town, South Africa. He chaired the Truth and Reconciliation Commission and uses his high profile to campaign for the oppressed. Tutu also campaigns to fight AIDS, homophobia, poverty, and racism.

Pamela Churchill Harriman (1920–1997), an English-born socialite linked to many important and powerful men, became a political activist and diplomat. Her only child, Winston Churchill, is named after his famous grandfather. Her esteemed father-in-law preferred her company to that of his own son, Randolph, who was infamous for his drinking, gambling, womanizing, and antisocial antics.

Harriman had friendships or affairs with Edward R. Murrow, Prince Aly Khan, Alfonso de Portago, Baron Élie de Rothschild, shipping magnate Stavros Niarchos, and many others. She paid close attention to all of her lovers' preferences and, typical of a Helper, would satisfy all their needs. Harriman's political career began in the United States through a marriage to an American, Averell Harriman, a businessman and ambassador to Russia and Britain. She became involved with the Democratic Party, creating a

to organize a reunion for five hundred alumni and alumnae from her business school. She squeezed in committee meetings and appointments with vendors for catering, flowers, photography, and the sound system after work. Her friends thought she was giving up too much precious free time, but the success of the event and the appreciation of the group made it worth it.

People Skills

You work on having a pleasing and comforting personality. You make friends, bring people out of their shells, and persuade them of your ideas by

new fund-raising system. In 1980 the National Women's Democratic Club named her Woman of the Year. President Bill Clinton appointed her ambassador to France in 1993.

Elvis Presley (1935–1977) pleased audiences with a combination of country and rhythm-and-blues styles, gospel, ballads, and pop. His charisma and ability to charm his audience aided his great success. He could "be whoever you want me to be" to his adoring fans by making them feel special as he sang love songs to them, seducing them with the curl of his lip, gyrating hips, and his wild clothes and throwing his trademark handkerchiefs to them. He earned a lot of money from recordings, movies, TV, and giving concerts in Las Vegas and elsewhere, and he had a reputation for using his money generously.

More examples of famous Helpers: Bill Cosby, Sophia Loren, Rachael Ray, and Nancy Reagan.

(Please note: Figuring out the career type of famous people is guesswork. Some project public personas that are different from how they behave in private life.)

using your smile, eyes, and voice. Small talk is probably easy for you. Tom goes one step further when he puts on his pinstriped suit and "charms the socks off" his parent-teacher association, being sure to provide explanations to the teachers in language they can understand. He learned part of this from observing colleagues, and the rest is innate.

Helped by his winning personality, Buck wheels and deals for his thriving custom construction business in a Texas city. "I always strive for a win-win. One of my secrets is to give the customers a little more than they bargained for." After a construction project is complete, Buck surprises them by throwing in some things that weren't listed in the contract just to make them happy when they move into their new home. He takes pride in excellent communication with parties he deals with, whether or not they are planning to do business with him again.

Tuned In to People's Needs

While not all Helpers are trained psychotherapists, many are good at counseling others because of their ability to tune in to other people. Dori, who *is* a therapist, says, "I can't be glib. I establish trust, which allows my clients to

talk and feel their emotions. I use nontalking approaches as much as possible. Art, music, and writing can sometimes be better ways to open up feelings."

Bent on pleasing, Helpers develop a chameleonlike ability to make themselves look the way others want them to look. "I can be a go-getter, relaxed, conversational, or whatever makes the other person happy," Cody says. "At work the boss loves this quality in me. I don't even *think* about what *I'd* like, and I'll drop everything else in order to be the one everyone can count on." Even though people sometimes abuse this quality in Helpers, their awareness of other people's needs can be a big asset for a company.

Amitav works in mergers and acquisitions for a worldwide bank, spending the majority of his time in front of financial spreadsheets or conducting due diligence on acquisition targets. He makes sure that co-workers' research reports and data are ready as soon as they are needed, he goes to great lengths to make sure he is well liked, and he keeps notes on their favorite books and hobbies so that he can give them just the right gift.

What a Helper Needs on the Job

Here are key things Helpers report they require to feel satisfied in their day-to-day work.

Looking Attractive

Helping others feel good includes making your appearance pleasing and surrounding yourself with things others will like, perhaps by putting up cheerful prints in your office. Amitav paid closer attention to his physique than did some of the other men in the bank's corporate development department. He spent long hours running, did pull-ups, lifted weights, and was usually the strongest man in the gym. He tweezed his eyebrows, came to work with a recent haircut and a clean shave, and had a tailor give his shirts an athletic cut with broad shoulders and a narrow waist. Although he was older than his boss, his boss assumed by his fitness that Amitav was the younger.

Some Helpers choose fields built around physical appearance and, like Paula Abdul and Richard Simmons, are seductive or entertaining. As a young woman, Shirley liked dressing up, putting on makeup, and striking poses, and she dreamed of earning a lot of money. She moved to New York City to pursue modeling. When that didn't work out, she became a photographer's studio assistant and learned the ropes of lighting, developing photographs, and working with models, agencies, designers, and hair salons.

Being Appreciated

Appreciation comes in many forms. You may like to be treated to dinners out or given bouquets. Perhaps having improved someone's life is reward enough. You won't be crass and call out for recognition, but you love to be thanked.

Helpers are so used to their role of doing things for others that they are sometimes surprised when the tables turn and others do things for them. When Tom the school principal received thank-yous from *two* different people for the same thing, he was floored. He doesn't like to be taken for granted, but simple thank-yous periodically will do. He also likes small gestures, such as when a teacher bought him a Halloween coffee mug to use in the lunchroom. When he was scheduled for surgery, the central office organized an interdenominational prayer circle for him, something he'll never forget.

Being Treated Well

You like to be the secret power behind the throne and to pay attention to those whom others might ignore, such as the janitors or the food servers behind the counter. In return, you receive favors that don't get done for people who aren't as nice, such as a free coffee in the cafeteria or access to certain places from the security guard.

Darlene gets to know the right people in high places by helping them with little things, such as filling out their form for an employee gym membership when they're too busy or giving them a tip on a great bakery. Anastasia owes her job to developing rapport with higher-ups, such as the directors of finance and human resources. After she took on extra projects that gave her wider experience than her colleagues had, they let her transfer to a more stable department during tough economic times. "My colleagues envied me a bit for it, but my extra efforts gave me more job security and a better office."

Shirley felt mistreated when a boss passed her over for a promotion and gave it to someone newer to the company. When she asked why, she learned it was because the other person had *asked* to be promoted. "I was so furious that I couldn't go to his promotion party. How people treat me deeply affects me."

Fitting In Socially

As a Helper, you value relationships above all else, so you try hard to fit in at work. You might undergo a style makeover if you work for a major fashion magazine or learn the technical aspects of the firm if you're on the office staff. You'll take time out of your busy day for coffee with co-workers to try to work out problems, and you'll offer help when a co-worker has a personal difficulty.

Dori wants to "bring us in closer alliance—to demonstrate a commonality and connect however I can." Cody volunteers to promote communities' causes, distribute e-mails, work on a political campaign, and fund-raise. He'll take on roles that require a lot of energy, like promoting a concert, because of his need to feel a part of the camaraderie. When he went camping one weekend with many co-workers and friends, his stepdaughter buried herself in a book, and he felt uncomfortable about it. He wanted her to be mingling with the folks—to be accepted and liked.

Making a Difference

How others are doing looms large in your consciousness, whether you feel concern for orphans, the homeless, helpless animals, or people whose

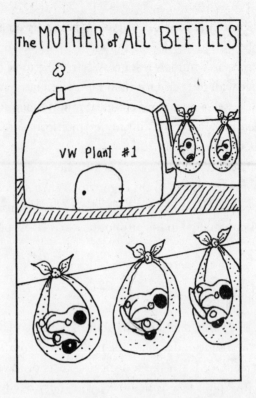

lives have been ruined in a war. If you can't lend a hand in your daily job, you at least don't want your career to work against your compassionate ideals.

Tom has a soft spot for people who are hurting inside, so the teachers confide in him as though he is their father. "I acknowledge their hurt and let them know they can come and talk to me about it. Once when a teacher's kid was picked up by the police, I went with her to the police station. In personal cases like that I never repeat to others what a teacher tells me. Discretion is important. A boss mustn't share things that shouldn't be shared."

Shirley was especially happy working at Charles Schwab brokerage because, even though the company's purpose was ostensibly to deliver value to the shareholders, the founder infused the workplace with his personal values of giving back to the community and helping even small customers. "Charles Schwab cared so much about customers' well-being that he gave them tools to take care of their money and never tried to pull the wool over anyone's eyes. I valued his integrity so much that I became very loyal. I need that in a job."

Darlene loved the community focus of her medical-billing employer. This minority-owned nonprofit in Philadelphia provided health care to a poor African American inner-city community who needed the coverage badly because of its high rate of disease. "We gave them access to level of health care they had never had."

The Other Side of Being a Helper

IT CAN BE HARD:

✓ to keep track of myself when concentrating on others.

✓ to avoid codependent relationships.

✓ when I let people take advantage of my wanting to please.

✓ to become overburdened when I can't say no.

I WORK ON:

✓ doing creative activities to help get in touch with myself.

✓ always checking in with myself about what I want.

✓ telling people, when they ask me for a favor, that I'll get back to them later in order to give myself time to think.

✓ receiving help from others.

Most pitfalls for Helpers involve being focused on other people's needs at the expense of their own. You can benefit from concentrating on activities that open you to your own real feelings and develop your opinions as separate from anyone else's. In the past two years Darlene has been working with an executive coach to help her explore what's important to her. She is becoming more comfortable with herself as she becomes more familiar with her own needs and feelings. As you contemplate your own career, keep in mind areas mentioned below where Helpers typically struggle.

From *Why Don't You Understand?* by Susie Leonard Weller; illustrated by Elizabeth Wagele (Parenting Press, 2009). Reprinted by permission.

Fear of Rejection

When you are afraid of rejection, you may try to change your feelings to match those around you so that you'll fit in and be liked. If others are somber, you will match their mood even if you started out feeling happy. But when you leave behind your own feelings in order to fit in, you practice a form of rejecting yourself. By instead recognizing your own feelings, you gain the freedom to be yourself no matter what the group around you is feeling. It's a wonderful opportunity to be yourself. It makes it easier to do your job.

Having Needs—Who, Me?

As a Helper, you are so busy thinking of others, you may not identify *your* personal needs. When he needed an apology from his co-worker, rather than asking for one, Tucker would privately retreat to his office to nibble on food or go to the restroom to pray for ten seconds, instead of looking out for himself directly.

It was easy for Darlene to forget about herself and try to make everyone else happy—to the point that she became sick. She was carrying the financial burden for her family, supporting her starving-artist husband while he pursued his dreams as an actor in Los Angeles. "In addition to a long day of work, I fed my family, got my kids to school on time, and attended all their extracurricular programs. I was also active in the PTA, a nonprofit minority women's organization, and my church. I was Superwoman, you know? Then one day I told my husband to take me to the hospital because I didn't feel right. The doctor told me my heart was palpitating from anxiety and if I didn't take care of myself I was at risk of soon developing hypertension and diabetes."

Overdoing for Others

Though helping others is commendable, you can overdo it to the point of ridiculousness. When Vicki was in her twenties she tried hard not to disappoint anyone, so she worked in either her mother's hair salon or her own until nine o'clock every night. "I didn't leave any time for myself. Finally, I've learned to set boundaries. One day I said to myself, 'Omigod, I don't have my own opinions!' I had surrendered myself to understanding my customers' lives and had neglected my own." Helpers sometimes overwork and suffer mental or physical stress; they then become ill and are forced to cut back.

This was the last meeting of HELPERS INC. With everyone OFFERING help, there was nobody NEEDING help.

It could have been a sad day, but everyone comforted everyone else before anyone was allowed to feel the loss....

Tom would go overboard for others as the principal of the school. He'd write the students' names on the attendance cards before distributing them, which the teachers usually did themselves, and provide teachers with prepackaged boxes of paper, pencils, and erasers to save them a trip to the supply room.

Buck was overinvolved in the employees' personal lives and did not set good boundaries with them. Approached by a brother-sister team down on their luck, he felt bad for them and—without checking references—gave the man a construction job and hired his sister to clean his house. Two weeks later he learned his lesson when they robbed a gas station. He wonders if he was too lenient to run a profitable business.

Giving Unsolicited Advice

Since you often think you know what is good for people, your natural inclination is to offer advice. But getting advice is something many people feel touchy about. You'll intrude less if you first ask them if they are looking for another opinion and give them an easy way to refuse it.

Marvin has been criticized for compulsively giving unsolicited advice. "Every time anyone asks me a question, even if it's about toothpaste or chewing gum, I tell them everything I know about the subject—even how to park the car in order to go to the drugstore to purchase the item." It's overkill.

Cody gives too much advice in the guise of wanting to help. "People tell me it can be incredibly irritating. I want to control but still be seen as a nice guy, so I'm not direct. Instead I'll say, 'It will be wonderful for the *project* if we do this. . . .'" This is the side of Helpers that others sometimes experience as manipulative.

When My Emotions Get the Better of Me

You have the strength of being in touch with your feelings, but sometimes feelings can be overwhelming. You might get exuberant when excited or break down in tears at a moment's notice. One Helper we interviewed mentioned becoming "rageful like Medusa" when not treated well. Many work situations require you to keep your feelings under wraps, however, in order to be professional. Some of you have no problem with this while others need to work on it.

Peggy was a teacher's aide in an elementary school. One day she needed to send a message to the teacher, so she called the phone in the classroom.

FEELINGS

The teacher informed her sternly that there was a rule not to call there while classes were in session but to phone only after school let out. "I was tired after working so hard that day and started crying. Then I felt so ridiculous."

Buck is a warm, expressive man who isn't embarrassed to shed tears at work because he's comfortable with his masculinity. He lives in the cowboy country in Texas, where men are expected to act especially tough. "Since I work in construction with a lot of rowdy, macho people, if it weren't for my size, at 6'4", I think I would have had my butt whipped a lot more often. But I feel good about being deeply emotional and not afraid to cry."

The Wagele-Stabb Career Finder for Helpers

Here are a few of the many possible areas for you to apply your talents in evaluating others' needs. Determining the results involves three easy steps: evaluating your strengths, selecting your dream careers from a table, and considering some practical concerns. The results are worth it! Follow the instructions below to identify your top strengths. You will then be asked to match them to career paths and to observe yourself, watching for which of them spark your greatest enthusiasm.

Try it once and see how easy it is. This test is engineered to coax your career preferences from the truest part of yourself. If you are uncertain about an answer, we suggest you stay with your first choice. Don't worry if you experience a little confusion; a certain amount frees you up to be all the more uninhibited in your choice. The key in steps 1 and 2 is *speed*.

Instructions for Using Career Tables

Step 1: My Strengths

First, read these five definitions. Rate them as they pertain to you and order your preferences in the box at the end.

Note: Any career type is capable of doing any job. The list of suggestions in the career table is not exhaustive, so we invite you to further investigate careers according to how well they use these five strengths.

Expressiveness

How do you rate your ability to communicate emotions successfully to one person or a group?   LO 1 2 3 4 5 HI

People Skills

How skilled are you at winning people over to your point of view, creating a comfortable environment, conversing, and being diplomatic?　　LO 1 2 3 4 5 HI

Perceptiveness

How aware are you of details about people and other complicated subjects?

LO 1 2 3 4 5 HI

Problem Solving

How do you rate your ability to use your store of knowledge and your intelligence to come to conclusions?　　LO 1 2 3 4 5 HI

Reliability

How much can others depend on you to be responsible and to do what you say you will do?

LO 1 2 3 4 5 HI

Now rank your strengths in importance from A to E, with A being your strongest trait. Write them in below, as in the example.

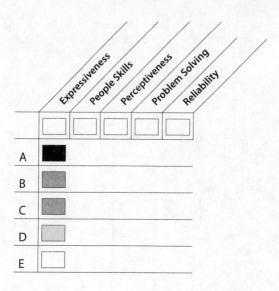

EXAMPLE

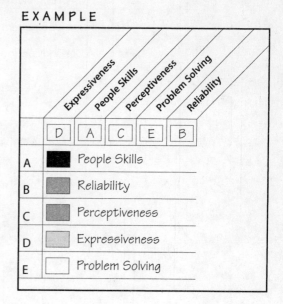

Step 2: My Favorite Career

Check the Career Tables below, starting with the ones that have the darkest-colored boxes (highest ratings) under your main strength. If you feel a special spark of excitement when you see one of the careers, write that one down. List up to four careers that most interest you:

Career _____

Career _____

Career _____

Career _____

Key: This chart shows the level at which each of the five strengths is used in each field (from the point of view of others who have held these jobs):

Exceptional	■
Significant	■
Somewhat	■
Minimum Requirement	□
Depends on Job	⠿

Business

	Expressiveness	People Skills	Perceptiveness	Problem Solving	Reliability
Accountant (independent CPA with private customers)	white	light	light	medium	black
Accounting staff (corporate accounting, budget analyst, etc.) # ®	white	white	white	medium	black
Administrative assistant (entry level) # ®	white	light	white	light	medium
Administrative executive secretary # ®	white	medium	light	light	black
Advertising specialist	medium	light	medium	medium	light
Business analyst (e.g., software implementation) $ # ®	white	white	medium	light	medium
Corporate executive (e.g., executive VP to the CEO)	medium	black	black	black	black
Customer support rep # ®	light	medium	light	light	light
Finance & accounting executive $ ®	white	medium	medium	black	black
Finance staff (corporate) # ®	white	white	light	medium	black
Financial advisor ↑	light	medium	medium	medium	black
Human resources manager	medium	black	black	medium	black
Investment banker/venture capitalist $	white	light	medium	black	black
Loan officer	white	light	medium	light	medium
Management analyst ↑ $ # ®	white	light	light	medium	medium
Management consultant $	white	light	medium	black	medium
Marketing manager $	medium	medium	medium	medium	light
Organizational psychology consultant (to human resources dept.) $	medium	black	black	medium	light
Product manager $ ®	light	medium	light	medium	medium
Project manager $ ®	light	medium	light	medium	medium
Recruiter ®	medium	black	black	medium	light

Business (continued)

	Expressiveness	People Skills	Perceptiveness	Problem Solving	Reliability
Retail banker (teller, representative, etc.) #	white	medium	white	—	medium
Sales executive $ ®	medium	black	black	medium	black
Sales representative/business development manager # ®	medium	black	medium	light	light
Small business owner	dotted	light	dotted	dotted	black
Tax preparer	light	light	white	medium	light
Training & development manager $	black	black	black	light	light

Construction & Manufacturing

	Expressiveness	People Skills	Perceptiveness	Problem Solving	Reliability
Carpenter (general construction) #	white	light	light	light	light
First-line supervisor of operations #	light	black	light	light	medium
General contractor	white	light	light	medium	black
Logistician (operations & materials coordinator) ↑	white	light	medium	medium	black

Education

	Expressiveness	People Skills	Perceptiveness	Problem Solving	Reliability
Adult literacy & GED instructor	medium	black	medium	medium	light
English-as-a-second-language teacher	medium	black	black	light	light
Principal or assistant principal	medium	black	black	light	black
Professor	medium	light	black	black	light
School counselor	medium	black	black	medium	light
Speech language pathologist ®	medium	black	medium	light	light
Teacher (K–12 #) ®; (postsecondary) ↑	medium	black	medium	medium	light
Teacher (preschool) ↑ ®	black	black	light	light	medium
Teacher's aide # ®	medium	black	light	white	light

Government & Nonprofit

	Expressiveness	People Skills	Perceptiveness	Problem Solving	Reliability
Activist (advocate for consumer rights, human rights, animal rights, etc.)	medium	light	medium	light	medium
Administrative services manager	light	medium	light	medium	medium
Chief of staff	light	medium	medium	medium	black
Civil service office worker	white	light	white	light	medium
Executive director (nonprofit)	light	light	medium	medium	black
Government contracts administrator ®	white	medium	light	medium	black
International relief agency workers	medium	black	black	light	medium
Ombudsperson	light	black	medium	medium	medium
Politician (city council member, governor, mayor, representative, senator)	medium	black	black	dark	dark
Program manager (nonprofit and govt.)	light	light	medium	light	medium
Social & human services assistant ↑ ®	light	medium	medium	medium	medium
Social justice worker (government)	medium	medium	medium	light	medium

Health Care

	Expressiveness	People Skills	Perceptiveness	Problem Solving	Reliability
Counselor/social worker ↑ # ®	light	medium	black	medium	medium
Dental hygienist ↑ ®	white	medium	light	light	light
Doctor (especially GP, internist, ob-gyn, pediatrics, physical medicine, rehabilitation) $	light	medium	black	dark	dark
Medical assistant (dentist's, occupational therapist's, physician's) ↑ ®	white	medium	medium	medium	medium
Nurse ↑ # ®	light	medium	black	medium	black
Nutritionist	white	light	medium	medium	light

Health Care (continued)

	Expressiveness	People Skills	Perceptiveness	Problem Solving	Reliability
Personal and home care aide ↑ #	gray	gray	black	white	black
Pharmacist $ ®	white	light gray	white	black	black
Pharmacy technician ↑	white	light gray	white	light gray	gray
Physical therapist ↑ ®	white	light gray	gray	light gray	light gray
Psychiatrist/psychologist ↑ $	light gray	gray	black	black	gray
U.S. Public Health Service officer	white	light gray	gray	gray	gray
Veterinarian ↑ ®	light gray	gray	black	black	black

Information Technology

	Expressiveness	People Skills	Perceptiveness	Problem Solving	Reliability
Database administrator ↑ $ ®	white	light gray	gray	gray	black
Desktop support/help desk rep	white	gray	gray	gray	light gray
Information systems manager ↑ $	white	gray	gray	gray	black
Information technology support engineer	white	light gray	gray	gray	gray
Security expert ↑	white	light gray	gray	gray	black
Software developer ↑ $ ®	white	light gray	gray	black	black
Technology executive $ ®	white	light gray	gray	black	black
Testing/quality assurance specialist ®	white	light gray	gray	light gray	black

Literature, Arts & Entertainment

	Expressiveness	People Skills	Perceptiveness	Problem Solving	Reliability
Actor	black	light gray	black	black	light gray
Agent (for artists and performers)	light gray	black	black	gray	black
Artist (painter, photographer, sculptor, etc.)	black	white	black	gray	dotted
Commercial artist (designer, events photographer, etc.)	black	gray	gray	light gray	light gray

Literature, Arts & Entertainment (continued)

	Expressiveness	People Skills	Perceptiveness	Problem Solving	Reliability
Journalist (advice columns, such as Miss Manners, Ann Landers, Dear Abby)	▒	■	■	▒	░
Journalist (hard news)	░	■	■	■	▓
Journalist (human interest)	▒	■	■	▒	░
Makeup artist (theatrical, performance) ↑	░	■	▒	□	░
Performer (dancer, instrumentalist, vocalist, etc.)	■	⦂⦂⦂	■	▒	□
Photographer (professional: ads, events, photojournalism, portraits, weddings)	▒	▒	■	▒	░
Speechwriter	■	□	■	▒	░
TV personality (e.g., anchor, radio broadcaster)	■	■	░	░	░
Writer (novels, poems, lyrics, scripts)	■	░	■	■	□

Math, Engineering & Science in Industry

	Expressiveness	People Skills	Perceptiveness	Problem Solving	Reliability
Mathematician	□	□	▒	■	░
Engineer					
Electrical engineer $ ®	□	░	▒	■	░
Environmental engineer ↑ ®	□	░	▒	■	░
Mechanical engineer ®	□	░	▒	■	░
Scientist					
Biologist	□	░	▒	■	░
Chemist, physicist	□	░	▒	■	░
Environmental scientist ↑ ®	□	░	▒	■	░
Epidemiologist	□	□	▒	■	░

Shading legend: □ = empty/white, ▢ = light gray, ▦ = medium gray, ■ = dark/black, ⦙ = dotted

Math, Engineering & Science in Industry (continued)

	Expressiveness	People Skills	Perceptiveness	Problem Solving	Reliability
Manager of research dept. (e.g., mentor young scientists and do PR for funding) $	▢	■	▦	■	■
Materials scientist & engineer	□	▢	▦	■	▢
Social scientist	▢	▦	■	■	▦

Service Industry

	Expressiveness	People Skills	Perceptiveness	Problem Solving	Reliability
Bartender	▦	■	▦	□	□
Child-care worker or nanny #	▦	▦	▦	▦	■
Concierge	▢	▦	▦	□	▢
Hairstylist or barber	▢	■	■	▢	▢
Horticulturist (gardener)	□	□	▦	□	□
Hotel or bed-and-breakfast manager	□	▦	▦	▦	▦
Interior designer	□	■	■	▦	□
Massage therapist ®	□	▦	▦	□	□
Personal organizer	□	■	■	▢	▦
Personal shopper	□	■	▦	□	□
Restaurant, banquet, or bakery staff #	□	⦙	▦	□	▦
Skin care specialist ↑	□	■	▦	▢	□
Store or restaurant manager #	□	▦	▦	▦	▦
Tour guide	▢	■	▦	▦	▦
Trainer (athletic, fitness, personal) ↑	□	■	■	▢	□

	Expressiveness	People Skills	Perceptiveness	Problem Solving	Reliability
Spiritual Field					
Funeral home director	gray	black	gray	light gray	gray
Meditation or yoga teacher	gray	gray	black	white	white
Monk, nun, yogi	dotted	dotted	black	dotted	dotted
Religious leader (chaplain, imam, pastor, priest, rabbi, etc.) ®	black	black	gray	gray	gray
Assistant religious leader (e.g., staff in a large congregation) ®	black	black	gray	gray	light gray
Uniformed Professions					
Aide (to admiral, general, etc.)	white	gray	gray	white	gray
Commanding officer	white	black	black	gray	black
Flight attendant	white	gray	gray	white	black
Pilot (airline, co-pilot, *Top Gun* fighter, flight engineer) $	white	gray	gray	black	black
Pilot (highway patrol) ↑	white	gray	gray	gray	black
Police dispatcher	white	gray	black	gray	black
Police officer	white	black	gray	gray	black
Support services noncommissioned officer (supply, transportation, etc.)	white	gray	gray	gray	gray
Other Fields					
Athlete	dotted	dotted	black	dotted	gray
Athletic coach	white	black	black	gray	gray
Coach (career, executive, life)	gray	black	black	gray	light gray
Interpreter or translator ↑	gray	light gray	black	gray	gray
Inventor	white	white	dotted	black	dotted

Other Fields (continued)

	Expressiveness	People Skills	Perceptiveness	Problem Solving	Reliability
Lawyer (especially public defender) $	■	■	■	■	■
Librarian	□	▨	▨	▨	▨
Maintenance & repair worker # ®	□	▨	□		▨
Stay-at-home parent	▨	■	■	▨	■

Step 3: Practical Considerations

After you've gone through the tables, note whether your favorite career fields match your needs for pay and security by checking for the following symbols in the Career Tables:

↑ = **Predicted Future Growth Area for Jobs**

$ = **High Pay**

= **Large Number of Present Openings**

® = **Recession-proof**

For more career ideas for the Helper,
see the recommended lists for the
Perfectionist and the Achiever.

CHAPTER THREE

The Achiever

Attaining a Successful Image

I F YOU ARE the third career type, you are *action oriented*. Being *efficient*, you will get the bulk of a job right and let the last 20 percent of perfection go, if necessary, in the name of effectiveness. When you rise to the *top* in an organization, it is because you are willing to work harder and longer than others around you, enjoying the *prestige* and satisfaction that come with success. Attractive roles are CEO, president, Olympic athlete, NFL football player, arts or media celebrity, corporate lawyer, investment banker, neurosurgeon, and top-grossing salesperson.

Industriousness, loving to perform and win, and other traits of this career type are pervasive in American culture. Being talented at managing their *image* and that of others, Achievers can contribute to public relations, be the figurehead for an organization, or navigate a challenging political landscape.

Getting to Know Yourself

If you have energy to burn compared to many of your friends and enjoy setting goals for yourself, you might be the Achiever career type. You're optimistic; there's not enough time not to be, for you have a lot to achieve.

No wonder so many heads of state are Achievers since they enjoy competing, presenting a positive public persona, communicating, and navigating complex political situations. Bill Draper, one of the foremost American entrepreneurs who defined venture capital in Silicon Valley, succeeded in investing and then made a second career in public service—meeting with leaders around the world—first as the chair of the U.S. Export-Import Bank under President Ronald Reagan and later as the CEO of the United Nations Development Programme.

The types next to yours, called your wings, can influence your working style. If your personality leans toward the Helper, you tend to be especially

people oriented and giving, while Achievers with a more developed Romantic wing may be especially interested in the arts, literature, or beauty.

Strengths Achievers Bring to the Workplace

As an Achiever, you are likely to be ahead of your time and tuned in to the prevailing cultural trends. Leave it to you, with your ingenuity, to find a way to make a better mousetrap.

Ability to Inspire People

Cindy, a senior vice president at a Fortune 500 company with a hundred people reporting to her, likes to kick-start an initiative by taking a complex concept, simplifying it, and getting everyone excited about it. "When our company had difficult decisions to make about how to invest in the right data systems, I figured out how to partner with the information technology department to solve this problem." She was efficient in the way she got the right people on board, asked the right questions, and soon had everyone moving in the same direction.

Early in his career, Patrick worked for a small publishing company, where he was in charge of a group of artists and writers who operated in a chaotic work environment. Normally, they'd be assigned to work in random pairs to collaborate on projects. When Patrick set out to make things run more smoothly and to find out what would make people's jobs more worthwhile to them, he learned that they each had different work styles. He realized that by pairing an artist with a writer whose style was compatible, their projects became more efficient and personally satisfying. He also instituted flextime, which was something he had wanted for himself. Flextime worked well for the employees, too, increasing their morale and productivity. Soon after Patrick instituted these major innovations in the system, several individuals blossomed in their careers.

Extremely outgoing, Ginger rose to chief operating officer of a corporate division by the age of twenty-five, primarily due to her vision and her ability to inspire employees. Her ability to communicate and her warm and effusive style helped her convince the employees to build a superior education business. She showed them she believed in them and had confidence in the business unit.

Ability to Read People

Lawyer Johnnie Cochran knew how to read a jury. You can't be a great trial attorney without the ability to pick up the subliminal messages given over

days, weeks, or months of watching them twitch, yawn, and grimace as they observe the proceedings. While there were many forces operating in the O. J. Simpson murder trial, Cochran's summation as Simpson's defense attorney was an outstanding moment and may have turned the tide in favor of Simpson's acquittal. Will jury members respond primarily to logic or to feelings? To a grand theory or to common sense? Johnnie, perhaps, knew. "If the glove don't fit, you must acquit," he said. And they did.

Richard is a radiologist who is aware of how he is received by people. "I am a good lecturer on breast self-examinations because I know they will make a difference in women's lives. I approach a lecture assuming everyone is with me, and I maintain eye contact with people in the audience. If I see a smile, I get charged up. If someone looks bored, it turns me off. I like to see that what I'm saying is useful, and I enjoy validation and thank-you notes, meaning a smile or applause."

Cindy thinks strategically to figure out where the unofficial power lies. "I read nonverbal reactions of people at meetings. You might think the most senior person is the only decision maker, but I notice the quiet influence of the observer, the vice president of finance, who talks privately after a meeting to the chief financial officer (CFO). The CFO talks regularly to the head of human resources, who has the ear of the top boss, the CEO. So I give special attention not just to the apparent decision maker but to those other players too."

True Story: The police had to be called to the Huntington Botanical Gardens Plant Sale because two lawyers got into a fight over a clivia.

Drive to Win

Businesses, including law firms, that are looking for someone with a competitive streak will do well to find an Achiever.

Achievers are usually obsessed with doing their best or winning. When Richard the doctor knew he couldn't bike the fifty miles a day necessary to complete the multiple sclerosis charity bike ride, he became one of the top-grossing fund-raisers for the event and stood out that way.

Priscilla anticipates competition on a daily basis, especially when she's trying to secure agreements in the financial services industry. There's always another bank ready to snatch up a deal if she doesn't. She says, "This industry is ruthless on a stick. There's no time to play games." And she thrives on that.

Tommy Lee *loves* the excitement of competition and winning. He remembers when his construction company in Oklahoma and several competitors in town were bidding on a large government deal to build a school gymnasium. "My main contender, Dumas Wiley, had an ego as big as all outdoors. The last guy in a negotiation always has a strategic edge because he has time to gather the most information, so Dumas Wiley 'graciously' let me go ahead of him for the negotiation. I was at a disadvantage, but I talked and talked with the vendor review team and told them about the special customized work I do. Before I walked out, they gave me the job without finishing their intended list of meetings. Dumas Wiley's ego shrank a couple of sizes that day."

Efficiency

With Achievers, quantity sometimes counts for more than quality. Getting where they're going fast is important too. They often drive fast cars and may not pay attention to parking meters if it slows them down too much. They want to get done with it so they can move on to the next thing. Priscilla says, "An Achiever may already be on his thirtieth deal while you're still painstakingly working out the details of your first one. And when you look at our scholastic achievement, we often will have not just one main subject, but three or five."

Manny had to be highly efficient to buffer his garment manufacturing business against sudden changes in cost controls. "Advertising and

Famous Achievers
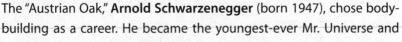

Oprah Winfrey (born 1954) is a television host, media executive, and philanthropist from a poor background. *The Oprah Winfrey Show* has earned Emmy Awards and is the highest-rated talk show in the history of television. She is also a book critic, an Academy Award–nominated actress, and a magazine publisher. She is a billionaire who is famous for her philanthropy, and some say she is the most influential woman in the world. She is admired for overcoming adversity to become a benefactor to others.

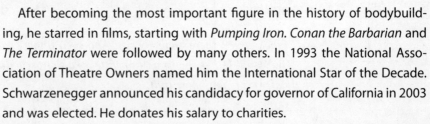

The "Austrian Oak," **Arnold Schwarzenegger** (born 1947), chose bodybuilding as a career. He became the youngest-ever Mr. Universe and won the title four more times.

After becoming the most important figure in the history of bodybuilding, he starred in films, starting with *Pumping Iron. Conan the Barbarian* and *The Terminator* were followed by many others. In 1993 the National Association of Theatre Owners named him the International Star of the Decade. Schwarzenegger announced his candidacy for governor of California in 2003 and was elected. He donates his salary to charities.

Maria Shriver (born 1955), who is married to Arnold Schwarzenegger, is the daughter of the politician Sargent Shriver and Eunice Kennedy Shriver, the sister of President John F. Kennedy. Maria Shriver coanchored the *CBS Morning News,* coanchored *Sunday Today* and weekend editions of *NBC Nightly News,* and was a contributing anchor on *Dateline NBC.* She took a leave of absence from *NBC Nightly News* when her husband became a candidate in the 2003 California recall election. Shriver has raised awareness of the contributions of women to California, worked on solutions to end cycles of poverty, and encouraged Californians to engage in acts of service to their communities. She has won Peabody and Emmy awards and is the author of six bestselling books.

More examples of famous Achievers: Tom Cruise, F. Scott Fitzgerald, Anthony Robbins, Sting, and Tiger Woods.

(Please note: Figuring out the career type of famous people is guesswork. Some project public personas that are different from how they behave in private life.)

entertaining were part of the game. It's important to wine and dine just the right people to move the business along. Still, I'd find ways to do this efficiently by attending style shows, where I could take groups of fifteen or twenty out twice a year."

Cindy's co-workers refer to her as a "nice bulldog" because she's not mean, but she is directive and keeps meetings and projects moving along. "I can navigate bureaucracy, but I feel tortured when I come up against unnecessary roadblocks. It's fun for me to take down obstacles and empower my team to get it done."

Hard Work

Mabel, honey, there's nobody else. And even if there was, how would I have the time? I operate on a tight schedule [kisses her]. You know that.

—from *The Best Man: A Play About Politics* by Gore Vidal

While any career type can work hard, many Achievers describe their work style as doing one thing in an intense spurt and then moving on to something else.

Richard, a chief of radiology, explains that at his clinic a computer system tracked how many patient files the radiologists would review in a day. "I would check the printout list of everyone's numbers before going home. Even though I didn't get a reward for working hard, such as an increase in salary or even others saying 'good job,' seeing that I had interpreted up to 120 patients' X-ray folders that day was my reward. One hundred to 120 were good for me compared to 30 or 40 for other doctors. As the chief, I liked to demonstrate exemplary behavior of hard work for the other doctors. Being the model was my big reward. I had internalized my father, who said, 'Be a hard worker because if you are you'll be the last one they fire when times are tough.' But times weren't even tough then!"

Priscilla explains that this propensity to work hard is hardwired or planted in her. "To date I have transacted $45 billion in deals. I can be cutthroat when the job depends on it. I defend my image and the reputation of the team at all costs. So if we have to stay up all night to rehearse for a big presentation, so be it. To get deals done I'm not going to coddle the team, and yes, that may mean we're working all Saturday and Sunday to get ready. I say, 'Go big or go home.'"

Risk Taking

Achievers will take risks. They are naturally optimistic that things will turn out well, and if that fails they are confident they can start over again in the same or a different field and they'll be fine. Isaac Dankyi-Koranteng, a customer account manager in Ghana and the financial supporter of his wife and children, is a good example. He heard that the first *Apprentice Africa* reality TV show was looking for contestants. Isaac left his stable job behind and traveled across Africa to Kenya to try to earn an apprenticeship with the CEO of a top advertising firm. He believed he could win by listening carefully to the seventeen other highly qualified contenders. He'd tap into their strengths and play on their weaknesses. Isaac won, achieving international fame and a well-paid executive job. His gamble paid off.

Manny took risks in the garment industry. If you buy thousands of yards of Hawaiian fabric, you can get stuck with it. But Manny had confidence in himself. "With conservatism in mind and a good sense of consumer tastes, I'd buy thousands of yards of Hawaiian fabric. I wouldn't think I could develop customers by introducing something *new* and hoping it would catch on. It was measured risk because I knew Hawaiian prints already had a proven market. Most of our customers were popular-priced stores like J. C. Penney's, for example, imitating high-priced stores like Saks Fifth Avenue and redesigning what they had."

What an Achiever Needs on the Job

Here are key things Achievers report they require to feel satisfied in their day-to-day work.

A Classy Image

Achievers are keenly aware of how they are seen by others, so they pay attention to their physique and the style of the moment in order to present themselves, their business, and their product in the best possible light. Mandy operates out of her house as an individual coach to Fortune 500 executives. Her clients are wealthy jet-setters, so she tries to live up to their standards. "How will executives believe I can help them if I show by the house I can afford that I'm not visibly succeeding in running my own business? I need to pay attention to the kind of car I drive and whether it's clean and well cared for. If I'm going to pick up a CEO client at the airport, it needs to say, 'She can earn a swanky living herself.'"

Priscilla doesn't wear flamboyant fashions, but the quality of her wardrobe selections is essential to her image. "I have a passion for clothes, such as a well-tailored Armani suit and a wristwatch with status. I'm not for the schlock handbag *ever*! My home makes a statement. It has an unobstructed view of Lake Michigan in a building in Chicago that's the equivalent of a Bentley car. Although I've acquired the kind of view that doesn't come available often, I don't own a jet—yet!"

Patrick is a less-common introverted Achiever and is not as interested in the way he dresses. He pays attention to the appearance of his publishing company's headquarters, however. "Our building started out looking nice, but now it looks like a rat maze. It has lost a lot of its style. I don't have to endure the crowding because I don't go in very often. We recently bought the building across the street, so a huge proportion of our people will get their own offices. That's important."

Dreams

What are *your* goals? What you can accomplish with money may be a start for many of you. Or your ideal may be a meaningful family life or the gift to others of your time. Perhaps instead you have dreams of greatness, fame, and adoration. In any case, Achievers never have small dreams; they intend to accomplish gigantic things.

Hank divides his time between Berkeley, Miami, and Paris. He is dedicated to the cause of bicycles. "I'm politically active in Miami, where I'm on the board of a new nonprofit organization, Green Mobility Network, which promotes alternatives to the automobile: mass transit, bicycles, and walking." His big dream is to model the bicycle master plan for Miami after that of bicycle-friendly Paris. "I'm also in the middle of a rapid transit project in Berkeley, where we already enjoy the results of my initiative from fifteen years ago, the Bicycle Boulevards, routes with special lanes marked for bikes throughout the city and an arching bridge for bikes over the large freeway."

Richard, who revolutionized his hospital's radiology department, began his career with big visions. In college he started a volunteer service organization, which now involves a thousand students a year doing acts of loving-kindness. Later, when he built an X-ray department in the hospital, he realized how important screening mammographies were. Fellow radiologists disagreed. "If each woman received a mammogram once a year, it would bankrupt society," they said. Yet Richard was sure they'd do an equivalent procedure if it saved *men's* lives. "Twelve out of thirteen chiefs of radiology voted no, so I did whatever it took to get it done. I finally established it in my hospital two years before the greater community did. I also went everywhere to teach about breast self-examinations. Now people come up to me and say, 'You saved my life.' "

Recognition

Success to Cindy means recognition. "It's not that I love working so hard; it seems I have no choice." Robin, the director of a Jewish funeral home, adds, "Recognition is great, and knowing in my heart I did well with that grieving family. When I was younger, raises and a title were important, but now all I need is to know I honored the deceased relative well."

Mandy gets teary when an athlete does something extraordinary and the crowd cheers. "I would cry when Jerry Rice, one of the greatest receivers in football history, caught a pass from Steve Young and the crowd went nuts. Someone told me that sometimes people get teary over what's missing in their own lives. I would love to have a whole stadium cheering me on. As an Achiever, that's how I know I'm lovable."

Stress Reduction

Though Achievers are often thought of as type-A personalities who work extremely long hours, most of those we interviewed are more balanced than the stereotyped workaholic. Many were also interested in projects outside of work, in having fun, and in taking time to be with their families.

Priscilla may be a true type A. Her transoceanic business trips take a lot out of her, so she needs to exercise regularly to minimize stress. When doing a road show in Asia, she discovered running was the perfect sport for her because all she needed was her running shoes and running clothes. She recently upgraded from marathons to ultramarathons as long as one hundred miles.

Cindy tells the classic Achiever story of being in the rat race for years until external forces compelled her to change. "I needed to slow down and focus on things besides work, but it wasn't easy. Then in an economic downturn my employer offered me an executive layoff package. It allowed me to take eighteen months off and spend time with my kids, renovate our house, take up Pilates, and do inner work. I'll be honest, stay-at-home parenting isn't the part I loved most; it was having more flexibility in my life. I finally learned not to feel rushed all the time to get everything done."

To Mentor and Be Mentored

Achievers often develop the skill of finding mentors and using their feedback to their best advantage. Throughout her career Mandy drew excellent mentors and thrived on their support. A turning point in her career was working with experts in the field of experiential learning methodology. She spent the next five years, including all her vacation time, at their institute to learn what these experts had to teach. Then she went out and trained corporate executives using best practices in experiential learning.

Priscilla actively sought out prominent mentors in finance or government. She spotted an opportunity when the former chair of the Federal Communications Commission offered a class in broadcast law and business. She got to know him during the course and bluntly asked, "May I stay in touch with you?" He agreed and has given her advice over the years. "I have also benefited from long-term mentorship from the managing director of a prominent investment bank in New York as well as a former U.S. Army general who is now a respected politician," she says.

Hank, who promotes alternatives to the automobile, places high value on student-teacher relationships as ways to maintain connection to the collective and to be remembered. He has given much extra help to young people over the years.

The Other Side of Being an Achiever

IT CAN BE HARD:

✓ to be patient with inefficiency or incompetent people.

✓ to distinguish who I am from my achievements. This is why intimacy is difficult.

✓ to not be overly competitive in all areas of my life, even when it isn't appropriate.

✓ to keep from getting exhausted from going and going.

I WORK ON:

✓ slowing down and setting limits on my working hours.

✓ staying emotionally present instead of focusing on my to-do list.

✓ broadening my interests to include more reading, relaxing, and creative endeavors.

Achievers often struggle with the following things.

Being Cut Off from Feelings

Being occupied with meeting work goals, getting ahead, and polishing your image can divert you from paying attention to how you feel. "It's easier to stuff your feelings," Patrick says. "Sometimes I know what my feelings are, but I decide not to act on them. Other times I don't even know how I feel. Playing music and writing poetry help me stay in touch, as well as working no more than three days a week. It also helps that working with feelings is the topic of a lot of the books my publishing company puts out."

Ginger learned early on that feelings can overwhelm her and are not safe. "Lately I've done a lot of journaling to try to *feel* my emotions and own them. All those years while I was a go-getter at the education company, I was grinding my teeth and had sleep apnea. At an unconscious level I was acting out my anger and sadness. I would stop breathing, which is dangerous because it can give you a heart attack. I went to a sleep clinic to be observed overnight. What's funny is that the next morning they said there was nothing wrong with how I slept. My fiancé pointed out, 'See, your body decided it was going to pass the test—so that night you didn't do your usual destructive behaviors.' It's true. I am an Achiever, and my goal was to pass the sleeping test, so I did!"

Dealing with Failure

Some Achievers report that when they are prevented from working (such as by a major failure or health problem), they feel they don't exist anymore. When one Achiever teacher fell chronically ill and had to rest at home a few months, she lost her sense of self-worth. She rethought her life, rebuilding an identity *not* based on doing, and felt happier. Manny the garment tycoon was depressed after his business shut down, but he picked himself up and found a new passion: English literature. When Achievers fail, they sometimes change game plans so that now something different constitutes achievement.

Robin hates dealing with failure. "It's not an option. I do whatever I have to in order to avoid it, whether it's being cleverer or more efficient.

If I'm passionate enough about a goal, I can do almost anything. I gave a nonprofit exactly one year of work because it had grand ideas and vision, but its director was not very good. After I helped the nonprofit get clarity about what it wanted to do, my passion subsided because it wasn't willing to make the difficult changes needed. Since it was bound to fail, I left."

Let Me Tell You About Myself . . .

An interesting thing about Achievers is that many of them will tell you about their achievements or prized possessions in the first few minutes after being introduced to you. "Hi. My name is Susan. I just talked to the mayor. Last month I met the governor. I drive a BMW, and I live in that pretty house you can see up there. And I write very well."

Patrick loved getting recognition in his field, which he missed when he moved to the country a few years ago. "I would do a disguised kind of bragging, like mentioning something I'm doing that people should know about. That's a problem when an Achiever retires. Where is your image of what you do?"

Ginger has pondered why many of the Achievers she knows seem to exaggerate their accomplishments. "What I find interesting about Achievers is that they manipulate their image. There are dual sides to us—a deep uncertainty and huge lack of confidence underlying the supreme confidence. I think in some ways every Achiever must feel like an actor because there isn't a human alive who is quite that confident."

Workaholism

Tommy Lee ran a successful manufacturing business in Texas. Then one day he woke up with an unusual medical condition that made his work twice as hard. Most people would have slowed down, but Tommy Lee kept persevering. "That year I had a big manufacturing job, so working through the illness created tons of stress. The project turned out fine, but I developed a full-blown heart attack."

Richard, the former chief of radiology, has no idea when he's overworking. "I have coronary artery disease because of it. If I were sick, I wouldn't know it. If I had a fever, people at the hospital would have to tell me I looked like I had one; only *then* could I go home. If I suddenly found myself with a free fifteen minutes, I'd fill it in. My wife would say, 'But what if it doesn't get done today?' trying to slow me down. The chief of radiology after me said, 'Richard, do you have to burn the candle at both ends?' I'd leave from work, fly to Frankfurt or Berlin or other places in Europe, and be back for work on Monday. Look how I maximized my time! Now I try to take it easier by talking with other doctors in the lunchroom, going for walks, or taking a nap in my home office. After I wound up with five stents in my heart, I found I could sleep in the middle of the day. I thought I had to be productive and had places to go. I was fooling myself."

She was the best in her yoga class, and she got stuck. We'll see what we can do.

The Wagele-Stabb Career Finder for Achievers

Here are a few of the many possible areas in which you can strive for success. Determining the results involves three easy steps: evaluating your strengths, selecting your dream careers from a table, and considering some practical concerns. The results are worth it! Follow the instructions below to identify your top strengths. You will then be asked to match them to career paths and to observe yourself, watching for which of them spark your greatest enthusiasm.

Try it once and see how easy it is. This test is engineered to coax your career preferences from the truest part of yourself. If you are uncertain about an answer, we suggest you stay with your first choice. Don't worry if you experience a little confusion; a certain amount frees you up to be all the more uninhibited in your choice. The key in steps 1 and 2 is *speed*.

Instructions for Using Career Tables

Step 1: My Strengths

First, read these five definitions. Rate them as they pertain to you and order your preferences in the box at the end.

Note: Any career type is capable of doing any job. The list of suggestions in the career tables is not exhaustive, so we invite you to further investigate careers according to how well they use these five strengths.

Ability to Inspire

How effective are you at encouraging others to transcend their usual efforts?

LO 1 2 3 4 5 HI

Drive to Win

How well do you thrive in a competitive atmosphere?

LO 1 2 3 4 5 HI

Efficiency

How quickly and effortlessly are you able to accomplish your tasks?

LO 1 2 3 4 5 HI

Problem Solving

How do you rate your ability to use your store of knowledge and your intelligence to come to conclusions?

LO 1 2 3 4 5 HI

Public Relations Skills

How do you rate your ability to promote yourself and those you represent?

LO 1 2 3 4 5 HI

Now rank your strengths in importance from A to E, with A being your strongest trait. Write them in below, as in the example.

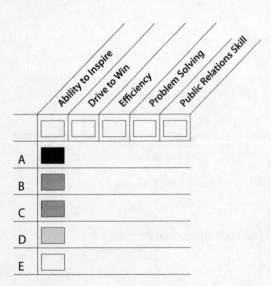

EXAMPLE

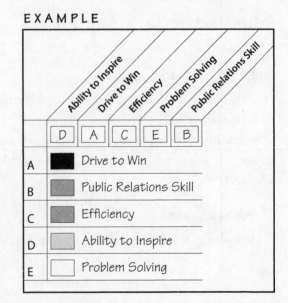

Step 2: My Favorite Career

Check the Career Tables below, starting with the ones that have the darkest-colored boxes (highest ratings) under your main strength. If you feel a special spark of excitement when you see one of the careers, write that one down. List up to four careers that most interest you:

Career _____

Career _____

Career _____

Career _____

Key: This chart shows the level at which each of the five strengths is used in each field (from the point of view of others who have held these jobs):

Exceptional	■
Significant	■
Somewhat	▢
Minimum Requirement	▢
Depends on Job	⸬

Business

	Ability to Inspire	Drive to Win	Efficiency	Problem Solving	Public Relations Skill
Accountant (independent CPA with private customers)	light gray	white	medium gray	medium gray	light gray
Accounting staff (corporate accounting, budget analyst, etc.) # ®	white	white	black	medium gray	white
Administrative executive secretary # ®	white	medium gray	light gray	light gray	white
Advertising agency consultant ↑ $	black	black	medium gray	medium gray	black
Advertising specialist	medium gray	medium gray	medium gray	medium gray	medium gray
Auditor (e.g., CPA in large accounting firm conducting audits of other companies) #	white	white	black	black	white
Brand manager	medium gray	black	medium gray	medium gray	medium gray
Business analyst (e.g., software implementation) $ # ®	white	light gray	medium gray	light gray	medium gray
Buyer (wholesale, retail)	white	black	black	light gray	light gray
CEO	black	black	black	black	black
Compensation and benefits manager	medium gray	light gray	light gray	light gray	white
Customer support rep # ®	light gray	light gray	light gray	light gray	light gray
Entrepreneur	dotted	black	medium gray	dotted	black
Finance & accounting executive $ ®	light gray	black	black	medium gray	medium gray
Finance staff (corporate) # ®	white	medium gray	medium gray	medium gray	white
Financial advisor ↑	light gray	medium gray	medium gray	medium gray	light gray
Financial analyst (equity research) ↑	black	black	black	black	black
Human resources manager	black	light gray	medium gray	medium gray	medium gray
Investment banker/venture capitalist $	medium gray	black	black	black	light gray
Management analyst ↑ $ # ®	white	medium gray	medium gray	medium gray	white
Management consultant $	light gray	black	medium gray	black	medium gray

Business (continued)

	Ability to Inspire	Drive to Win	Efficiency	Problem Solving	Public Relations Skill
Marketing manager $	▨	▨	▨	▨	■
Organizational psychology consultant (to human resources dept.) $	■	▨	▨	▨	■
Product manager $ ®	□	▨	▨	▨	▨
Project manager $ ®	▨	□	■	▨	□
Public relations specialist	■	▨	▨	▨	■
Recruiter (especially executive recruiter) ®	■	▨	▨	▨	■
Retail banker (teller, representative, etc.) #	□	□	▨	□	■
Sales executive $ ®	■	■	▨	▨	▨
Sales representative/business development manager # ®	■	■	□	□	■
Small business owner	⋯	■	▨	⋯	▨
Training & development manager $	■	□	□	□	□
Web designer (user interface) $	□	□	□	▨	□

Construction & Manufacturing

	Ability to Inspire	Drive to Win	Efficiency	Problem Solving	Public Relations Skill
Construction manager	□	□	▨	□	□
First-line supervisor of operations #	▨	□	□	□	□
General contractor	▨	■	▨	▨	▨
Manufacturing business owner	■	■	■	▨	■
Plant manager	■	■	■	▨	□

	Ability to Inspire	Drive to Win	Efficiency	Problem Solving	Public Relations Skill
Education					
Principal	black	light	medium	medium	black
Professor	black	dark	light	black	light
Teacher (K–12 #) ® ; (postsecondary) ↑	black	light	light	light	light
Government & Nonprofit					
Administrative services manager	black	light	dark	medium	medium
Executive director (nonprofit)	medium	medium	medium	medium	black
Government contracts administrator ®	white	light	medium	medium	white
Government service executive $	medium	medium	medium	medium	black
Politician (city council member, governor, mayor, representative, senator)	black	black	medium	black	black
Treasurer or comptroller $	medium	medium	black	medium	medium
Health Care					
Chiropractor ↑	light	light	light	light	light
Counselor/social worker ↑ # ®	black	white	white	medium	light
Dentist $	light	medium	medium	medium	light
Doctor (especially emergency, ob-gyn, plastic surgery, surgery) $	medium	black	medium	dark	light
Health services manager	light	light	black	medium	medium
Nurse ↑ # ®	medium	light	medium	medium	white
Pharmacist $ ®	light	light	medium	black	white
Psychiatrist/psychologist ↑ $	black	light	white	black	light
Veterinarian ↑ ®	medium	medium	medium	black	light

Information Technology

	Ability to Inspire	Drive to Win	Efficiency	Problem Solving	Public Relations Skill
Computer systems analyst ↑ $ ®	☐	░	█	█	░
Database administrator ↑ $ ®	☐	░	█	▒	☐
Information systems manager ↑ $	▒	░	█	▒	☐
Security expert ↑	☐	░	█	▒	☐
Software developer ↑ $ ®	☐	▒	▒	█	☐
Technology executive $ ®	░	█	█	█	▒

Literature, Arts & Entertainment

	Ability to Inspire	Drive to Win	Efficiency	Problem Solving	Public Relations Skill
Actor (especially Hollywood films)	░	▒	☐	█	▒
Agent (for artists and performers)	▒	█	▒	░	█
Art or museum curator ↑	▒	░	░	░	█
Artist (painter, photographer, sculptor, etc.)	☐	⁙	☐	░	⁙
Copywriter (ads, brochures, Web sites)	☐	░	░	▒	☐
Critic (books, movies, music)	▒	░	░	█	▒
Editor (copy, books, newspaper)	█	░	░	▒	⁙
Fashion designer	☐	█	░	▒	█
Journalist (hard news)	▒	█	█	▒	▒
Journalist (human interest)	░	▒	▒	▒	█
Journalist (opinion)	░	▒	░	▒	▒
Managing editor $	█	▒	▒	░	█
Musician (conductor)	█	█	▒	█	█
Musician (instrumentalist, vocalist)	☐	⁙	▒	▒	▒

	Ability to Inspire	Drive to Win	Efficiency	Problem Solving	Public Relations Skill
Literature, Arts & Entertainment (continued)					
Photographer (professional: ads, events, photojournalism, portraits, weddings)	□	▦	▦	▦	■
TV personality (e.g., anchor, radio broadcaster)	■	■	■	▨	■
Writer (lyrics, nonfiction, novels, poems, scripts)	⊡	▦	▨	■	⊡
Math, Engineering & Science in Industry					
Mathematician	□	▨	■	■	□
Engineer					
Aerospace engineer $	▨	▦	■	■	□
Biomedical engineer ↑ $	▨	▨	■	■	□
Computer hardware engineer $	▨	▦	■	■	□
Electrical engineer $ ®	▦	▦	■	■	□
Environmental engineer ↑ ®	▨	▨	■	■	□
Materials scientist & engineer	▨	▨	■	■	□
Mechanical engineer ®	▨	▨	■	■	□
Nuclear engineer $	▨	▦	■	■	□
Petroleum engineer $	▨	▦	■	■	□
Scientist					
Biologist	□	▨	■	■	□
Chemist	□	▨	■	■	□
Manager of research dept. (e.g., mentor young scientists and do PR for funding) $	▨	▦	■	■	▦

	Ability to Inspire	Drive to Win	Efficiency	Problem Solving	Public Relations Skill
Math, Engineering & Science in Industry (continued)					
Physicist $	dotted	light gray	black	black	white
Social scientist	light gray	light gray	light gray	black	black
Service Industry					
Chef	light gray	gray	black	light gray	light gray
Hotel or bed-and-breakfast manager	light gray	light gray	gray	gray	gray
Interior designer	black	gray	light gray	light gray	black
Store or restaurant manager #	gray	light gray	gray	gray	light gray
Spiritual Field					
Human potential seminar leader	black	black	light gray	gray	black
Meditation or yoga teacher	light gray	white	white	white	dotted
Monk, nun, yogi	light gray	white	dotted	dotted	white
Religious leader (chaplain, imam, pastor, priest, rabbi, etc.) ®	gray	light gray	gray	gray	black
Uniformed Professions					
Aide (to admiral, general, etc.)	white	gray	gray	white	gray
Astronaut	light gray	gray	gray	gray	white
Commanding officer (especially combat infantry officer, swift-boat captain, etc.)	black	black	gray	gray	light gray
Drill instructor	black	black	gray	white	white
Flight attendant	light gray	white	gray	white	light gray
General or admiral	black	black	black	black	gray
Intelligence briefer	white	gray	light gray	light gray	black

Uniformed Professions (continued)

	Ability to Inspire	Drive to Win	Efficiency	Problem Solving	Public Relations Skill
National Oceanic and Atmospheric Administration (NOAA) expedition leader	■	▨	■	■	■
Pilot (airline, co-pilot, *Top Gun* fighter, flight engineer) $	□	■	■	■	□
Pilot (highway patrol) ↑	□	▨	■	▨	□
Police officer	■	▨	■	▨	■
Public affairs officer	▨	▨	□	□	■

Other Fields

	Ability to Inspire	Drive to Win	Efficiency	Problem Solving	Public Relations Skill
Agent (for artists, performers, athletes)	■	■	▨	□	■
Athlete	⠿	■	■	⠿	⠿
Athletic coach	■	■	▨	▨	■
City planner	□	□	▨	▨	▨
Coach (career, executive, life)	■	□	□	▨	▨
Inventor	⠿	⠿	⠿	■	⠿
Judge $	■	■	■	▨	□
Lawyer (especially civil [torts & personal injury], corporate, prosecuting) $	■	■	▨	■	■
Stay-at-home parent	■	■	■	▨	▨
Transportation manager	▨	▨	▨	▨	▨

Step 3: Practical Considerations

After you've gone through the tables, note whether your favorite career fields match your needs for pay and security by checking for the following symbols in the Career Tables:

↑ = **Predicted Future Growth Area for Jobs**

$ = **High Pay**

= **Large Number of Present Openings**

® = **Recession-proof**

For more career ideas for the Achiever,
see the recommended lists for the
Helper and the Romantic.

CHAPTER FOUR

The Romantic

Expressing Individuality

I F YOU ARE the fourth career type, you are highly motivated to look for *meaning* within yourself. You have the ability to express *individuality* and bring *human values,* such as *compassion* and *originality,* to the workplace. Typical careers where you are appreciated for being *unique* include graphic designer, retail space designer, actor, producer, writer, musician, painter, chef, pastor, and therapist. You may enjoy being a gardener, secretary, health professional, or craftsperson. In the corporate world you are valued as the creative director, who sets a distinctive look for the company's brand standards, or the change management consultant offering insights dealing with human issues of mergers, acquisitions, and layoffs. Your ideas of what "could be" are important resources for an organization. You excel in roles that require you to create an appealing work atmosphere, brand image, written collateral, or conference program.

If you haven't found your perfect medium already, you may need to explore several different ones before you hit upon what's best for expressing your voice.

Romantics are often noticed for their pensive yet dramatic appearance.

As a Romantic, your rich interior life of thoughts and feelings contributes wisdom and meaning to others' worlds. You may feel a certain melancholy, but you also have a vision of how to make life more significant and elegant. Since you value authenticity, you express your moods honestly, whether they are sad, mad, subtle, or tempestuous. It puzzles you that others limit themselves to trying to appear happy most of the time. Others value you for exploring both the dark and bright sides of a situation, and they enjoy your ability to see life with an ironic twist.

Perhaps you have a disdain for the mundane and routine—"dull reality." You crave intensity and drama and are attracted to crises. Being around you frees others to get in touch with what's important to *them,* to search for deeper truths, and to explore their own emotions.

Being a Romantic, you are a deep, reflective caretaker of humanity and an empathic and sensitive listener. Romantics sometimes prefer jobs that, though they may or may not be personally fulfilling, allow them to save energy for important artistic or otherwise soul-enriching activities outside work. J.T. has a tech job by day to earn a living. "My acting, which I do at night, is my real career; being onstage is the way I enter into the world of beauty and fantasy."

Getting to Know Yourself

Self-expression is not only your special gift, it is also a necessity, like air, without which Romantics would suffocate. If you have not maximized your unique voice to its full potential, do not give up. Keep experimenting and follow your passions to see where they lead you. If you have an artistic bent, you may consider reading *The Artist's Way* by Julia Cameron. In her chapter "A Course in Discovering and Recovering Your Creative Self," she talks about "shadow artists" who hold back from fully developing their talents. They may stand in the shadow of someone who is perceived to be a "real" artist while they play a supportive or secondary role in the arts. If you have never been encouraged to explore your artist self or were told you aren't good enough, now may be the time to give yourself the encouragement you need to strike out on your own.

It's important to have a career that suits your nature. For example, you may be a Romantic doctor who's especially talented at dealing with emotional situations and whose gifts are more suited to the emergency room or a clinic other than the particular one in which you work.

Perhaps you're a professional football player noted for knocking heads together. But you have a sensitive soul, and you feel most of your teammates wouldn't understand this side of you. An athlete who is a poet at heart needs to make contacts with other like minds. Consider submitting your work to poetry journals, going to poetry readings, or even changing your career.

Bringing originality to what you do is one of your greatest strengths. If you don't have your own personal creative outlet for this, try to bring originality to your work situations.

The types next to yours, called your wings, can influence your personality. If you lean toward the Achiever side, you tend to be more sunny, optimistic, and outgoing while if you lean toward your Observer wing, you are likely to be on the shy side, and you might have an interest in an intellectual or scientific career due to the thinking influence of the Observer. Achievers tend to be extraverted while Observers tend to be introverts, as do Romantics.

Strengths Romantics Bring to the Workplace

The careers of great artists and musicians of all time, among them composer Claude Debussy, writer Gustav Flaubert, and filmmaker Ingmar Bergman, are characterized by *beauty* and *creativity,* two strengths often associated with Romantics. All artists are not Romantics (and vice versa), however.

Compare your own strengths to the typical strengths of this career type.

Authenticity

Only the shallow know themselves.

—Oscar Wilde

If you are a Romantic, the emotional depth you bring to your work shows in the outer world as your inability to accept a cheap substitute.

Your insightful comments show you have thought profoundly about your work. You shun light chitchat as too superficial, preferring to engage in significant matters, and you strive to find fresh ways of expression. Having you on the staff or in a social gathering adds a sense of gravitas.

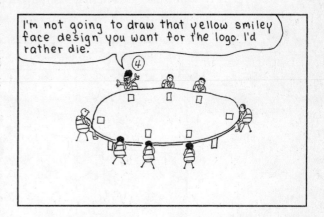

Many Romantics appreciate the value of the unconscious rather than always trying to reason things out to get to the truth. As ministers and psychologists, they can also discern information and feelings on an intuitive level. Kate, a pastoral counselor, worked with a woman who was suffering from insomnia. Kate encouraged her to scrawl in a journal whatever came to mind in the middle of the night. The woman did that a couple of nights and discovered much of value she hadn't known was on her mind. Opening herself up this way, she was able to alleviate stress and begin to sleep better and feel better.

Compassion

Whether your job description calls for it or not, co-workers will value you for conveying compassion when a caring tone is needed. Since you are the person many of us would want to go to in a crisis for understanding or for dealing with a difficult situation, management would do well to appoint you to bring the news about layoffs or other hardships.

You maintain a strong heart connection because your rich internal life helps you share others' emotional experiences. Medical professional Isabel felt such compassion and suffering for her patients that it was sometimes hard to hold back her tears. Betty was able to drink in the aesthetic experiences of her Romantic friend and intuit his feelings when he faced death from AIDS. He wanted to *live* as he was dying, and he wanted her to meet him on an emotional level. When he was near death, he needed nursing care, he needed to be hugged, and he needed honesty—and she could do that too. She could talk about death, which most of his other friends were unable to do.

Hilde always helps blind people trying to cross the street and brings home stray animals from work. She's so sensitive, she used to cry watching Greenpeace commercials, and she gets depressed by the news.

Creativity

If you are a Romantic, you will probably be inventive in either practical or imaginative assignments. Matthew is creative in a down-to-earth way. One morning he woke up full of energy and enthusiasm for remodeling his bathroom. He'd make it the most beautiful and functional room in his house. Overtaken by this flash of inspiration, he finished in almost no time at all. Jesse uses the combined imagination of a whole group for her best creative work in product development. Her favorite time is starting off a meeting with a blank piece of paper and beginning the process of bouncing ideas off one another.

Interpreting Meaning

Romantics who are especially gifted at interpreting meaning include orchestra conductors, mediators, and theater critics. In business, they may take a complex technical system and translate it for the sales force to understand by adding attractive visuals and putting the subject on a more accessible level.

Catherine was good at writing handbooks because of her ability to empathize with the readers and make her writing understood. She turned to novels to show how people could lead lives that had more meaning than self-gratification. Her characters would start out being self-centered but in the end would learn that chari-

table actions not only help others but also influence those around them to be generous and aware of those in need. Meanwhile, she created meaning through the art itself.

When Kate worked in a cemetery, she helped people understand the choices they were making. She would explain the difference between having a memorial or a bronze plaque. Should they put Grandpa in the ground? Would it be okay to put him in a triple grave or a double grave? She would interpret what the symbolism meant. "I'd help them understand what they'd be giving and receiving."

Dauntlessness

Some of you are dauntless. Your courage can inspire others, stir things up, and lead people where no one has gone before. You'll quit your job or change careers if something does not fit your values, and you'll speak up if the subject means enough to you. The risk-taking actions you perform may come at key turning points in your career, accompanying your momentous breakthroughs. A bold move can seem necessary in order to claim your identity, express the truth, or facilitate a compassionate act.

Since Tiffany is drawn to drama, life and death, joy and grief, and to the macabre, unusual, and offbeat, she has no problem working in crime-scene cleanup or in a mortuary. She doesn't want to keep the realities of life hidden. Elgar, too, has an interest in the offbeat. Owing to their unusual palette of ink colors, his posters were singled out among many submissions to be printed in a lovely coffee-table art book. He had carefully culled his palette from hundreds of photos of real suicide and murder victims in varying stages of decay. He sampled the colors of their putrefying flesh and wove them into cheery posters.

Romantics never plod through life or shy away from intensity. Some might face danger or even death working in a country undergoing a revolution if it means making the world a better place. Allan faced dangers when he performed acts of compassion around the world: "I worked in countries where people were being killed and had to think fast or I might be killed myself. I have also worked with tribal people who have AIDS."

The following composer/pianist, dancer, and actor have all taken professional risks in their quests for self-expression.

Famous Romantics

Film celebrity **Johnny Depp** (born 1963) chooses unusual and risky roles, such as the title roles in *Edward Scissorhands* and *Ed Wood*. In *Pirates of the Caribbean* he risked his movie-star image by creating a wacky, unique character reminiscent of the Rolling Stones's Keith Richards. When he performed in the remake of the children's film *Charlie and the Chocolate Factory,* he turned the beloved Willie Wonka into a creepier rendition of the character. Depp walked away from a very lucrative *21 Jump Street* role to do an offbeat movie, *Cry-Baby.*

David Del Tredici (born 1937) is a self-typed Romantic composer and an eloquent voice in the gay community. He is dauntless in his music and in flaunting his sexual orientation through his choice of musical subjects. Pulitzer Prize winner and recipient of a Guggenheim and other fellowships and commissions from around the world, Del Tredici was composer in residence with the New York Philharmonic. James Joyce in *The Modern World* writes, "He is probably the most prominent, and possibly the most adamant, neo-Romantic composer to reject received academic technique in years. Del Tredici's music is always complex, intelligent, and highly individualistic."

Isadora Duncan (1877–1927) was an innovative dancer who met a tragic death. Riding in Paris in an open car, she was strangled when her long scarf became entangled in one of the car's wheels. She is reported to have dropped out of grammar school because she found it to be constricting to her individuality. In her private life she was anything but traditional. Rebellious and a dreamer by nature, at the age of twelve she vowed not to marry. Later she bore two children by different men. In her last United States tour in 1922–23, in an era of concern about communism, she bared her breasts on stage and waved a red scarf proclaiming, "This is red! So am I!"

More examples of famous Romantics: Björk, John Lennon, Yukio Mishima, and Tennessee Williams.

(Please note: Figuring out the career type of famous people is guesswork. Some project public personas that are different from how they behave in private life.)

What a Romantic Needs on the Job

Here are key things Romantics report they require to feel satisfied in their day-to-day work.

Authenticity as a Guiding Principle

If you are a Romantic, you want to work for a company whose policies you agree with or to sell a product you believe in. This principle extends to preferring natural materials too: cottons, silk, and wool over synthetics. In other words, what is real trumps the artificial, superficial, or trite.

Ann lives in a house that is listed in a register of historic places, and she is restoring it to its bona fide old self, doing such things as removing wallpaper to find the original stenciled walls. With her love of what is genuine, she would have felt as cheesy and fake as J.T. did pressuring people he knew to spend way too much on a set of knives when he couldn't find any other part-time job during college. Just graduating from college, Loki landed a job that was considered fairly prestigious, but acting interested in consumer-packaged goods was painful for him because it was a lie. "If the job does not reflect me, it's just horrible," he said.

Beauty

As a Romantic, you may be especially drawn to beauty and the excitement it brings, which is far preferable to the tediousness of everyday life. Careers can be built around beauty in the fields of visual displays, the arts, and audio and video production. Writer and professor Harold Bloom is himself a work of art. He puts his Romantic personality on view with style and grandiloquence:

[It's a mistake] to believe that miserable is a bad thing to be. [Harold] Bloom, in his lyric sadness, his grandiloquent fatigue, and his messianic loneliness, is a great soul. "He did not seem happy," a former student says, "but happiness seemed a trivial quality

compared to whatever Harold was." Bloom is not low so much as over the top. In his misery, he is magnificent.*

To Gloria, how she does her work, and in what setting, is as important as what she does. Having beauty around her makes everything about her life easier. Gary used to give reports in grammar school in rhyme and from as far back as he could remember was attracted to small stones, jewels, crystal perfume bottles, glistening found objects, and music. It's no wonder he became an oil painter for a living. Beauty is so important to Aretha that she will cry if someone lives in an ugly setting because she imagines what it might do to that person's spirit.

Romantics are probably the easiest to identify of the nine career types because their style gives them away. Projecting a certain image is how Georgia expresses herself. "When I was younger, I dressed in gothic style. Now that I'm twenty-five, my style has changed." While she works in a clothing store now, it's likely she'll find a career in fashion to be best for her.

Creative Outlets

As a Romantic, you may have an insatiable need to express yourself through art, music, or acting—to reveal your inner worlds most honestly by means of the creative process. There are many ways to be creative, however, including approaching life decisions in creative ways and pouring your imagination into almost anything you do. Some Romantics feel the day is a waste if they don't spend a few hours after work doing something creative. Dylan keeps a firm boundary between work and home, not taking home either papers or problems so he can feel free to paint a picture or put together a sculpture out of scraps of wood he gathered from his property.

*Larissa MacFarquhar, "The Prophet of Decline," *The New Yorker,* September 20, 2002.

Living Out My Ideals

Romantics evaluate how they feel about their experiences. They think seriously about the meaning of life, including the role their career plays: "What can I contribute and learn through my job? Am I working for an honorable company that is adding something to the world?"

Adria left her administrative job to make ice cream for a living. She chooses only locally grown ingredients; uses no mixers, fillers, or preservatives; and has created a mobile ice-cream parlor so inviting that the whole neighborhood meets there to enjoy its ambience. Her unique flavors and her original parfait truck help make a day in Seattle more meaningful and joyous.

Andrew, a short-story writer, was determined to express his passion for life exactly as he felt it, not as he thought his culture was telling him to feel. He wished to express the real love and intensity that could come only from accurately observing himself. The task he gave himself was to capture his slightest nuances of feeling as well as his large and explosive ones.

Dave's goal is not to become rich or famous but to see how competent he can be. Learning and growing—his spiritual development—matters to him most.

Time Apart from Others

If you are a Romantic, you are most likely introverted and need to work in private for part of the day. Corporate jobs that require you to run from meeting to meeting or be creative on demand might not appeal to

About Ingmar Bergman's Movie _The Seventh Seal_

Long ago a man served as a Knight. When Death was ready to take him, the Knight challenged him to a game of chess, and the Knight won a temporary stay. He wasn't trying to get out of his death. Instead, he wanted to see if he could perform at least one meaningful act before he died.

you. When you have enough time alone each day, you can use it to collect your thoughts, get in touch with your feelings, and store up some ideas for future use. Being in a group might be unpleasant for you, like being part of a herd and losing touch with your individuality.

Sometimes so many people at Kate's workplace come to her with desires or agendas that she needs to remove herself for a while. She goes to the canyon before or after work and walks two miles up and back listening to just the rustling of the trees or sits happily in her car as a necessary balance to her workday.

When Kate felt depleted at work she took breaks away from people by driving to a park and listening to music.

The Other Side of Being a Romantic

As you contemplate your own career, keep in mind these areas where Romantics typically struggle.

IT CAN BE HARD:

✓ to be present to the outside world; I often would rather get lost inside my own mind.

✓ to feel anonymous (though when needing to be alone I can take refuge in anonymity).

✓ to be stuck in depression (though a little melancholy isn't bad).

✓ to be regarded as reacting too dramatically to life.

I WORK ON:

✓ becoming more disciplined about getting work done.

✓ appreciating what I *do* have.

✓ pausing, when I feel misunderstood, to get more information about the situation.

✓ learning to appreciate the ordinary too.

Diva Attitude

You may experience a roller-coaster of contrasting feelings and attitudes about yourself, including sometimes feeling entitled. Loki said, "It's a shameful indulgence, but my confidence was based on my sense of being better than those around me, so that I would stand out for being good at what I do."

J.T. admits he can be a bit of a diva when doing something creative: "I feel like I am always the most talented and best actor in the plays I am in. I know the best way to do everything, and I get annoyed when the director goes off on a stupid tangent that has nothing to do with the show. I am less of a diva when I have a good director or am surrounded by quality people. When something magical happens and everyone is clicking, I focus less on being the most gifted here and more on creative aspects that are getting fulfilled."

Envy

Romantics are familiar with the all-consuming experience of feeling resentful from wanting what another has. Haythorp is tall and handsome and is a brilliant, top-notch speaker on science. The ladies all puff themselves up when he enters the room. He has what Evan wants, and Evan hates him for it.

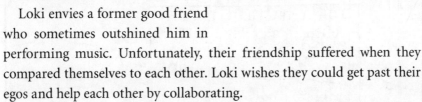

Loki envies a former good friend who sometimes outshined him in performing music. Unfortunately, their friendship suffered when they compared themselves to each other. Loki wishes they could get past their egos and help each other by collaborating.

A mathematician acquaintance set out to solve the most difficult problem Helga had ever seen. She had thought she could prove this theorem after just a little more preparation, but this guy seemed to have so much more innate talent than she that she realized no training would ever compensate for it. Their mutual friends were in awe of his abilities, but she found herself seething with negative emotion.

Longing

As a Romantic, you may sometimes lament that something you had in the past is missing from your life. This longing can take you away from the here and now and hinder you from staying on task.

J.T. feels as though he's been getting stuck with stage directors who don't know what they're doing . . . or if he were in a different play things

would be better . . . or perhaps he should have taken that other role several months ago or . . .

Melancholy

Dark moods are not uncommon for Romantics. They may feel attached to a sad feeling that stops short of depression, a mood often referred to as "sweet melancholy." Some are also prone to serious forms of depression.

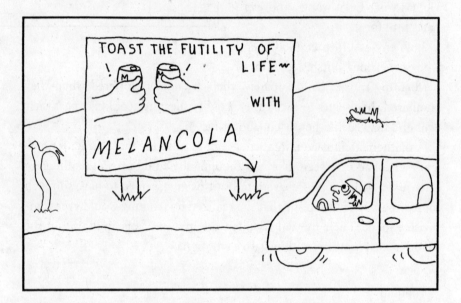

Here are some job preferences that Romantics express. Do their perspectives sound familiar?

- "I prefer working side by side at my job, or I tend to get depressed."

- "I easily absorb moods. When I realized how much I could be brought down by those around me, I found different people to interact with."

- "I feel melancholy when things can't move forward, so I chose working for myself, which I control."

The hardest thing about being a Romantic, to some, is the feeling of being on the outside looking in—as if they are not living their "true" life. But Romantics who are engaged in their work feel that their life has meaning.

As a Romantic, you may find that slipping into a bit of melancholy is not necessarily a bad thing for you. You may enjoy this emotion or feel that something creative is coming out of it. But the people you work with may experience melancholy as negative or too depressing. There are cases in corporate America where melancholy Romantics were pushed out of the company because they were misunderstood as "drama queens" or "bad apples." Talking about the negatives at work gave their bosses the often-erroneous impression that they were not committed to solving problems.

Self-Doubt and Shame

As a Romantic, you may find that sometimes your self-esteem plummets so low it seems things will *never* go your way.

For example, at a meeting Annabel started talking to a man who turned out not to be who she thought he was—a case of mistaken identity. Instantly she felt ashamed, even though she realized that mistakes like this happen to everyone. Similarly, if anybody at work got cranky or if anything went wrong, Hai would feel it was his fault even though usually it wasn't. Many Romantics have a tendency to feel they have let somebody down or have not done a good job—that they could have done more or should have done less.

Julianne used to get depressed when she heard about peers who were doing so much with their lives. She would wonder if she had neglected to develop her talents in design, music, dance, and acting. Then one day she said to herself, "Why can't I do that when I see others seizing the opportunity?" So she started a program of taking classes, going to psychotherapy, and exploring new careers.

The Wagele-Stabb Career Finder for Romantics

Here are a few of the many possible avenues for using your talents and expressing your individuality. Determining the results involves three easy steps: evaluating your strengths, selecting your dream careers from a table, and considering some practical concerns. The results are worth it! Follow the instructions below to identify your top strengths. You will then be asked to match them to career paths and to observe yourself, watching for which of them spark your greatest enthusiasm.

Try it once and see how easy it is. This test is engineered to coax your career preferences from the truest part of yourself. If you are uncertain about an answer, we suggest you stay with your first choice. Don't worry if you experience a little confusion; a certain amount frees you up to be all the more uninhibited in your choice. The key in steps 1 and 2 is *speed*.

Instructions for Using Career Tables

Step 1: My Strengths

First, read these five definitions. Rate them as they pertain to you and order your preferences in the box at the end.

Note: Any career type is capable of doing any job. The list of suggestions in the career table is not exhaustive, so we invite you to further investigate careers according to how well they use these five strengths.

Ability to Discern

How do you rate your ability to be insightful, to perceive, and to make clear distinctions?

LO 1 2 3 4 5 HI

Aesthetic Sense

How developed is your sensitivity to beauty, style, and taste? LO 1 2 3 4 5 HI

Compassion

To what degree do you resonate with the tender feelings of others?

LO 1 2 3 4 5 HI

Imagination

How able are you to create out of your own vision or to experiment with new ideas and ways of doing things?

LO 1 2 3 4 5 HI

Sense of Meaning

How important are your sense of purpose and the ideals you apply to your work?

LO 1 2 3 4 5 HI

Now rank your strengths in importance from A to E, with A being your strongest trait. Write them in below, as in the example.

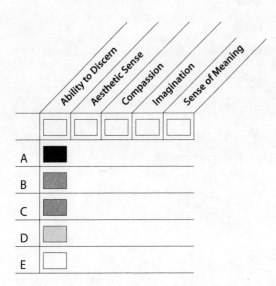

E X A M P L E

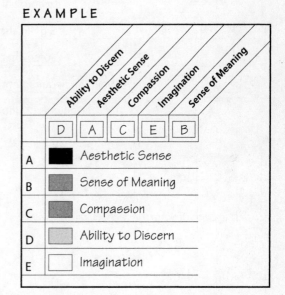

Step 2: My Favorite Career

Check the Career Tables below, starting with the ones that have the darkest-colored boxes (highest ratings) under your main strength. If you feel a special spark of excitement when you see one of the careers, write that one down. List up to four careers that most interest you:

Career _____

Career _____

Career _____

Career _____

Key: This chart shows the level at which each of the five strengths is used in each field (from the point of view of others who have held these jobs):

Exceptional	■
Significant	■
Somewhat	■
Minimum Requirement	□
Depends on Job	⊞

Business

	Ability to Discern	Aesthetic Sense	Compassion	Imagination	Sense of Meaning
Administrative assistant (entry level) # ®	░				
Administrative executive secretary # ®	░				
Advertising agency consultant ↑ $	▒	▒	⋯	█	▒
Advertising specialist	░	░	⋯	░	
Brand manager	█	⋯		▒	▒
CEO	█	⋯	░	▒	▒
Customer support rep # ®	░		░		▒
Entrepreneur	▒	⋯	⋯	█	⋯
Financial advisor ↑	▒		⋯		░
Human resources manager	▒		▒	░	█
Management consultant $	█			▒	▒
Marketing manager $	▒	⋯			⋯
Organizational psychology consultant (to human resources dept.) $	█	░	▒	░	█
Product manager $ ®	▒	⋯		▒	⋯
Project manager $ ®	▒				
Recruiter ®	▒		░		▒
Sales executive $ ®	▒			░	░
Small business owner	░	⋯	⋯	█	⋯
Training & development manager $	▒	▒	░	▒	█
Web designer (user interface) $	▒	█	⋯	▒	░

	Ability to Discern	Aesthetic Sense	Compassion	Imagination	Sense of Meaning
Construction & Manufacturing					
Carpenter (finish woodworker)	light gray	dark gray	white	dark gray	white
General contractor	light gray	dotted	white	dotted	white
Tile or marble setter	light gray	dark gray	white	medium gray	white
Education					
English-as-a-second-language teacher	light gray	light gray	light gray	medium gray	medium gray
Professor	black	dotted	light gray	medium gray	medium gray
School counselor	medium gray	white	medium gray	light gray	black
Teacher (K–12 #) ®; (postsecondary) ↑	medium gray	dotted	medium gray	medium gray	black
Government & Nonprofit					
Executive director (nonprofit)	medium gray	dotted	light gray	medium gray	black
International relief agency workers	medium gray	white	black	light gray	black
Politician (city council member, governor, mayor, representative, senator)	black	white	light gray	medium gray	black
Program manager (nonprofit and govt.)	medium gray	dotted	light gray	medium gray	black
Social & human services assistant ↑ ®	light gray	white	black	light gray	black
Health Care					
Counselor/social worker ↑ # ®	medium gray	white	black	medium gray	black
Doctor (especially emergency, internist, pediatrics, physical medicine, plastic surgery, rehabilitation) $	black	white	medium gray	medium gray	black
Hospice worker	white	white	black	medium gray	black
Nurse ↑ # ®	medium gray	white	black	light gray	medium gray

Health Care (continued)

	Ability to Discern	Aesthetic Sense	Compassion	Imagination	Sense of Meaning
Psychiatrist/psychologist ↑ $	■	□	■	▨	■
Veterinarian ↑ ®	■	□	■	░	■

Information Technology

	Ability to Discern	Aesthetic Sense	Compassion	Imagination	Sense of Meaning
Computer systems analyst ↑ $ ®	■	▨	□	▨	□
Database administrator ↑ $ ®	▨	▨	□	□	□
Information systems manager ↑ $	■	▨	□	░	□
Software developer ↑ $ ®	■	▨	□	▨	□
Technology executive $ ®	▨	□	□	▨	░

Literature, Arts & Entertainment

	Ability to Discern	Aesthetic Sense	Compassion	Imagination	Sense of Meaning
Actor	■	■	■	■	■
Architect	■	■	□	■	■
Art director (marketing dept. or independent studio) $	▨	■	⊡	■	▨
Artisan/craftsperson	▨	■	□	■	⊡
Artist (painter, photographer, sculptor, etc.)	■	■	■	■	■
Casting agent	■	▨	░	░	□
Commercial artist (graphic designer, product designer, etc.)	▨	▨	□	▨	⊡
Copywriter (ads, brochures, Web sites)	■	▨	□	▨	□
Critic (books, movies, music)	■	■	□	▨	■
Dancer	▨	■	■	▨	■
Director (plays, motion pictures, radio, TV)	■	■	■	■	■
Editor (copy, books, newspaper)	■	■	⊡	▨	▨

Literature, Arts & Entertainment (continued)

	Ability to Discern	Aesthetic Sense	Compassion	Imagination	Sense of Meaning
Entertainer (figure skater, magician, mime, etc.)	▦	■	⠿	■	⠿
Essayist	■	▦	⠿	▦	■
Fashion designer	■	■	□	■	⠿
Film editor	■	▦	▒	■	■
Illustrator, cartoonist	■	▦	⠿	■	⠿
Journalist (hard news)	■	▦	□	▦	■
Journalist (human interest)	■	▦	▦	▦	■
Journalist (opinion)	■	▦	⠿	■	■
Landscape architect	■	■	□	■	▒
Makeup artist (theatrical, performance) ↑	□	▦	▒	▦	▒
Managing editor $	■	▦	⠿	▦	■
Multimedia artist or animator ↑	▦	▦	⠿	■	▒
Musician (composer, conductor, vocalist, instrumentalist)	■	■	▦	■	■
Photographer (professional: ads, events, photojournalism, portraits, weddings)	■	▦	⠿	▦	■
Set designer	▦	■	□	■	▦
Speechwriter	▦	▦	□	▦	■
Technical writer ↑	■	▒	□	□	□
Writer (lyrics, nonfiction, novels, poems, scripts)	■	■	■	■	■

Math, Engineering & Science in Industry

	Ability to Discern	Aesthetic Sense	Compassion	Imagination	Sense of Meaning
Mathematician	■	▨	□	▨	▨
Engineer					
Aerospace engineer $	■	▨	□	▨	▨
Biomedical engineer ↑ $	■	▨	▨	▨	▨
Electrical engineer $ ®	■	▨	▨	▨	▨
Environmental engineer ↑ ®	■	▨	□	▨	▨
Mechanical engineer ®	■	▨	▨	▨	▨
Scientist					
Atmospheric scientist $	■	▨	□	▨	▨
Biologist	■	▨	□	▨	▨
Chemist	■	▨	□	▨	▨
Environmental scientist ↑ ®	■	▨	▨	▨	▨
Epidemiologist	■	▨	□	▨	▨
Manager of research dept. (e.g., mentor young scientists and do PR for funding) $	■	▨	▨	▨	▨
Materials scientist & engineer (e.g., nanotechnology) $	■	▨	□	▨	▨
Physicist $	■	▨	□	▨	▨
Social scientist	■	▨	□	▨	■

Service Industry

	Ability to Discern	Aesthetic Sense	Compassion	Imagination	Sense of Meaning
Concierge	▨	⠿	⠿	▨	▨
Hairstylist or barber	▨	■	▨	▨	▨
Hotel or bed-and-breakfast manager	▨	▨	⠿	□	□

	Ability to Discern	Aesthetic Sense	Compassion	Imagination	Sense of Meaning
Service Industry (continued)					
Interior designer	light gray	black	gray	gray	gray
Owner/creator of service or business (vintage clothing, artisan foods, etc.)	gray	gray	dotted	black	gray
Restaurant or bakery staff #	gray	dotted	dotted	gray	white
Store or restaurant manager #	light gray	dotted	dotted	dotted	gray
Spiritual Field					
Funeral home director	light gray	light gray	black	light gray	black
Human potential seminar leader	gray	light gray	gray	gray	black
Meditation or yoga teacher	gray	light gray	black	light gray	white
Monk, nun, yogi	gray	light gray	black	light gray	dotted
Religious leader (chaplain, imam, pastor, priest, rabbi, etc.) ®	gray	light gray	gray	gray	black
Uniformed Professions					
Commanding officer	dotted	white	gray	gray	black
Equal-opportunity specialist	gray	white	white	white	gray
Flight attendant	white	white	gray	white	white
Judge Advocate General Corps (JAG) (especially defense counsel)	black	white	dotted	gray	black
Overseas embassy military attaché	gray	light gray	gray	white	gray
Military band musician (especially the distinguished marine corps band)	black	black	dotted	black	black
Military intelligence analyst	black	white	white	gray	gray

Other Fields

Other Fields	Ability to Discern	Aesthetic Sense	Compassion	Imagination	Sense of Meaning
Athlete	▨ (gray)	⁞⁞⁞ (dots)	☐ (white)	⁞⁞⁞ (dots)	☐ (white)
Athletic coach	▨ (dark gray)	⁞⁞⁞ (dots)	▨ (gray)	⁞⁞⁞ (dots)	▨ (gray)
Coach (career, executive, life)	▨ (gray)	☐ (white)	■ (black)	▨ (gray)	■ (black)
Environmental science & protection technician ↑ ®	▨ (gray)	☐ (white)	☐ (white)	☐ (white)	☐ (white)
Inventor	⁞⁞⁞ (dots)	⁞⁞⁞ (dots)	⁞⁞⁞ (dots)	■ (black)	⁞⁞⁞ (dots)
Lawyer (especially defense attorney) $	■ (black)	☐ (white)	▨ (gray)	▨ (gray)	■ (black)
Librarian	▨ (gray)	▨ (gray)	☐ (white)	▨ (gray)	▨ (gray)
Sound & lighting engineering technician	■ (black)	▨ (gray)	☐ (white)	☐ (white)	☐ (white)
Stay-at-home parent	▨ (gray)	⁞⁞⁞ (dots)	■ (black)	■ (black)	■ (black)

Step 3: Practical Considerations

After you've gone through the tables, note whether your favorite career fields match your needs for pay and security by checking for the following symbols in the Career Tables:

↑ = **Predicted Future Growth Area for Jobs**

$ = **High Pay**

= **Large Number of Present Openings**

® = **Recession-proof**

For more career ideas for the Romantic,
see the recommended lists for the
Achiever and the Observer.

CHAPTER FIVE

The Observer

Acquiring Knowledge

I F YOU ARE the fifth career type, you are *curious*. You *think* a lot, often *focusing* on one thing at a time; you enjoy *time alone;* and you relish your *independence*. Some of you like to *analyze* and conduct extensive research or study systems—the more complex or abstract the better—while others prefer to keep track of practical information, such as transportation or meteorology. You are invaluable to an organization for your ability to make sense of vast amounts of data.

It's common for people of your career type to be *introverted, idiosyncratic,* and *shy*. You prefer to meet with others to discuss an issue and then work on it alone. Some of you prefer communicating through writing—such as research reports, medical journals, peer-reviewed publications, and e-mail. Some of you are at ease in public settings and are stellar public speakers when talking about your area of expertise. You still require plenty of *privacy* to think your thoughts and to concentrate on your projects.

Typical roles of Observers are as scientists, professors, research analysts, photographers, and librarians. Other common occupations are as computer programmers, lawyers, surveyors, biologists, chemists, psychologists, writers, and artists.

Getting to Know Yourself

If you sometimes take a detached, ironic stance or consider yourself a nerd, a geek, or a dork, you might be an Observer. You come in many varieties, however, and not all are nerdlike. While working with math or computers suits some of you, others are interested in the more concrete areas of bikes, cars, cooking, or working with children. A good symbol for you is the delicate glasswing butterfly because in your core you are sensitive, gentle souls, you dislike conflict, and you tread lightly.

While it might seem contradictory that a gentle soul could be this way, you also appear to others to be harsh or overly critical at times. This is related to your ability to be acutely discerning, a valuable asset in your life. You don't mean to be aggressive or dismissive; you're just trying to get at the truth of the matter. So you can become impatient with those around you who don't seem as logical or informed as you are. If you have superior knowledge, you can appear arrogant. Observers don't always blend in well with other people.

If you are a young and very bright Observer, chances are you are on top of the latest thinking in your field of interest. If others seem to find you weird for a time, remember that struggling to be who you are helps you develop empathy as well as other important inner resources for dealing with life. Stick to your guns, have faith in yourself, and look for others like you for friends.

One of the problems in Observers' careers is a lot of knowledge concealed behind a mild-mannered exterior. Observers rarely have flamboyant, dazzlingly stylish, bombastic, commanding personalities. However,

there are a few examples, such as astrophysicists and actors, who are extremely attractive and successful professionally because of their ability to communicate their incredible expertise. For the most part, Observers are intensely and quietly humble. As Lao-tzu said, "He who knows does not speak. He who speaks does not know." Though there are exceptions, Observers don't usually flaunt their knowledge and abilities, and as a result others sometimes undervalue them. Their thoughts and observations are valuable, though, and they can be creative forces for positive change when they dare to chime in.

The types on each side of yours, called your wings, often influence your career type. If you lean toward the Romantic, you tend to be more humanistic and possibly more interested in the arts than are Observers with a more developed Questioner wing, who are more likely to have careers in intellectual or scientific areas.

Strengths Observers Bring to the Workplace

As an Observer, you are valued for your *knowledge* and your ability to see *different angles* and an *objective* perspective on the workplace. Most Observers like a *quiet* place to work—the optimum atmosphere in which to focus *in depth*.

Ability to Grasp Structure

Your ability to perceive how things fit together enables you to predict likely outcomes. "When you write mystery novels, there are twenty themes that move along like little tributaries," Jaki Girdner explains. "You have to juggle many balls in your head and make sure the end of the book matches the beginning. You have to be aware of the structure—not so different from when I wanted to be an architect."

Chuck has worked for thirty-six years as a land surveyor, establishing the precise location of roads, property corners, fire hydrants, and even lightbulbs. His work requires attention to detail within a structure of mathematical relationships. "You can't be wrong *ever,* or someone's property will be off. You start out surveying a big dirt field, and over time you build something [on that field] that you designed in the office on computer-aided design software. It's like painting; I feel artistic when I determine for contractors where to build things." When Chuck drives around the San Diego Bay, where empty lots once stood, he now sees all the airport runways, terminal buildings, hotels, convention centers, and city parks that he helped build.

Focus

Observers stay with a project until it's completed and rarely go off on tangents. "A lot of people say they'd write if . . . , but they can't focus enough to keep the ideas lined up in their head while they're working." The actual process of writing and focusing is exhilarating to Jaki. She loves "editing it, perfecting it, brushing its hair, and making it beautiful."

Chuck has so much ability to focus on his work, nineteen hours a day wouldn't bother him a bit. Others are tired after eight hours. Driving home from work, he is still playing back in his head any calculations he might have missed, shortcuts he could try next time, and ways his logic can be improved.

Objectivity

Co-workers, students, and clients appreciate having Observers around who can see things in an unbiased, nonjudgmental way. At one point in his career, David worked for Bread and Roses, singer Mimi Fariña's nonprofit, which sends musicians into psych wards, old folks' homes, children's wards, AIDS hospices, and so on. "I felt at home in the heavy-duty psychiatric lockdown wards with people whose minds had stopped trying to impose order upon reality—who just broke down and let reality flow on top of them, unparsed, unwinnowed," he said. "The attendant nurses would be winking and tsk-tsk-ing at me not to believe the outlandish tales the

Larissa concentrated so hard on the dung beetles, she didn't know a whole city had sprung up around her.

psychotics would tell me, but I enjoyed following these people into the kaleidoscopic windmills of their minds. I didn't argue with them or gainsay their fantastic 'explanations' of reality. Observers don't have to be told that the world is ultimately polysemous. No one person has dibs on what's real, and we understand how the merest detour of a synapse can send a person's reality in a different direction."

Original Way of Looking at the World

Looking at the world differently from most people is the source of much of Observers' creativity. On one hand, if they're too idiosyncratic, they become alienated from those around them. On the other hand, their idiosyncrasies can reveal a variety and richness that others may not have noticed.

Franz Kafka (1883–1924) found innovative ways to criticize bureaucracy and to show how it is possible to get trapped in red tape or go crazy from trying to deal with modern technology. In *The Metamorphosis* a salesman is turned overnight into an insect and spends most of the novella on his back painfully trying to turn over. The author from Prague is also known

for his novels *The Trial* and *The Castle,* in which troubled individuals try to cope in a terribly impersonal world. *Kafkaesque* is a word that means a nightmarish atmosphere—suggestive of his writing. Kafka studied law and worked for an insurance institute. He was described as boyish and neat, with austere good looks, a quiet and cool demeanor, obvious intelligence, and a dry sense of humor.

Sensitivity

Most Observers have an inherently gentle and sensitive nature. Since awareness of others is hugely important in a work situation, their interest in observing or reading other people can be useful in fields such as teaching or sales, where they can observe a whole class or an individual's needs.

When Observers are doctors, their gift is not showing patients they are considering worst-case scenarios. For example, they would never scare a patient with a cold by saying there was a slight chance a swollen gland could be lymphoma. Instead, they would request a return visit to see for themselves that all was well. Observers need to experience things themselves or see the evidence. They're not easily convinced.

Gus, a schoolteacher, enjoyed the inspirational speech that Herb Cole, an author on education, gave to two thousand teachers the day before school started one fall. Most of the teachers thought students basically need a firmer hand, and when Cole said, "We should love our students more," some of them booed him. "I thought their reaction was so bad. I really agreed with Cole," Gus said. "A few years later I was invited to start a class of children with disabilities partly because I had been a sensitive teacher in a neighborhood with a lot of low-achieving, disadvantaged kids. My class was successful. One girl said it was the best time of her life because I really listened to the kids."

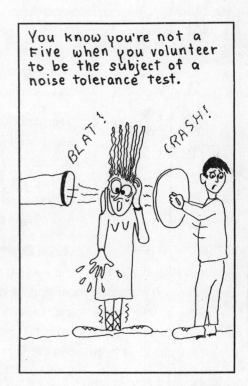

You know you're not a Five when you volunteer to be the subject of a noise tolerance test.

From Elizabeth Wagele's *The Happy Introvert* (Ulysses Press, 2006). Reprinted by permission.

Famous Observers

Albert Einstein (1879–1955) was introduced to Kant's *Critique of Pure Reason* and *Euclid's Elements.* In 1921 Einstein was awarded the Nobel Prize in physics "for his services to Theoretical Physics, and especially for his discovery of the law of the photoelectric effect." Einstein's research following the development of his theory of general relativity consisted of attempts to generalize his theory of gravitation in order to unify and simplify the fundamental laws of physics, particularly those of gravitation and electromagnetism.

Georgia O'Keeffe (1887–1986) was an independent-minded artist who combined natural elements with abstraction in her paintings of huge flowers, dry bones, rocks, shells, and landscapes. She was a loner who loved the quiet, wide-open spaces found in Texas and New Mexico. She had an untraditional relationship with the photographer Alfred Stieglitz.

Daniel Day-Lewis (born 1957), who won Academy Awards for Best Actor in 1989 and 2007, is quiet and introverted. He was mocked as an outsider while growing up in England. Instead of socializing, he developed a rich fantasy life, which later helped him to delve deeply into his characters. He particularly enjoys the nonverbal aspects of theater or characters who are struggling to express themselves, especially Robert De Niro's early work. Promoting films is his least favorite part of the process of filmmaking.

More examples of famous Observers: Marie Curie, Emily Dickinson, Bill Gates, Alfred Hitchcock, and Jhumpa Lahiri.

(Please note: Figuring out the career type of famous people is guesswork. Some project public personas that are different from how they behave in private life.)

What an Observer Needs on the Job

Here are key things Observers report they require to feel satisfied in their day-to-day work.

Independence

You have a laissez-faire attitude toward others and would appreciate the same attitude from them. Since you trust yourself to make your own decisions and see no reason to involve yourself in theirs, it would be logical if others likewise did not meddle in yours.

Gus liked having a classroom that was in a remote corner of the school property. "Hardly anyone went out there. When I taught learning-disabled students, the people who ran the school wished that the kids who were slow or had problems and their teachers didn't exist. The less they heard about them or were reminded of them, the better. That was a benefit to me because it kept them from intruding on my class."

With the most longevity of all the employees in his firm, Chuck has created a situation that allows him almost complete independence. "I've

Academia Nuts #2

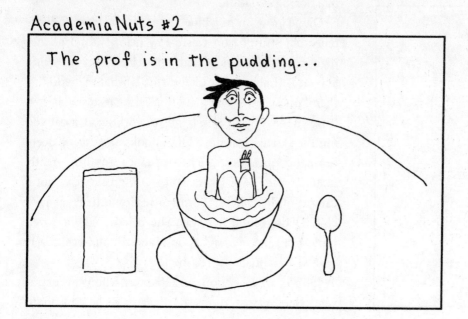

The prof is in the pudding...

had twenty different bosses who don't really know what I do, including my current one, who understands maybe 2 percent of it. Now I'm my own boss and my own motivator." Chuck's first boss after college had interviewed hundreds of applicants for the apprentice land surveyor position. Finding Chuck was "like finding a needle in a haystack," the boss said, because he needed someone with superb math skills to check his work and Chuck was by far the best. But now that Chuck's the boss, he works independently from the employees under him—and no one checks Chuck's calculations. "Being the head of the surveying crew, I'm confident dealing with large-scale risk every day; in thirty-six years I haven't made a mistake that has cost the company anything."

Intellectual Stimulation

Observers have interesting and full internal worlds and usually don't need extra stimulation from the outside. They can easily engage in work that is interesting to them. Trouble comes when they are prevented at work from being engaged at the depth they enjoy. Most of them have little patience for small talk, and they try never to be trapped in a boring situation.

Diane grew up in a blue-collar family for whom intellectual stimulation was a low priority, and all her high school friends ended up working in factories. She said, "I always felt like, if this is what the world is, then I'm on the wrong planet!" Feeling lost, she drifted from managing a punk band to working as a caterer, but she started reading a lot of books and asking deep, dramatic questions, such as, "Does anything really matter?" Her co-workers said, "Oh, great, we've got a caterer-philosopher!" Through her own internal process, Diane found her way. She discovered she loved philosophy, set her sights on Harvard, and eventually earned a graduate degree there.

John is an exception: an Observer who is an extravert. He's very studious and learns all he can about renewable energy and psychology, but he is also outgoing, which goes to show you can't tell a book by its cover. John applies what he learns intellectually to real situations, improving the air people breathe and also their emotional well-being. He has brought renewable energy to his community and state by starting weatherizing programs, creating community gardens, and landing grants to heat city buildings with solar power. "I follow through on what I do in private until I get it done," he says. "I always need something important to sink my teeth into."

So many thoughts—
so little time.

Time Alone

Observers need to ruminate on what they have observed—to assimilate information—in solitude. Psychologist Tom spreads out his client hours and structures his day to achieve this. Gus gets periods off as a teacher and goes across the street to the library to read. As a consultant, Diana has found a perfect balance between disappearing into herself while working at home and interacting with people while working in an office. "I wouldn't like being in a high-visibility managerial role where I had to interact with people eight hours every day. When work requires it, I can counter my natural tendencies and go into the office. In the meantime, I don't mind being pinged by e-mail at home."

For Jeffrey, having time alone to enjoy his hobbies in peace "is not nice or helpful—it's absolutely required." At work, he doesn't go to the water cooler or kitchen because he doesn't enjoy it. "I stay at my desk, where I'm comfortable and contribute the most." Observers don't need outside stimulation; they need the lack of unpleasant outside stimulation.

Time to Respond

Bosses receive a more considered response when they let Observers take plenty of time to figure out what they think and feel and how to express it. Kirby isn't able to accommodate his students or family members who request a swift response. He prefers a few days to think over a topic and to get all its parts into a larger panorama before he answers. "Even smaller questions, such as whether or not to have broccoli or turnip greens as the side dish, are not something I can decide right away. I have to go into a private space way down deep, and during that time I lose my ability to remain social. This is why I prefer to argue on the Internet rather than in person, even with close friends, students, or family members."

As a psychotherapist, Tom doesn't have the luxury of taking time to respond. Sometimes in a session with a client he'll say, "Give me a minute to think about that," but he can't wait beyond the hour. Actually, doing psychotherapy has helped him reduce the need for mulling over his responses.

To Be Perceived as Being Self-Directed

Observers are interested in their internal success: the sense that "I've done a good job" or "I'm really fascinated by what I'm doing." They want their security needs to be taken care of, but great wealth and prestige are usually not their primary values.

When Jaki started writing, she had a friend, also a writer, who said she had to force herself to write. Jaki said, "Don't you just love to write?" When the friend replied that she wanted to be rich and famous, Jaki was surprised. "People want to win the writing prizes," Jaki observed. "I never thought about it—I just wanted someone to pay me to write because that's what I enjoy spending my time doing.

Chuck is not materialistic. "I don't think about the money or recognition," he says. "My boss tells me, 'By law we have to pay you for extra hours worked,' but I don't even turn in overtime sheets. I just enjoy doing what I do well. My wife and I don't spend much or go to expensive restaurants; we're pretty simple. When friends ask me to help them with building projects I do it, but I don't accept money. Once a lady from church paid me four hundred dollars for helping her with her house project, but I gave the money away to Build a Miracle in Tijuana, Mexico." When he retires,

Chuck says he doesn't need recognition or a party—he'll just walk out the back door with a sense of satisfaction over a job well done.

The Other Side of Being an Observer

When the work itself is challenging, the difficulties for an Observer can be minimal. Psychotherapist Tom, for example, is his own boss and likes his work. He helps people, has time to be alone scheduled between clients, and doesn't feel beholden to anyone. When he has a client who is especially intelligent—possibly smarter than he is—he enjoys the stimulation. In a nutshell, his career works "miraculously." Here are some potential pitfalls, however, that Tom and others have experienced in other work settings.

IT CAN BE HARD:

✓ to feel awkward instead of comfortable in social situations.

✓ to be a "hothouse plant" and more sensitive than many to loud noises and too much emotion, including confrontation.

✓ to have such high standards for impeccable logic that I can get out of sorts when others seem illogical.

✓ to feel overly intruded upon.

I WORK ON:

✓ making sure I give and take in conversations and resist giving lectures on subjects I know a lot about.

✓ realizing experiences count for a lot too, not just knowledge in my head.

Difficulty Dealing with Confrontation

Observers dislike conflict and try to avoid it. However, they may enjoy an intellectual argument. What they really don't like is emotional confrontation, but if it's on an intellectual plane it can be fine.

Rather than disciplining the employees under him when they don't do a job properly, which feels too emotional to him, Chuck thinks he can do it better and quicker himself, even though it means a larger workload. He admits that avoiding confrontation is one of his primary motivations. Part of his job responsibilities as a surveyor include becoming involved in court cases where he must prove that an accident did not take place on company property or a building does not encroach on the property line. He has never made such a mistake, but an error in the calculations could result in tremendous liability. "There's always some part of it that is controversial, and I would much rather avoid the conflict."

"Deer in the Headlights" Fear

Observers specialize in having thoughts about potential threats far in the future. They do well to pay attention to what could be the source of their fears and to try to resist letting fear paralyze them. Many can be good at keeping a poker face, even while inside they feel anxious, rather like a deer that freezes when caught in the headlights. Others' anxieties can infect the Observer easily, so proximity to a nervous co-worker can be unsettling.

Jaki's main experience in life is feeling frightened. "I'm afraid of everything. I'm afraid of hurting someone's feelings, stepping on a fly. In serious situations I can usually focus and take care of myself, but when something little comes up I'm scared."

Many Observers, including Chuck, are too cautious to take chances. "In my field there's always that liability that could drive you crazy," he says. "I'm not a gambler or a risk taker at all. I hate to do things I'm not really good at, such as types of surveying that are out of my area of expertise. I stay in the areas of my profession I know well."

Jim was singing in a chorus performance and standing in the front row when someone's music dropped down beside his foot. "When we got to a series of rests, I saw that a person was on the floor. I went to take his pulse, and he didn't have one. I laid him flat and felt a pulse. We called 911, and the oratorio ended. I'm a doctor, but I dread things like that."

Hypervigilance Against Intrusion

Observers sometimes so greatly dread people's intrusions that they end up hurting people's feelings. Many have learned ways to avoid it so the actual intrusion doesn't happen very often. Chuck goes partway—letting people ask him questions without stopping what he's doing. "When I'm working on the computer and people come by to talk to me, I should stop and make eye contact. Instead I look at the computer for two seconds, up at them for one second, then back at the computer for two seconds, and so on."

When friends call Jaki and they don't pay attention when she tells them she's writing, she often does not insist on her solitude but later feels resentful. "Instead I should make strong boundaries. I get really mad at solicitors, but I should just shut the door whether their foot is in it or not."

Negative Thoughts

One reason Observers focus on the negative is that they often feel misunderstood, given that they are by nature introverts in an American society based largely on extraverted values. (The Finnish society, by contrast, is based primarily on introverted values.) Observers can be annoyed by intrusion, ignorance, and lazy thinking. Also, their busy minds examine all sides of an issue, including the dark side, and pessimism creeps in from a tendency to focus on future worries. At the extreme, Observers are contrarians. Flaubert said that when he saw a beautiful woman's face he couldn't help seeing the skull underneath. "We [Observers] don't put much store in what everyone else takes seriously," Gus says. "To me, extraverts are always busy spinning their wheels. An aversion to that pointless socializing influences our lives a lot."

Jaki often talks back with mean voices in her head, but never out loud. "I may think, 'What kind of stupid asshole are you?' Or, 'If I was stupid I'd say that too!' It's a lifetime habit of bad thoughts and comebacks. But you'd never know it. I have characters in my novels say those things instead of saying them myself. If I'm infuriated with someone who has a lot of power over me, I'll imagine them having a snake coming around their neck or something. Having an overactive imagination takes the sting out of stuff. I consider things before I really say them."

Social Discomfort

Most Observers feel uncomfortable in large groups, preferring to be with one or two friends or alone. Some are socially phobic. Gus says, "In some situations I feel comfortable. In others I don't. I liked my job for many years because I had a group of good friends, but by the time I retired from teaching, my best friends had left. I don't make new ones easily. The faculty would have deadly get-togethers where wives and husbands would come and everyone would act genteel. I didn't like those and didn't go."

Observers' problems come when they have to deal with people. Relationships that are structured, such as the doctor-patient relationship, are sometimes easier to handle. In unstructured situations, they often don't know what to do or what to talk about. Jim feels uneasy about where to sit at big dinners because he doesn't want to intrude on anyone. He only goes places where he knows people. He's planning on going to his fiftieth Yale reunion and is overwhelmed by it.

Social hour at the Joneses' —

The Wagele-Stabb Career Finder for Observers

Here are a few of the many possible areas in which you can work to assimilate information. Determining the results involves three easy steps: evaluating your strengths, selecting your dream careers from a table, and considering some practical concerns. The results are worth it! Follow the instructions below to identify your top strengths. You will then be asked to match them to career paths and to observe yourself, watching for which of them spark your greatest enthusiasm.

Try it once and see how easy it is. This test is engineered to coax your career preferences from the truest part of yourself. If you are uncertain about an answer, we suggest you stay with your first choice. Don't worry if you experience a little confusion; a certain amount frees you up to be all the more uninhibited in your choice. The key in steps 1 and 2 is *speed*.

Instructions for Using Career Tables

Step 1: My Strengths

First, read these five definitions. Rate them as they pertain to you and order your preferences in the box at the end.

Note: Any career type is capable of doing any job. The list of suggestions in the career table is not exhaustive, so we invite you to further investigate careers according to how well they use these five strengths.

Ability to Focus

To what length can you concentrate on a single activity? LO 1 2 3 4 5 HI

Complex Thinking

How do you rate your capacity to comprehend and work with complicated information?

LO 1 2 3 4 5 HI

Objectivity

How fair, impartial, and nonjudgmental can you be?   LO 1 2 3 4 5 HI

Sensitivity

How would you rate your kindness or your responsiveness to refined expressions of feelings in others?   LO 1 2 3 4 5 HI

Working Independently

To what degree are you self-directed, preferring to work on your own projects for long periods of time?   LO 1 2 3 4 5 HI

Now rank your strengths in importance from A to E, with A being your strongest trait. Write them in below, as in the example.

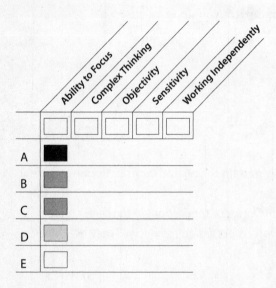

EXAMPLE

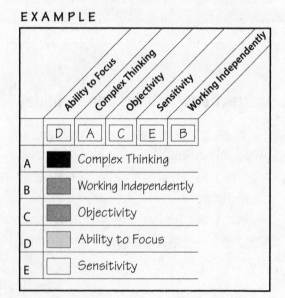

Step 2: My Favorite Career

Check the Career Tables below, starting with the ones that have the darkest-colored boxes (highest ratings) under your main strength. If you feel a special spark of excitement when you see one of the careers, write that one down. List up to four careers that most interest you:

Career _____

Career _____

Career _____

Career _____

Key: This chart shows the level at which each of the five strengths is used in each field (from the point of view of others who have held these jobs):

Exceptional	■
Significant	▨
Somewhat	▢
Minimum Requirement	□
Depends on Job	⣿

Business

	Ability to Focus	Complex Thinking	Objectivity	Sensitivity	Working Independently
Accountant (independent CPA with private customers)	medium	light	medium	white	medium
Accounting staff (corporate accounting, budget analyst, etc.) # ®	black	medium	black	white	medium
Actuary ↑	black	black	black	white	medium
Advertising specialist	light	light	light	light	light
Auditor (e.g., CPA in large accounting firm conducting audits of other companies) #	black	medium	black	white	medium
Brand manager	light	medium	medium	light	light
Business analyst (e.g., software implementation) $ # ®	black	medium	medium	light	light
CEO	medium	medium	black	light	light
Compensation and benefits manager	medium	medium	medium	light	light
Entrepreneur	medium	dotted	medium	dotted	medium
Finance & accounting executive $ ®	light	black	black	light	light
Finance staff (corporate) # ®	black	black	black	white	light
Financial advisor ↑	medium	light	medium	light	light
Financial analyst (equity research) ↑	medium	black	black	light	dotted
Investment banker/venture capitalist $	medium	black	black	dotted	light
Management analyst ↑ $ # ®	black	medium	black	white	light
Management consultant $	black	black	black	light	light
Organizational psychology consultant (to human resources dept.) $	medium	medium	medium	black	light
Product manager $ ®	light	medium	medium	light	light
Project manager $ ®	light	light	black	light	light

Business (continued)

	Ability to Focus	Complex Thinking	Objectivity	Sensitivity	Working Independently
Real-estate appraiser	light gray	light gray	medium gray	white	medium gray
Retail banker (teller, representative, etc.) #	medium gray	light gray	medium gray	medium gray	light gray
Small business owner	dotted	dotted	white	dotted	light gray
Tax preparer	black	light gray	black	white	
Web designer (user interface) $	black	light gray	medium gray		medium gray

Construction & Manufacturing

	Ability to Focus	Complex Thinking	Objectivity	Sensitivity	Working Independently
Carpenter	medium gray	white	light gray	light gray	medium gray
Logistician (operations & materials coordinator) ↑	medium gray	medium gray	medium gray	light gray	light gray
Manufacturing operations analyst	black	black	black	white	light gray

Education

	Ability to Focus	Complex Thinking	Objectivity	Sensitivity	Working Independently
Educational researcher	black	black	black	light gray	dotted
English-as-a-second-language teacher	white	light gray	medium gray	black	medium gray
Principal	white	medium gray	medium gray	black	white
Professor	black	black	medium gray	medium gray	medium gray
Teacher (K–12 #) ®; (postsecondary) ↑	white	dotted	black	black	medium gray

Government & Nonprofit

	Ability to Focus	Complex Thinking	Objectivity	Sensitivity	Working Independently
Civil service office worker	medium gray	light gray	light gray	white	light gray
Detective (police or private) ↑	medium gray	medium gray	medium gray	light gray	light gray
Forensic science technician ↑	black	light gray	medium gray	light gray	black
Government contracts administrator ®	black	white	black	white	light gray

Legend: ■ = filled (black), ▨ = dark gray, ▦ = medium gray, ░ = light gray, □ = empty (white), ⦂ = dotted

	Ability to Focus	Complex Thinking	Objectivity	Sensitivity	Working Independently
Government & Nonprofit (continued)					
Natural science manager (e.g., to advise regulatory agencies on land use, animal, medical & engineering issues) $	■	■	■	░	░
Politician (city council member, governor, mayor, representative, senator)	■	■	■	▦	□
Treasurer or comptroller $	■	▦	□	□	▦
Treasury or office of the comptroller staff	■	░	■	□	▦
Health Care					
Counselor/social worker ↑ # ®	▦	▦	▦	■	□
Doctor (especially cardiology, endocrinology, hematology, internist, medical faculty, neurology, radiology, research) $	▦	■	■	■	⦂
Hospice worker	▦	□	░	■	□
Nurse ↑ # ®	▦	▦	■	░	□
Pharmacist $ ®	▦	▦	▦	□	□
Pharmacy technician ↑	▦	░	░	□	□
Psychiatrist/psychologist ↑ $	▦	■	■	■	▦
Information Technology					
Computer systems analyst ↑ $ ®	■	■	■	□	■
Database administrator ↑ $ ®	■	■	■	□	■
Desktop support/help desk rep	░	▦	■	░	□
Information systems manager ↑ $	■	■	■	□	■
Information technology support engineer	░	■	■	░	□
Network/systems administrator ↑ $ ®	■	■	■	□	■

	Ability to Focus	Complex Thinking	Objectivity	Sensitivity	Working Independently

Information Technology (continued)

	Ability to Focus	Complex Thinking	Objectivity	Sensitivity	Working Independently
Security expert ↑	■	■	■	□	■
Software developer ↑ $ ®	■	■	■	□	■
Technology executive $ ®	▥	■	■	▥	□
Testing/quality assurance specialist ®	■	▦	■	□	■

Literature, Arts & Entertainment

	Ability to Focus	Complex Thinking	Objectivity	Sensitivity	Working Independently
Actor	▦	▥	▥	■	⠿
Architect	▦	■	■	□	▥
Art director (independent studio) $	▦	▦	□	■	■
Art director (marketing department)	▦	▦	⠿	▥	□
Art or museum curator ↑	□	▦	⠿	■	⠿
Artisan/craftsperson	▦	□	⠿	■	■
Artist (painter, photographer, sculptor, etc.)	▦	▥	⠿	■	■
Commercial artist (graphic designer, product designer, etc.)	▦	▥	▥	▥	▥
Copywriter (ads, brochures, Web sites)	▦	▥	⠿	■	⠿
Critic (books, movies, music)	▦	■	⠿	■	■
Director (plays, motion pictures, radio, TV)	▦	▦	⠿	■	⠿
Editor (copy, books, newspaper)	■	▦	⠿	■	▥
Entertainer (figure skater, magician, mime, etc.)	▦	□	⠿	■	⠿
Film editor	■	▦	⠿	■	▥
Illustrator, cartoonist	▦	⠿	⠿	⠿	■
Journalist (hard news)	■	■	■	▦	■
Journalist (human interest)	▦	▥	⠿	■	■

Literature, Arts & Entertainment (continued)

Legend: ■ = full · ▥ = partial (gray) · ⋮⋮ = dotted · □ = empty

	Ability to Focus	Complex Thinking	Objectivity	Sensitivity	Working Independently
Journalist (opinion)	▥	■	▥	▥	■
Multimedia artist or animator ↑	▥	⋮⋮	⋮⋮	⋮⋮	■
Musician (composer, conductor)	■	■	□	■	⋮⋮
Musician (instrumentalist, vocalist)	■	▥	□	■	⋮⋮
Photographer (professional: ads, events, photojournalism, portraits, weddings)	■	▥	⋮⋮	■	⋮⋮
Technical writer ↑	■	■	■	□	■
Writer (lyrics, nonfiction, novels, poems, scripts)	■	■	⋮⋮	■	■

Math, Engineering & Science in Industry

	Ability to Focus	Complex Thinking	Objectivity	Sensitivity	Working Independently
Mathematician	■	■	■	□	■
Engineer					
Aerospace engineer $	■	■	■	▥	■
Biomedical engineer ↑ $	■	■	■	▥	■
Electrical engineer $ ®	■	■	■	▥	■
Environmental engineer ↑ ®	■	■	■	▥	■
Mechanical engineer ®	■	■	■	▥	■
Product safety engineer	■	■	■	▥	■
Scientist					
Astronomer $	■	■	■	□	▥
Biologist	■	■	■	□	▥
Chemist	■	■	■	□	▥
Environmental scientist ↑ ®	■	■	■	□	▥

Math, Engineering & Science in Industry (continued)

	Ability to Focus	Complex Thinking	Objectivity	Sensitivity	Working Independently
Epidemiologist	black	black	black	white	dotted
Manager of research dept. (e.g., mentor young scientists and do PR for funding) $	black	black	black	medium gray	medium gray
Materials scientist & engineer (e.g., nanotechnology)	black	black	black	white	medium gray
Physicist $	black	black	black	white	medium gray
Social scientist	black	black	black	light gray	dotted

Service Industry

	Ability to Focus	Complex Thinking	Objectivity	Sensitivity	Working Independently
Horticulturist (gardener)	light gray	light gray	dotted	light gray	black
Insurance adjuster	medium gray	light gray	black	light gray	light gray
Store or restaurant manager #	medium gray	medium gray	dotted	light gray	medium gray

Spiritual Field

	Ability to Focus	Complex Thinking	Objectivity	Sensitivity	Working Independently
Meditation or yoga teacher	black	white	white	black	white
Monk, nun, yogi	medium gray	white	white	black	dotted
Religious leader (chaplain, imam, pastor, priest, rabbi, etc.) ®	medium gray	medium gray	medium gray	black	white

Uniformed Professions

	Ability to Focus	Complex Thinking	Objectivity	Sensitivity	Working Independently
Commanding officer	light gray	light gray	medium gray	medium gray	white
Engineering school instructor	medium gray	medium gray	medium gray	medium gray	white
Military intelligence analyst	light gray	black	medium gray	white	medium gray
National Security Agency code breaker	medium gray	black	white	medium gray	dotted
Naval submarine officer	medium gray	medium gray	medium gray	light gray	white

Uniformed Professions (continued)

	Ability to Focus	Complex Thinking	Objectivity	Sensitivity	Working Independently
Pilot (airline, co-pilot, flight engineer) $	■	▩	□	□	□
Postal worker (USPS, military, etc.)	□	□	□	▩	■
Technician (electronics, shipboard oil lab, etc.)	▩	□	▩	□	■

Other Fields

	Ability to Focus	Complex Thinking	Objectivity	Sensitivity	Working Independently
Air traffic controller $	■	■	■	□	□
Athlete	■	▩	▩	⊡	⊡
Athletic coach	■	⊡	▩	▩	□
Coach (career, executive, life)	▩	▩	▩	■	□
Environmental science & protection technician ↑ ®	■	▩	▩	□	▩
Interpreter or translator ↑	■	■	■	■	▩
Inventor	■	⊡	⊡	⊡	■
Judge $	■	■	■	□	□
Lawyer (constitutional) $	■	■	■	□	▩
Lawyer (corporate, patent) $	■	■	■	□	■
Lawyer (tax, wills, trust) $	■	■	■	▩	▩
Librarian	▩	▩	▩	▩	⊡
Maintenance & repair worker # ®	■	□	▩	□	▩
Mechanic (airplane, car, motorboat, ocean liner)	■	■	▩	□	▩
Sound & lighting engineering technician	■	▩	▩	▩	▩
Stay-at-home parent	▩	▩	▩	■	⊡
Surveyor ↑	■	■	■	□	▩
Transportation inspector	■	▩	▩	□	▩

Step 3: Practical Considerations

After you've gone through the tables, note whether your favorite career fields match your needs for pay and security by checking for the following symbols in the Career Tables:

↑ = **Predicted Future Growth Area for Jobs**

$ = **High Pay**

= **Large Number of Present Openings**

® = **Recession-proof**

For more career ideas for the Observer,
see the recommended lists for the
Romantic and the Questioner.

CHAPTER SIX

The Questioner

Reducing Risk

I F YOU ARE the sixth career type, your *safety* is of utmost importance, so you are in the habit of *analyzing* situations. You probe for weaknesses in systems and potential dangers to yourself or others. You look for legal liability, a defect in a design, a bug in software, a disorder in a personality. Of all the career types, you feel fear the most palpably and frequently, so you formulate *worst-case scenarios* to plan how you would handle threats before they arise.

Questioners are often difficult to identify as a career type. The same person can behave in two opposite ways, which are both responses to fear: phobic (behaving timidly and showing their fear) and counterphobic (behaving assertively or going against their fear). These may be manifest in *fight-or-flight* reactions to threats. In the "flight" or *phobic* style, the person appears unsure or worried and may double-check with others for certainty. Comedian and filmmaker Woody Allen represents this style when he asks endless questions and has a fretful expression on his face. The "fight" or *counterphobic* style is an effort to be perceived as strong and to scare off any-

Chris the chrysalis was timid, like a cautious Questioner. He wanted to be sure he would be as protected as a butterfly as he had been in his previous cocooned existence. But once out in the world, Chris was brave and showed the predators he was tough.

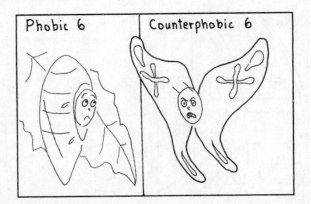

one who has bad intentions. President George W. Bush represented this style when he took a strong stance after the September 11 attacks on the World Trade Center and said, "You're either with us or against us." In counterphobic mode, Questioners may become overly aggressive in order to cover up their underlying sense of *uncertainty* or anxiety. While Questioners often present one of these personas and try to hide the other, sometimes they vacillate back and forth between the two.

Getting to Know Yourself

You like examining things from many angles, and you look for the truth—perhaps in the form of science. You may be both drawn to and repelled by authority—the authority within and outside yourself.

Some Questioners make sure those in power do not abuse it while others are eager to cooperate with authority. You can be a good team player when you feel safe under the protection of a strong leader. You have strong *investigative* capabilities, have a reputation for *loyalty* and *dependability,* are alert and *energetic,* and are often known for your *wit.*

You may lean toward the career types on each side of yours, which are called your wings. Questioners who are more influenced by the Observer type tend to be more reserved and introverted; Questioners who lean toward their Adventurer wing are often outgoing.

Strengths Questioners Bring to the Workplace

As a Questioner, you are highly valued by bosses, co-workers, and clients for your *dedication.* Some of you display *compassion* while others have more *analytical skills;* some stand out in the organization for your *common sense* about the here and now while others have valuable *intuition* about future ventures.

Being Exact

Thanks to being careful, you're more likely to get that promotion, deal, or partner and less likely to get a heart attack.

Dominic, a pitcher, is so exacting he is the team's best closer. In contrast to many of his teammates, who relish competition, Dominic works hard because he's motivated primarily by the *fear of losing*. You can imagine what went into developing his skills—hitting targets over and over and over with a baseball.

The same internal voice that helped him get good grades in school shouted in his ear with every throw of the ball: "Hit the bull's-eye! Failing would be a disaster."

To design the safest roller-coaster ride in the world, hire a careful Questioner as the engineer. Growing up, Michael trusted the power of his own rational thought and the scientific method, dedicating years to one of the most exacting engineering majors available at a top university. Literally a rocket scientist, he completed a PhD at a young age and worked in the defense industry for a few years. Still young, he courageously left his safe employee position to co-found an engineering consulting firm. One year an accident occurred on the Space Mountain roller-coaster at Disneyland, injuring nine passengers, and he was awarded the contract and redesigned the ride. He raised the bar for being exact in the system design. Through extensive tests and analysis, Michael determined the root cause of the problem and made the ride safer. He also helped Disneyland minimize costs and ride downtime.

Skepticism

Skepticism, an ingredient in Questioners' DNA, is an asset in many work situations. It's essential for getting at the truth of something, whether in an audit, in the courtroom, or in a lunch-break discussion.

Things that are not visible to the naked eye fascinated Roger. He wanted to be either an astronomer or a physicist. Now he's working in the field of nanotechnology: controlling matter on an atomic or molecular

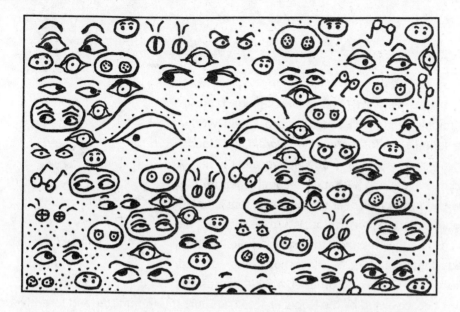

scale. That he's especially concerned about the environmental impact of nanomaterials suits his skeptical personality. It is known that when silver nanoparticles are used in socks to reduce foot odor, they can end up destroying helpful bacteria in waste treatment plants. A study of rats showed that nanoparticles settled in their brains and lungs, increasing biomarkers for inflammation and stress responses. Even some lipsticks may contain toxic nanoparticles! So Roger is combining his skepticism with his knowledge of science to investigate nanoparticle products' safety. Had he chosen astronomy, would he be analyzing every unidentified piece of space matter to see if it were an asteroid heading our way?

Greta, an artist and wildlife activist, has devoted much of her life to protecting endangered wolves by fighting gun and hunting lobbyists. She's skeptical about whether the factors endangering wolves in America will ever be adequately addressed, but she perseveres anyway. "Important environmental issues get pushed to the background when the government and news media focus the public's attention on other pressing issues. Due to a recent delisting of wolves as endangered species and other new laws, hunters are killing them in large numbers again. We keep suing the agencies and winning. But if we lose future cases, wolves will be killed again."

Famous Questioners

Yusuf Islam, aka Cat Stevens (born 1948), is a rock megastar from the 1970s loved for his thoughtful songs such as "Wild World," "Trouble," and the sound track for the cult film *Harold and Maude*. He exudes nervousness typical of many Questioner career types.

As a rock musician, Stevens had hesitations about his stardom. In 1976 he nearly drowned and, while near death, prayed that if his life was spared he would devote his life to God. When he survived, he became a Muslim and changed his name to Yusuf Islam. For twenty-five years he raised a family, founded Muslim schools, and donated music proceeds to help orphans and other charitable causes. He was given the Man of Peace award by the Nobel Peace Prize Laureates Committee and recently has reappeared on the music scene, using his fame to fuel humanitarian relief work.

Erin Brockovich (born 1960) is a legal clerk and environmental activist who, with no formal law school education, was instrumental in bringing a case against the Pacific Gas and Electric Company (PG&E) of California in 1993. An unemployed single mother of three, she was working as a file clerk when she ran across some files on a pro bono case involving PG&E and discovered a systematic cover-up of the industrial poisoning of a community's water supply. Through her persistence, PG&E was eventually found responsible for the pollution and brought to justice. This was portrayed in the Hollywood movie *Erin Brockovich*.

Loyalty

Questioners are often loyal members of the military, unions, law enforcement, and charitable and political groups with a high level of commitment to the group's goals. Their sense of duty and service makes them dependable work partners.

Chase will do anything for his boss and has let him know in many ways that he can be trusted to work with the company's books and bank accounts. As long as Rose's housecleaning clients treat her with respect, keep

Robert Kennedy (1925–1968) was one of U.S. president John F. Kennedy's younger brothers and his advisor, including during the Cuban Missile Crisis. He also contributed to the American civil rights movement. As attorney general, Kennedy pursued Teamsters president Jimmy Hoffa

on account of Hoffa's corruption in financial and electoral actions. After John F. Kennedy was assassinated in late 1963, "Bobby" continued as attorney general under President Johnson for nine months. He was elected to the Senate from New York and broke with Johnson over the Vietnam War, among other issues. Kennedy announced his own campaign to run for the nomination of the Democratic Party for president in 1968. He was committed to social justice, especially racial equality, in his presidential campaign. Kennedy defeated Eugene McCarthy in the California primary but was shot and killed shortly afterward.

More examples of famous Questioners: Sigmund Freud, Dustin Hoffman, Spike Lee, Richard M. Nixon, Kristin Scott-Thomas. (See also many famous comedians under "Wit," page 162.)

(Please note: Figuring out the career type of famous people is guesswork. Some project public personas that are different from how they behave in private life.)

their schedules, and pay her on time, she will be loyal. "I'll clean up the most challenging messes they leave for me, including barf on the wall. But if someone is rude, critical, or mean and doesn't appreciate my efforts, I won't work there anymore."

When Olivia was a director of product strategy, she stayed on even through her company's multiple reorganizations. At first she had reported to vice presidents, but later she reported to directors who were barely senior to her and finally to a woman at the same grade level. She was careful not to become insubordinate to her colleague. "I was loyal, made the best of what I was given, and found something to do that excited me."

Catherine pursued a PhD in social welfare out of loyalty to the New York City welfare system, which gave her and her disabled single mother support when they were poor. She wanted to serve communities like the one she grew up in. "Working for the government and applying public funds to public problems was my ideal." So Catherine has felt fulfilled working hard for years on a modest salary to distribute government funds to help at-risk children.

Problem Solving

Many Questioners have a skill similar to many Observers, which is to excel at reviewing and making sense of large amounts of complex information. Olivia, a director of product strategy, created a detailed five-year road map for her company, identifying all the technology systems and operational processes they needed to fix within their $400 million budget. "I led a cross-departmental committee to identify the top ten 'pains' in our operations and systems. Then the e-business department and information technology (IT) department had a heated debate about whether we should

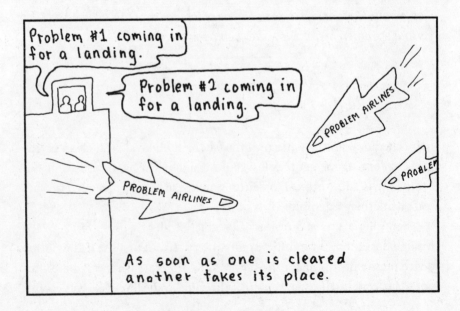

build or buy the key technology solution. My job was to identify the best path and lead the company to a consensus. Since the scales were dead even, I looked for the raindrop that would tip one side. It was torturous trying to decide between giving IT meaningful work developing the software and [giving the company] the hard business advantage of speed-to-market by buying it. I made the business decision to buy based on my analysis that our company had neither the resource capacity nor adequate technical skill sets to build."

Jennifer is an interaction designer for the investment Web site of a major bank. "I take complex banking concepts and make them easy to use and understand, problem-solving within the constraints of usability, technical, and business considerations. English isn't the first language for many of our fifteen million customers, and it's hard to come up with Web page layouts of account details that work for every financial portfolio composition. The medium I'm working in now is the Internet, but interaction design is applicable for interior design, architecture, software design, editing a book, designing a remote control, drafting, and so on. I used it to design the house I live in. I'm going to use interaction design when I get a PhD in library science too, solving problems in researching for information."

Protectiveness

You might think a phobic Questioner would need a counterphobic persona to scare people away, but phobic Questioners can think of creative ways to protect themselves. They just might not come out and challenge someone to a fistfight.

Adrianna, an attorney, fights hard for women's rights. She provided legal advice to battered women and helped them keep their jobs when domestic problems caused absences from work. Her friends joked that in those days she scared a lot 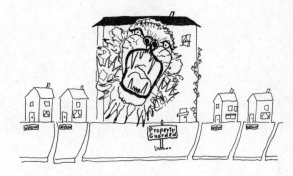 of nice men off on the first date by saying, "Don't try anything with me because I legally represent battered women!" At the Legal Defense and

Education Fund of the National Organization for Women she worked on a Supreme Court case fighting immigration laws that discriminated based on gender. Despite the fact that she felt she sold out for a few years when she left nonprofit work to help defendants on Wall Street in white-collar cases, she did take care of her own security needs, buying herself a condo and building up her retirement account. After her short stint in the for-profit world, Adrianna studied international law in Geneva to expand her expertise to all types of human rights and volunteered to represent a prisoner held at Guantánamo Bay.

Wit

Many famous comedians are or have been Questioners (Jason Alexander, Woody Allen, Lewis Black, Albert Brooks, George Carlin, Billy Crystal, Rodney Dangerfield, Larry David, Ellen DeGeneres, David Letterman, Richard Lewis, Gilda Radner, Don Rickles, Chris Rock), and it's no wonder. Good Questioners need to have their finger on the pulse of their audience in order to know what will make them laugh. This skill is connected both to watching for dangerous situations and to making friends.

The creative spark individual Questioners bring to the world of entertainment also comes from finding ways to cope with fear and anger and liking to thumb their noses at authority. Other sources of humor include having the ability to combine incongruous situations and to see past phoniness and point to a truth most of us haven't perceived, as does Jon Stewart.

What a Questioner Needs on the Job

Here are key things Questioners report they require to feel satisfied in their day-to-day work.

Certainty

While some career types might want spontaneity or unpredictability built into their workday, Questioners, especially those of you who tend to be phobic, need to know what lurks around the corner before you venture out. Too many possibilities leave you wondering which one is the surest thing. Your active mind can go off course speculating about anything that is unspoken, confusing, or smacks of manipulation.

Jennifer is conservative when it comes to finances. "I'm not a risk taker. I fell into the work I do [interaction design] rather than take chances that may have brought me more enjoyment or financial success. I stayed in a stable job and like to plan for my goals and future promotions. I'm creative by finding clever ways to work within the rules and structure. When I burned out on the med school track, I entered the dot-com field when jobs and money were plentiful. I left my job because I made so much money being a dot-com person I thought I would never have to work again. That didn't make me happy, though, because work gives me the structure I need. My finances changed too, and I had to get another job anyway. Now I'm going to get an advanced degree in library science online, which should bring in even more money. I'll keep my present job while getting my degree to be safe."

Monty loves the certainty he gets when people are direct with him. "If you don't like me, say so. Nothing drives me crazier than someone who sits back and says nothing; I don't know whether they're for or against me or whom I'm dealing with. My boss is like that sometimes—so quiet, it's torture. Sometimes I'll just out-and-out ask, 'What are you *thinking?*' because I can't take not knowing any longer."

Fighting for a Cause

You understand what it's like to feel vulnerable, so some of you are attracted to careers in which you protect the underdog or do relief work. If your career is unrelated to a cause, you might participate in similarly gratifying activities in your free time.

After Greta graduated from a design school, she earned her living as an artist, teaching in New York City and working at the Metropolitan Museum of Art, but she felt undirected about her career. Learning about the plight of the wolves, however, gave her focus. She always felt close to animals, especially all kinds of dogs, and kept a file on them. "After college I picked up a book about wolves and went on my lunch hour to see one." Soon she connected with activists, took a leave of absence, and drove to remote Minnesota, where wolves were most in danger, to help the North American Predator Conservation group create a program to defend wildlife.

Rose had been interested in nature—backpacking, canoeing, and hiking—since high school. She volunteered at a drop-off recycling center in the late sixties, long before curbside pickups. Then she moved to the woods of northern California, where there was more dirt than cement. Opposing wasteful consumerism, she worked in health food stores, lived on a shoestring, built a cabin of recycled materials, cooked on a wood stove, and lived off the grid. Eventually she started a housecleaning business for a living but did not feel well at the end of the day after using standard toxic cleaning products. So she eliminated bleach, ammonia, and other caustic chemicals. Now she has a cleaning company known for using green and eco-friendly solutions, reducing poisons to humans, other living beings, and the earth.

Intellectual and Physical Stimulation

Your nervous system needs a way to discharge energy, both physically and mentally, so avoid taking jobs where you might be expected to look busy when you have nothing to do. You thrive in careers that keep you challenged and active.

Jennifer's co-workers are bright, so she's always being pushed and challenged by them. "It's exhausting! But that's also why I'm happy there." She rides her bike to work, takes walks during her breaks, and rushes around in the large building she works in. "I really need that because of my abundant energy. At my last job I didn't have physical outlets, and I felt stunted. I'm an extravert and the main person in my group who plans social activities. My job fulfills a lot of needs beyond financial."

After years as a stay-at-home mom, Karla was bored. "I was excited to get a job in medical billing. When my first assignment was too easy, I requested a more difficult one. I followed my curiosity and read through accounts to figure out what happens to patients, for example, those with brain damage. I don't mean to sound morbid. Finding the causes—and the social work side of it—fascinates me. Some people might think I'm weird, but my passion is figuring out how killers think. I read true-crime books and watch at least one forensic case a day on TV. Accounts of serial killers don't scare me. I don't think, 'That could happen to me.' Instead, it's stimulating to try to figure out how and why they could do such things. For example, Jeffrey Dahmer, the serial killer, had a normal childhood, so I wonder, 'Was he born that way?'"

Physical Security

In physician Oliver Sacks's book *Musicophilia,* he says, "The brain needed to stay incessantly active. . . ." This may be more true with Questioners than with any other type and may explain why this type is more prone to panicking when there is a lack of activity.

At meetings, Cromwell prefers to sit with his back to the wall. "That way I'm sure no one can sneak up behind me." Elsie adds, "I'd never work where I had to have an office above the fourth floor. It's about being able to escape in case of a fire." Laura feels secure when she wears clothes to work that are sexy and attract compliments. She explains her logic: "If people notice me, it guarantees they won't leave me out if something dreadful happens, like a disaster. I need to be taken care of. Will I be saved?

Unfortunately, I've been given warnings by my boss four times that my dress is too low in front or not long enough at the hem."

When Rose cleans houses, she wants to be told if anyone in the household is sick so she can reschedule or take precautions. She often wears latex gloves to protect herself from germs in the daily exposure of cleaning homes. Precariously balanced objects or faulty electrical wiring aren't good either. Once some clients let their large pit bulls put their jaws with sharp teeth around her arm. She was upset that the owners wouldn't put the dogs in another room, so she quit that job.

Reassurance

When danger is present, if you can't scare it away you might decide to run. Another option is to have someone you trust—better yet a whole army of people you can trust—protect you and reassure you that all is well.

Bret, a structural engineer, says he feels suspicious whenever he deals with corporate clients and receives little support from his boss, the president of the firm, a tough, imposing man who often talks to him in an accusatory way. But recently that changed. "My job on one project, which involved coordinating ten different sets of drawings, was to tell the big corporate client what wasn't working. My lack of confidence set in, and I had trouble getting started. My project manager sensed the delay and reassured me that I am good at finding the critical flaws in drawings. My boss acknowledged the work was mind-bending and sent an e-mail to the client saying we needed another day to finish the work. With this support and reassurance, relating to business people no longer seemed like such a hurdle."

Bahubali is concerned about his financial security, so he monitors his investment accounts online daily. "When the economy was strong, I kept double-checking with my financial advisor to ensure they were all FDIC insured. She probably thought I was paranoid. Later during the major economic downturn, I was redeemed when the unimaginable happened—

household names like Lehman Brothers going out of business. I told her, 'However much I used to check on my accounts, I was right to do so!'"

The Other Side of Being a Questioner

As you contemplate your own career, keep in mind these areas where Questioners typically struggle.

IT CAN BE HARD:

✓ to feel anxious and to have fears, such as the fear of public speaking.

✓ to get into trouble because I said something sarcastic or otherwise showed my anger inappropriately.

✓ to be too cautious and hesitant.

✓ to do just the opposite and jump in recklessly, trying to prove I'm not afraid.

I WORK ON:

✓ not automatically taking the devil's advocate position or arguing too much.

✓ keeping my pessimistic thoughts to myself.

✓ thinking about what I'm about to say before I blurt out something I'll regret.

✓ not blaming others when I make a mistake or am criticized.

✓ my habit of trying to control *everything*.

Anxiety

Even though thinking through potential risks to a large-scale software project is Olivia's job description in product strategy and one of her top skills, thinking of too many worst-case scenarios can immobilize her. She keeps extensive resource spreadsheets and five-hundred-page functional specifications. She prepares for everything so that nothing can knock her over, but it doesn't always work. Obsessing over so much information can lead to "analysis paralysis," so when it's time to take certain business risks, her efficient Achiever boss lets her know it's okay to take action.

Public speaking makes Karla nervous, so instead of getting up in front of the class in school, she tells the teacher to give her an F. Eduardo's angst comes up every year before the annual conference. "Two days before I speak to a thousand people, my anxiety eats me up in a thousand different ways. I feel as though I'm going through a meat grinder. But once I'm there, an inner peace comes over me and I begin to feel courageous."

Authority Issues

Some of you are fearful of the higher-ups at work while others have an antiauthoritarian attitude and are eager to buck the system. Many of you feel both of these things at the same time. You might think you could do a better job at leading, but you don't want to be a target either.

Olivia is a bit subservient. When any of her superiors asks her a question, if she doesn't have the answer she feels herself going into a panic. Monty admits, "Anyone who makes it to the top or has power can set me off." He used to argue with his boss until one day he realized that he wanted to be the authority. He was blaming his boss for being in charge because he wasn't in charge himself.

Asma gets tense when setting up paleontology exhibits at the university. He has a love-hate relationship with the museum director, and when he gets nervous, he raises his voice and goes on the attack. Then he feels guilty and is afraid the director is angry with him, so he disappears for a while.

Questioners sometimes feel uncomfortable being the authority. When it comes to communicating about his research to others, Eduardo says he likes to "play second fiddle" to his research partner. "But now my partner is taking time off, and I'm in the limelight. When I am the authority, I feel as though there's a bulls-eye on my back and people will shoot arrows at me." Catherine feels uncomfortable with the limelight too. Her natural inclination at fund-raising events is to hang out modestly at a side table. However, because she represents the charity's largest donor, she recognizes that her presence is important to the attendees. She forces herself to get on the microphone to say how proud her organization is of them.

Doubt

Eduardo often feels uncomfortable forming an opinion on an issue because he knows it's not possible to build a watertight case. "If I stick my neck out with certainty about my position on the matter, my mind will prepare for an onslaught of attacks against it. When everyone is going around the table giving ideas, if I have something original to say and they put me on the spot, I tell them I'll go second. I'd rather bolster someone else's ideas than expose myself first. I also don't want to be the one to step forward and say, 'You're not getting it right,' because what if *I'm* not right? When I finally do jump into the debate I get an adrenaline rush."

Jennifer says she often doubts others. "In a lot of ways I'm trusting of people I have a good impression of, but sometimes I worry that people are talking about me behind my back."

Bret has always doubted his interview skills. "Thank goodness I landed my job after only two interviews. I'm so shy that going through many interviews would have been a nightmare." When Karla decided to go back to work after ten years as a stay-at-home mom, she doubted anyone would want to hire her. "I was a nervous wreck when I finally drove to potential jobs to inquire whether they were hiring. I'd sit in the car fighting myself about whether to walk in to request an application. My résumé embarrassed me; I imagined employers thinking to themselves, 'Oh, yeah, she stayed home doing nothing for ten years.' Since I had worked in a doctor's office and dealt with medical insurance I could take advantage of a friend's help to get me my current job in that field."

Testiness

Oscar Levant (1906–1972) either was witty or had a big mouth, depending on your perspective. He once said to his friend George Gershwin, "Tell me, if you had it to do over, would you fall in love with yourself again?" Levant was a Questioner movie actor, pianist, and composer who appeared on his own radio show and quiz shows and suffered from real and imagined illnesses, stage fright, and an active mind that combined wit with inflammatory remarks. Levant was quoted as saying, "I once said cynically of a politician, 'He'll double-cross that bridge when he comes to it,'" and "Once I make up my mind, I'm full of indecision."

Olivia describes what she feels inside when she acts testy at work: "You know how they say that if a car lands on top of her child, a 5'2", one-hundred-pound mother will be able to lift the car powered by her adrenaline and fear? Well, in a business environment, when someone speaks to me in a way that I perceive as threatening, the same kind of adrenaline rush occurs in me. I could get fired, but otherwise it's not life threatening!"

Vacillation

In Karla's performance review, her boss said she should make more confident decisions. "There's no handbook on billing patients, so I review each situation and decide whether I should bill Medicaid or the patient or just write the whole thing off. Then I worry I'll get in trouble, and I second-guess myself. I walk to my boss's desk and go over the details of the case with her, asking if I should have chosen a different path. Typically my boss responds, 'Well, what do *you* think?'"

Jennifer makes a decision immediately and sticks to it while trying to discern internally if she's right or not. Olivia says she got gray hairs while trying to make the decision for the e-business group on whether to buy or build the new software. "It should have taken no more than a week to analyze. Instead, it took us four months, and another two months to argue about it. I want to take in all the information and understand everyone's point of view. It's torturous."

The Wagele-Stabb Career Finder for Questioners

Here are a few of the many possible areas in which you can work to reduce risk. Determining the results involves three easy steps: evaluating your strengths, selecting your dream careers from a table, and considering some practical concerns. The results are worth it! Follow the instructions below to identify your top strengths. You will then be asked to match them to career paths and to observe yourself, watching for which of them spark your greatest enthusiasm.

Try it once and see how easy it is. This test is engineered to coax your career preferences from the truest part of yourself. If you are uncertain about an answer, we suggest you stay with your first choice. Don't worry if you experience a little confusion; a certain amount frees you up to be all the more uninhibited in your choice. The key in steps 1 and 2 is *speed*.

Instructions for Using Career Tables

Step 1: My Strengths

First, read these five definitions. Rate them as they pertain to you and order your preferences in the box at the end.

Note: Any career type is capable of doing any job. The list of suggestions in the career tables is not exhaustive, so we invite you to further investigate careers according to how well they use these five strengths.

Critical Thinking

How skilled are you in perceiving and carefully judging all aspects of difficult questions or problems you are working out?   **LO   1   2   3   4   5   HI**

Exactness

How do you rate your preference for being detail oriented and/or meticulous?

LO 1 2 3 4 5 HI

Identifying with Others

To what degree can you put yourself in the place of other people?

LO 1 2 3 4 5 HI

Skepticism

To what degree do you have a doubting or questioning mind?   LO 1 2 3 4 5 HI

Taking Precautions

How watchful and proactive are you when it comes to avoiding possible injuries, losses, or mistakes?   LO 1 2 3 4 5 HI

Now rank your strengths in importance from A to E, with A being your strongest trait. Write them in below, as in the example.

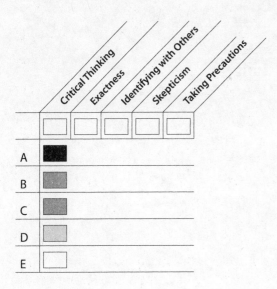

EXAMPLE

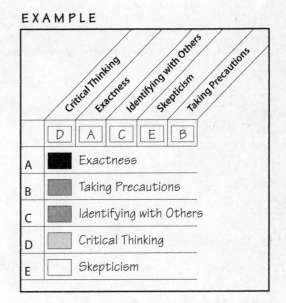

Step 2: My Favorite Career

Check the Career Tables below, starting with the ones that have the darkest-colored boxes (highest ratings) under your main strength. If you feel a special spark of excitement when you see one of the careers, write that one down. List up to four careers that most interest you:

Career _____

Career _____

Career _____

Career _____

Key: This chart shows the level at which each of the five strengths is used in each field (from the point of view of others who have held these jobs):

Exceptional	■
Significant	■
Somewhat	■
Minimum Requirement	□
Depends on Job	⊞

Business

	Critical Thinking	Exactness	Identifying with Others	Skepticism	Taking Precautions
Accountant (independent CPA with private customers)	light gray	black	white	gray	gray
Accounting staff (corporate accounting, budget analyst, etc.) # ®	light gray	gray	white	black	black
Actuary ↑	black	black	white	gray	black
Administrative assistant (entry level) # ®	white	gray	light gray	white	dotted
Administrative executive secretary # ®	light gray	gray	light gray	light gray	light gray
Advertising specialist	light gray	gray	gray	white	light gray
Auditor (e.g., CPA in large accounting firm conducting audits of other companies) #	light gray	black	white	black	black
Brand manager	gray	gray	gray	gray	light gray
Business analyst (e.g., software implementation) $ # ®	gray	black	light gray	gray	light gray
Buyer (wholesale, retail)	gray	black	light gray	gray	gray
CEO	black	gray	black	gray	gray
Compliance officer (e.g., brokerage, health care) $	white	black	white	light gray	black
Customer support rep # ®	light gray	light gray	black	light gray	dotted
Entrepreneur	black	dotted	dotted	gray	black
Finance & accounting executive $ ®	black	black	gray	black	black
Finance staff (corporate) # ®	gray	black	light gray	black	gray
Financial advisor ↑	gray	gray	black	light gray	black
Financial analyst (equity research) ↑	black	black	gray	black	black
Human resources manager	gray	light gray	black	light gray	black
Investment banker/venture capitalist $	black	black	gray	black	black
Management analyst ↑ $ # ®	gray	black	light gray	black	light gray

	Critical Thinking	Exactness	Identifying with Others	Skepticism	Taking Precautions
Business (continued)					
Management consultant $	black	dark gray	medium gray	black	light gray
Marketing manager $	medium gray	medium gray	black	light gray	light gray
Product manager $ ®	medium gray	medium gray	black	medium gray	medium gray
Project manager $ ®	light gray	medium gray	medium gray	medium gray	black
Real-estate broker or agent	medium gray	medium gray	medium gray	medium gray	medium gray
Recruiter ®	light gray	light gray	black	medium gray	medium gray
Retail banker (teller, representative, etc.) #	white	black	medium gray	medium gray	black
Sales executive $ ®	light gray	light gray	black	light gray	light gray
Sales representative/business development manager # ®	light gray	light gray	black	light gray	light gray
Small business owner	medium gray	medium gray	black	medium gray	black
Tax preparer	light gray	black	light gray	medium gray	black
Web designer (user interface) $	black	medium gray	medium gray	medium gray	medium gray
Construction & Manufacturing					
Carpenter (finish woodworker)	light gray	black	white	white	light gray
Carpenter (general construction) #	light gray	medium gray	white	white	medium gray
Construction manager	light gray	light gray	light gray	white	black
General contractor	medium gray	light gray	light gray	medium gray	black
Manufacturing operations analyst	black	black	black	white	light gray
Education					
Educational researcher	black	medium gray	light gray	black	light gray
Principal	medium gray	medium gray	black	medium gray	medium gray

	Critical Thinking	Exactness	Identifying with Others	Skepticism	Taking Precautions
Education (continued)					
Professor	black	dotted	gray	black	dotted
School counselor	gray	white	black	light gray	gray
Teacher (K–12 #) ®; (postsecondary) ↑	gray	dotted	black	light gray	light gray
Government & Nonprofit					
Administrative services manager	gray	gray	gray	light gray	light gray
Civil service office worker	white	gray	white	white	light gray
Consumer rights advocate	black	light gray	black	black	black
Detective (police or private) ↑	black	black	white	black	gray
Investigator	black	black	black	black	black
Judge $	black	black	white	black	black
Paralegal ↑	gray	black	light gray	gray	black
Politician (city council member, governor, mayor, representative, senator)	black	light gray	black	light gray	light gray
Social & human services assistant ↑ ®	light gray	light gray	black	light gray	light gray
Union organizer	gray	light gray	black	black	black
Health Care					
Clinical laboratory technician	gray	gray	white	gray	black
Counselor/social worker ↑ # ®	gray	light gray	black	light gray	gray
Dental hygienist ↑ ®	light gray	black	light gray	light gray	black
Doctor (especially anesthesia, GP, ob-gyn, neurology, pediatrics, public health, medical faculty, neurology, radiology, research, surgery) $	black	black	black	black	black

Health Care (continued)

	Critical Thinking	Exactness	Identifying with Others	Skepticism	Taking Precautions
Health services manager	■	▒	▒	▒	▒
Nurse ↑ # ®	▒	■	■	░	■
Pharmacist $ ®	■	■	□	▒	■
Pharmacy technician ↑	▒	■	░	░	■
Physical therapist ↑ ®	▒	▒	■	░	▒
Psychiatrist/psychologist ↑ $	■	░	■	▒	■
Veterinarian ↑ ®	■	■	■	■	■

Information Technology

	Critical Thinking	Exactness	Identifying with Others	Skepticism	Taking Precautions
Computer systems analyst ↑ $ ®	■	▒	░	▒	▒
Database administrator ↑ $ ®	■	▒	□	▒	▒
Desktop support/help desk rep	■	▒	▒	▒	▒
Information systems manager ↑ $	■	▒	▒	▒	▒
Information technology support engineer	■	▒	▒	▒	▒
Network/systems administrator ↑ $ ®	■	▒	□	▒	▒
Security expert ↑	■	▒	□	▒	▒
Software developer ↑ $ ®	■	▒	⠿	▒	▒
Technology executive $ ®	■	▒	▒	▒	▒
Testing/quality assurance specialist ®	■	▒	□	▒	▒

Literature, Arts & Entertainment

	Critical Thinking	Exactness	Identifying with Others	Skepticism	Taking Precautions
Actor	■	▒	■	□	░
Agent (for artists and performers)	▒	▒	▒	■	■

Literature, Arts & Entertainment (continued)

	Critical Thinking	Exactness	Identifying with Others	Skepticism	Taking Precautions
Architect	medium	light	black	light	light
Artist (painter, photographer, sculptor, etc.)	black	dotted	dotted	white	white
Art director (marketing dept. or independent studio) $	medium	medium	medium	dotted	
Art or museum curator ↑	light	light	medium	dotted	
Comedian	black	dotted	black	black	dotted
Commercial artist (graphic designer, product designer, etc.)	medium	black	medium	light	medium
Copywriter (ads, brochures, Web sites)	black	medium	black	dotted	light
Critic (books, movies, music)	black	medium	black	black	
Director (plays, motion pictures, radio, TV)	black	medium	black	dotted	medium
Editor (copy, books, newspaper)	medium	black	medium	dotted	
Illustrator, cartoonist	black	dotted	black	light	white
Journalist (hard news)	black	black	black	black	black
Journalist (human interest)	medium	medium	black	medium	
Journalist (opinion)	black	medium	black	medium	light
Musician (composer, conductor)	black	black	dotted	light	light
Musician (instrumentalist, vocalist)	medium	black	dotted	light	
Photographer (professional: ads, events, photojournalism, portraits, weddings)	light	black	medium	light	medium
Technical writer ↑	black	black	medium	light	medium
Writer (lyrics, nonfiction, novels, poems, scripts)	dotted	dotted	black	dotted	white

Math, Engineering & Science in Industry

	Critical Thinking	Exactness	Identifying with Others	Skepticism	Taking Precautions
Mathematician	■	■	□	■	▨
Engineer					
Aerospace engineer $	■	■	░	■	▨
Biomedical engineer ↑ $	■	■	░	■	▨
Civil engineer ↑	■	■	░	■	▨
Computer hardware engineer $	■	■	░	■	░
Electrical engineer $ ®	■	■	░	■	▨
Environmental engineer ↑ ®	■	■	░	■	■
Industrial engineer ↑	■	■	░	■	▨
Mechanical engineer ®	■	■	░	■	▨
Nuclear engineer $	■	■	░	■	▨
Petroleum engineer $	■	■	░	■	▨
Product safety engineer	■	■	■	■	▨
Scientist					
Atmospheric scientist $	■	■	□	■	▨
Biologist	■	■	□	■	░
Chemist	■	■	□	■	▨
Environmental scientist ↑ ®	■	■	□	■	▨
Epidemiologist	■	■	░	■	▨
Manager of research dept. (e.g., mentor young scientists and do PR for funding) $	■	■	▨	■	▨
Materials scientist & engineer (e.g., nanotechnology)	■	■	□	■	▨

Math, Engineering & Science in Industry (continued)

	Critical Thinking	Exactness	Identifying with Others	Skepticism	Taking Precautions
Physicist $	black	black	white	black	gray
Social scientist	black	black	light gray	black	gray
Troubleshooter	black	black	light gray	black	gray

Service Industry

	Critical Thinking	Exactness	Identifying with Others	Skepticism	Taking Precautions
Chef	light gray	black	gray	light gray	black
Child-care worker or nanny #	light gray	gray	black	gray	black
Gaming supervisor, investigator ↑ ®	light gray	gray	gray	black	black
Hairstylist or barber	light gray	black	gray	white	light gray
Hotel or bed-and-breakfast manager	light gray	light gray	black	light gray	gray
Insurance adjuster	light gray	gray	light gray	gray	gray
Massage therapist ®	white	white	black	white	light gray
Restaurant or bakery manager	gray	gray	black	light gray	black
Store or restaurant manager #	light gray	gray	black	light gray	light gray

Spiritual Field

	Critical Thinking	Exactness	Identifying with Others	Skepticism	Taking Precautions
Funeral home director	gray	gray	black	white	gray
Monk, nun, yogi	dotted	dotted	dotted	dotted	dotted
Religious leader (chaplain, imam, pastor, priest, rabbi, etc.) ®	gray	light gray	black	light gray	light gray
Yoga instructor, meditation teacher	dotted	black	dotted	dotted	dotted

Uniformed Professions

	Critical Thinking	Exactness	Identifying with Others	Skepticism	Taking Precautions
Air traffic controller $	black	black	white	black	black
Astronaut	black	black	gray	black	black

Uniformed Professions (continued)

	Critical Thinking	Exactness	Identifying with Others	Skepticism	Taking Precautions
Commanding officer	light gray	gray	gray	light gray	black
Firefighter	black	gray	gray	black	black
Flight attendant	gray	gray	white	white	gray
Judge Advocate General Corps (JAG) investigator	gray	gray	white	black	gray
Military contract administrator	gray	white	light gray	white	black
Noncommissioned officer	light gray	gray	gray	white	white
Pilot (airline, co-pilot, flight engineer) \$; (highway patrol) ↑	gray	black	white	gray	black
Police officer	gray	gray	light gray	black	gray
Project officer (weapons systems, supplies, etc.)	black	white	white	white	gray
Safety inspector (Coast Guard marine safety, etc.)	gray	gray	light gray	black	gray

Other Fields

	Critical Thinking	Exactness	Identifying with Others	Skepticism	Taking Precautions
Animal trainer ↑	light gray	light gray	black	light gray	black
Athlete	gray	black	light gray	gray	black
Athletic coach	gray	black	light gray	white	black
Coach (career, executive, life)	gray	light gray	black	light gray	light gray
Environmental science & protection technician ↑ ®	black	black	light gray	black	black
Interpreter or translator ↑	light gray	black	black	white	light gray
Inventor	black	dotted	dotted	black	dotted
Lawyer (e.g., corporate, tax, patent, wills, trust, DA) \$	black	gray	white	black	light gray
Librarian	light gray	gray	light gray	dotted	light gray
Maintenance & repair worker # ®	white	gray	white	black	black
Mechanic (airplane, car, motorboat, ocean liner)	black	black	light gray	black	black

Other Fields (continued)

	Critical Thinking	Exactness	Identifying with Others	Skepticism	Taking Precautions
Paralegal ↑	medium	black	white	light	medium
Stay-at-home parent	medium	medium	black	light	black
Transportation inspector	black	black	white	black	black

Step 3: Practical Considerations

After you've gone through the tables, note whether your favorite career fields match your needs for pay and security by checking for the following symbols in the Career Tables:

↑ = **Predicted Future Growth Area for Jobs**

$ = **High Pay**

= **Large Number of Present Openings**

® = **Recession-proof**

For more career ideas for the Questioner,
see the recommended lists for the
Observer and the Adventurer.

CHAPTER SEVEN

The Adventurer

Exploring Possibilities

I F YOU'RE THE seventh career type, you are an eternal *optimist,* eager for new *options,* with a sense of *enthusiasm* and *fun.* Some call you a *generalist* because of your many activities and interests. You are *flexible,* prefer minimal supervision, and many of you will bypass the hierarchy if it stands in your way.

An Adventurer might be a marketing director putting a new spin on the positioning of a company, a travel guide scouting out new venues for ecotourism, a product developer adding new features with the latest technology, or an executive coach helping clients explore their full career potential. If you have a technical orientation, you design or improve practical products, such as sports cars or a library Web site. Other occupations where Adventurers are found are as a craftsperson, explorer, tennis pro, fix-it shop owner, food critic, magazine ad salesperson, prospector, safari leader, transportation operator, and travel writer. Teaching positions with long vacations are particularly appealing. Many of you gravitate to roles where you can develop new skills or bring together existing skills in interesting ways. Nobel laureate in physics Richard Feynman was also a juggler, an amateur painter, and a bongo player, and he studied biology and Mayan hieroglyphs. He loved solving puzzles and picking locks, had a large circle of friends from all walks of life, wrote books, and liked to play pranks.

Getting to Know Yourself

If you are an Adventurer, you like to use *all* of your strengths or abilities, either simultaneously or in a sequential or rotating way. So how do you find the right work situation? Would you like to be an innkeeper, which can combine storytelling with being a designer, historian, travel guide, and chef? If you like to write and take photographs, you might decide to be a journalist, but would you feel too confined as a newspaper employee? If you have a short attention span, how about being a freelance journalist? Accepting short assignments would appeal to a desire for instant gratification much more than would being an accountant or polishing stones all day. Repetitive work on an assembly line would be your worst nightmare; don't do it!

The types before and after yours, called your wings, are likely to influence your personality. If you lean toward the Questioner, you may be more cautious in your adventures while your Asserter wing influences you to be brasher.

Strengths Adventurers Bring to the Workplace

As an Adventurer, you are valued for your *upbeat* and *inventive* approach to life, your *broad range of interests* and *knowledge,* and your *love of life,* which rubs off on others. Many of you have an ample supply of chutzpah.

Exploring New Ventures

Adventurers can be pioneers in practical or conceptual ways. Larry is a "serial entrepreneur" in Silicon Valley, having founded multiple start-ups such as an e-commerce Web site for motorcycles and a virtual community where friends can kibitz during baseball games. He's that guy who will say "why not?" and jump off the cliff. "People who shun change and fear failure look at me as though I'm crazy. At first they saw me as simply wanting everything my way. Now they understand that my thirst for trying things gets them moving too."

David was a pioneer in the space industry and explored avenues for his company that included bouncing sound waves off the moon to determine the safest place for the first spaceship to land. In retirement, he became involved in saving redwood forests, helping disadvantaged children, doing hospice work, teaching ecology to kids, and traveling to new places. His exploration of space turned into exploring how he could help humanity.

Multitasking

You have a quick thought process and are well suited for jobs that require flexibility, versatility, and the ability to juggle several activities at once. Fast-paced work environments might be too taxing for other career types, but you are comfortable in an active setting. Project manager Adrienne's job fits her. She deals with information coming in from many directions, which wouldn't be appropriate for a slow, methodical thinker.

Jamal, an executive assistant for an entertainment law firm, does a lot of juggling as well. Every film that makes it to the theater requires an incredible amount of legal work behind the scenes. Every actor must have a contract, every set involves vendors, every borrowed Rolex watch requires a written agreement, and the unions are watching to make sure each rule is followed. Jamal monitors these agreements from the start of negotiation until they are finalized eighteen months later; he may have two hundred different documents pending on several films at once. His outgoing personality helps him build good relationships with agents and production offices to expedite getting the contracts signed in a timely manner.

Networking

Most of you are facile at conversation, gathering information, and making connections. You probably gravitate toward crowds and love parties. In general, you like yourselves, so people like to be with you.

Chris's job requires relationship building with other departments in order to win their support on projects. When he realized his company operates in a culture of informal agreements made outside conferences rooms rather than through formal processes, he increased his social skills and became a master networker. Getting to know people after work at happy hour has become a successful investment in more ways than one. He's bought so many drinks for co-workers that when he first arrives the bartender often says, "Hey, Chris, this one's on me."

Doralee adores meeting new people. She'd rather go to a party full of people she's never met than to one full of old friends; it's a more exciting adventure that way. She can start a friendship with someone of any age, even with a stranger in an elevator. Meeting each new person is like sampling an attractive piece of candy—gratifying her like a sugar rush. After savoring one, she likes moving on to the next delicacy.

Optimism

You are the one who says, "I know we can do it," and your quick smile lightens people up. Life is a celebration. Your co-workers value you for generating excitement, and your belief in what is possible (and impossible!) can raise a project to new heights. Optimism was Parker's key to success when she worked in advertising sales. "I loved cold-calling as long as it was for a product that I respected. If one person rejected me, I could always move on to the next."

Harriet has been so cheerful and optimistic her whole life that her family and friends call her "Happy." She *knows* there's light at the end of every tunnel. She *knows* it's a matter of a couple of days and the business will be fine. She might worry about details but not about the eventual outcome. She went bankrupt once, but she knew she would get back on her feet—and she did.

When Nancy, a nurse, doesn't like something that is happening at the hospital, such as cords all over the floor, she takes positive action. "If you go to the appropriate person—the engineer—he'll put them up on the IV poles. If you go in with clear ideas on how procedures could be changed, you get somewhere. Nurses have a tendency to accept what is handed to them, but you *can* change any workspace, even in a hospital."

Playfulness

Adventurers find ways to get the most out of life. Being playful and having a sense of humor are strengths for salespeople, performers—especially comedians, motivational speakers, or masters of ceremonies—writers, certain artists, teachers, doctors, and other careers that deal with people.

Findlay is a concert pianist extraordinaire and the chair of a university music department. Once at a noontime solo recital attended by hundreds, he ended his classical music program with a piece by George Gershwin, "An American in Paris." Halfway through the piece he stepped away from the piano bench while the piano music kept going; he had recorded himself playing from this point, and the transition was flawless. He broke into a tap dance to his own playing to finish the performance. Faculty and students were overjoyed to see a six-foot-four-inch debonair professor dancing on the stage and having the time of his life. They were all chuckling as they gleefully danced off to their afternoon classes and work.

Famous Adventurers

Leonardo da Vinci (1452–1519) was the archetype of the "Renaissance man." His *Mona Lisa* and *Last Supper* are the most reproduced portraits and paintings of all time. He was also a scientist, mathematician, engineer, inventor, anatomist, sculptor, architect, botanist, musician, and writer. His notebooks contain valuable drawings, scientific diagrams, and ideas on the nature of painting. Many consider him the most talented person ever to have lived. Leonardo introduced concepts for the helicopter, the tank, solar power, the calculator, and the double hull on ships to Europe. He contributed to plate tectonics theory, anatomy, civil engineering, optics, and hydrodynamics.

Steve Jobs's (born 1954) innovations range from the first type fonts used on Macintosh computers to the award-winning interface of music iPods. Jobs, with Apple co-founder Steve Wozniak, created one of the first commercially successful personal computers. Among the first to see the commercial potential of the mouse-driven graphical user interface, Jobs also later served as CEO of Pixar Animation Studios. He is one of the idiosyncratic, individualistic Silicon Valley entrepreneurs who understands the importance of design and the crucial role aesthetics play in public appeal. His products are both functional and elegant.

Rock singer and actress **Tina Turner** (born 1939) is known for her energetic, zippy stage presence, powerful vocals, career longevity, and widespread appeal. She has won numerous awards, and her achievements in the rock music genre have led to her being referred to as the Queen of Rock 'n' Roll. She has sold more concert tickets than any other solo music performer in history.

More examples of famous Adventurers: Lucille Ball, Steve Martin, Wolfgang Amadeus Mozart, and Tracy Ullman.

(Please note: Figuring out the career type of famous people is guesswork. Some project public personas that are different from how they behave in private life.)

What an Adventurer Needs on the Job

Here are key things Adventurers report they require to feel satisfied in their day-to-day work.

Being Liked

You hold your special dual commodity, "What Is Positive" and "What I Do to Be Liked" high in the air to preserve them from any negative contamination that may be swirling around near the

Social Butterflies

ground. You give affirmation generously and surround yourself with co-workers who support you and give you a sense of security on the job.

Nurses enjoy applause for their work, like getting candy and gifts from grateful patients and families. "They *love* us," Nancy says. "For the most part, we are the ones that relieve their suffering. It's extremely important to us to have that appreciation."

Violet, an actress who later opened a speakeasy, enjoyed the experience of running the bar because it was a home base for the neighborhood. When a city blackout happened or when the heat would get turned off in people's apartments, neighbors would meet there. She kept everyone's stories straight as the "big mama" of the group. The whole world felt like her friend.

Entertaining Others

Adventurers like to give parties, tell stories, and hang out with friends, family, and business colleagues. Some need to recharge their batteries after a schmooze-fest by being alone for a while. "I'm a people pleaser," says Happy. "I like cooking, and yet I know what makes a good party, and it isn't the food—it's the mix of who's going to get along with whom. I please myself first and foremost. If it's going to be a musical party, the invitees have to be musical. If it's a Shabbat dinner, will there be too much ritual for some of the guests? I wouldn't want anyone to be anxious to leave."

Erin amuses others at the annual Burning Man project, an international festival in the Nevada desert where Adventurers make up a high percentage of the attendees. Once she created a suit made entirely out of pieces of mirrors. "I rode a motorcycle covered in the same reflective material. People would see themselves as I went by—so I was one big mirror moving through the desert. I thought of myself as invisible. That's the way in which I love being the center of attention."

Fun and Excitement

Excitement . . . is precisely what you should strive to chase.
It is the cure-all. When people suggest you follow your
"passion" or your "bliss," I propose that they are, in fact,
referring to the same singular concept: excitement.

—Timothy Ferriss, bestselling author of *The 4-Hour Workweek*

You spice up work with new, creative situations. You may feel a rush of fear at first before you know what's going on, and then a thrill when you begin to master it. You may also find fun in practicing something over and over to get it right or solving a stimulating problem.

Rob was a professional ice skater for five years with the Ice Follies, always in different cities. When he arrived in a new town, he'd go out and find utilitarian contacts, friends, or both. "I'm the most social person in the world," he says. "I can remember meeting about three thousand people.

The people I like to connect with are good fun and have good taste; they come up with fantastic ideas for activities that I wouldn't have thought of. In the skating world I didn't like my colleagues. I'd rather be by myself than with someone I don't like."

Damon, an entrepreneur, musician, writer, and surfer, enjoys himself by getting engrossed in his work. He tries to see that those around him are enjoying themselves too. Chris earned the reputation as "the most fun person in the office." Being liked not only fulfilled his own need for enjoyment but also provided him job security. Because he was a maverick, not seeing eye to eye with the management could have resulted in being forced out. But all the twenty-something employees at the startup loved him. "So the executive management team couldn't get rid of me," he said. "There would have been a revolt." Then on his birthday when he opened his office he found it filled with balloons, soft drinks, potato chips, Red Vines, and a two-by-three-foot "Happy Birthday" card.

Lack of Limits

As Adventurers, you hate to say no and love to plan alternatives so you won't be stuck if your plans don't work out. You think, "What else can I do in the neighborhood? I would *not* want make the trip in vain." If you are a salesperson or venture capitalist, the idea of uncapped riches is exciting. If you are a research professor, you hope for unlimited prospects for discovery. Being a therapist with an independent practice, you like controlling your own schedule.

Adrienne likes to do contract work that allows her to switch jobs every three months. This gives her the feeling of freedom. Nancy feels frustrated that nurses must work twelve hours a day instead of eight, but she knows she can always quit, so she doesn't feel trapped. "I stay on because I feel lucky I have so many choices in this profession; I could work in a hospice, home care, school, go back to school, go off to Africa, or join the Peace Corps. There are always jobs for nurses, and you can do anything. I have so many possibilities—I can switch from a hospital setting to a clinic, for example."

Idealism

Some Adventurers are incapable of doing anything they don't feel passionate about. Passion could mean joining a revolution in the jungle somewhere, as Norris did traveling all over South and Central America in the seventies, or joining a political cause at home. As a nurse, Nancy saves the world at work almost every day. "That you can relieve pain and suffering is an ideal job."

Federico brings knowledge about the housing market to his real-estate business and makes people happy. Violet's heart goes out to the homeless in her local park in New York City. She takes time off work to deliver them meals. Parker, a financial advisor, gives 1 percent of her revenue to an environmental protection organization and encourages her clients to leave good values to their children.

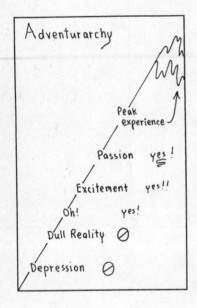

Other Adventurers might have as their ideal being in nature, working for world peace, or having a peak experience listening to music—whatever turns them on or takes them out of their everyday life into a transcendent dimension. Jonas said, "When I am at my best is when I'm totally absorbed in a task, all cylinders firing, wondering where the time has gone. Job satisfaction means being able to function in that place at least part of the time." Happy says, "Playing and singing count as idealism to me. I'm skeptical that there could be world peace. If there could be, that would be my ideal."

Living a balanced life and savoring time away from the job are how the Adventurer lives out her ideals. Many of our interviewees meditate to calm down. Larry, Elaine, Happy, and Nancy all play music. Besides being a nurse, Nancy tours Europe with a recorder ensemble. Happy sings in a chorus. Damon surfs. Adventurers often study subjects like astronomy for fun. Whitey the geologist roams the earth on his mountain bike. "Being at rest, not feeling pulled one way or the other—as I feel when I'm doing tai chi— is integrating. I'm moving in a direction without conflict. Also, humor and laughter are reassuring ways of exchanging feelings with others. Laughter is close to crying to me. Holding a grandchild is up there too."

The Other Side of Being an Adventurer

Jonas, a naval officer, would rather not think about his weaknesses, but he admits it is a good idea to hear about potential traps an Adventurer could fall into if he is not vigilant. "I'd like to catch myself when I'm dismissive of negative feedback and say to myself, 'Not so fast, champ. This might come around and bite you in the butt.' Or when I tune out and plan my next trip to Costa Rica when I'm supposed to be listening to an important speech

They tell me I'm too happy to have any problems....

by the CEO, I should catch myself and say, 'Better pay attention now—this might be important even though it is boring.' Instead of running away, I need practical advice on how to deal with the aspects of any job that Adventurers detest."

IT CAN BE HARD:

✓ to deal with negativity and conflict.

✓ to be patient when I'm feeling bored.

✓ to stick with one career track when I see all the enticing options around me.

✓ to return my thoughts to the present situation instead of planning future possibilities.

I WORK ON:

✓ scaling back the number of activities I get involved in.

✓ refraining from taking up all the airtime and instead listening to others.

✓ being aware of when I display an off-putting attitude of superiority that I didn't intend.

✓ accepting no for an answer.

Attraction to Going to the Edge

Many Adventurers like the thrill they feel from taking chances even though they have an aversion to death and are the most likely type to want to stay young forever. Rob had a high tolerance for the emotional tension of performing nightly in the Ice Follies before fifteen thousand people. The pressure of having to do difficult leaps and jumps perfectly for five years in a row would strike terror in the hearts of most people. "If you fall too much you get fired. You get used to it."

The most exciting time for Violet, an actress, painter, and poet living in New York City, was when she worked for an online media company as an event planner and performance artist improvising intricate creations. Her masterpiece was a millennium party lasting a month. With a large budget, Violet rented a ten-thousand-square-foot loft. She used in-line skates to get from end to end and set up 120 sleeping pods and 80 cameras throughout, calling it a "human experiment." The party streamed live over the Internet. On camera was a clear plastic shower containing naked partygoers! Guests dined on 100 types of cereal and huge platters of lobsters, oysters, roasted ducks, and profiteroles. Navy SEALs and sexy girls with guns managed a shooting range on one end. In the pods a guy trained by the CIA pretended to interrogate people. In a paintball gallery guests squirted people dressed up as Santa and his reindeer. And the five borough presidents played a giant game of Risk against a team of artists for dominion over the world. Reflecting later, Violet felt she had a lot of fun, but it didn't help her build a nest egg for her family or achieve any career advancement.

Fear of Fully Committing to a Career

Since you love freedom and variety, the thought of sticking with one job for the long haul may cause you some anxiety. If you find yourself liking to change jobs frequently, consider that the downsides can be not sharpening your skills through repetition, not being taken seriously professionally, missing advancement opportunities, and not building lasting work relationships.

The next exciting possibility always distracts Parker. In this case, the possibility is an online wine marketing company one of her clients founded. "I'm intrigued with the food and wine industry," Parker said. "When I heard my client's presentation, I thought, 'Wow, I wish I had done something like that.' I'm meeting with her to discuss the open position for a director of customer acquisition, which I'd love to do part-time. But why am I entertaining this idea when I already have a full-time job? [Laughing.] If I wasn't already building a business and raising kids, I'd do it in a heartbeat. Here I am finally building expertise in one area, and I'm tempted to leave it all behind. I've got to stay committed to my present job, though."

Jamal's fear of commitment prevents him from becoming a full-fledged film producer, which is what he'd most like to do. He has the experience and skills to do the job, but if he stays in a legal assistant role he is spared the responsibility. "This way, I'm involved in a lot of productions and my work is necessary," he says, "but I don't get so personally involved that it overwhelms me."

Fear of the Negative

You may be driven by your fear at times but not realize it. Notice when you are doing something in a frenzied fashion; it may mean there is something you are trying to avoid. When we asked Adventurers about fear and their dark side, we heard responses like, "I don't do grief"; "I don't *have* a dark side"; "I only have a fear of falling down"; or "I was afraid everyone would look at me differently and feel sorry for me when my brother died." Ted Turner, who has many characteristics of an Adventurer, said in a 2008 interview with Charlie Rose that when his father died he started working eighteen hours a day to keep from thinking about it.* It's nearly impossible for Nancy to escape fear of making mistakes that could cost people their lives. Nursing is a good career for Adventurers who want to experience all types of emotions from joy to dread to grief.

Moments of fear fed into Violet's decision to sell her neighborhood bar. "If I still had to worry about the bottom line every night I ran the bar, I'd be scared for my family. When money was tight, I'd try to work out a budget for when our son would be born, but I'd dissolve into tears because it seemed impossible. Then I figured out how to change the paradigm and took an employee position. I still have images from that time of not existing anymore or living in pain."

While Adventurers like Violet appear confident, it is useful for them to realize to what degree fear drives their choices. Violet develops her more quiet and serious side in order to make prudent choices for her family and remain loyal to her current employer.

Gluttony for Something New

Sometimes Adventurers have tons of projects in the almost-finished state. They easily become distracted by anything new that may be more exciting, so they pile it on top of everything else and become overwhelmed. Some avoid this by modeling their behavior after the self-discipline of the Perfectionist or the laser focus of the Observer. Another way to stay focused is to hire a project manager to help you stick to a timeline. It's too much to ask an Adventurer to ignore exciting possibilities altogether, though—like asking a fish not to swim.

Parker used to hold monthly seminars to generate new business. Usually when she collected the feedback forms she would find ten people had checked the box, "Yes, I'd like to meet with you to review my portfolio." But with some of them Parker would never follow up! Instead, she would

---

*Interview on *Charlie Rose*, PBS, April 1, 2008.

get involved in the excitement of planning the next seminar and what she wanted to do next.

"'A monkey leaping from pole to pole' applies to me," Elaine said. "I'm a taster. I took a writing class but never finished anything. I start writing stories in my head all the time, but I never write them down." Elaine carries out most of her exciting travel plans, however. Right now she's considering Hawaii, the Philippines, and Tahiti.

Talking Too Much

Some Adventurers are compulsive talkers. One said he didn't have the *courage* to shut up. While talking too much is a way to avoid feeling anxious, it can also be a matter of grabbing more than one's share of attention. Adventurers can try various on-the-job strategies to become better listeners, including watching others' body language and taking "active listening" classes offered by human resources.

According to Rob, Adventurers have an improvisatory nature. "We don't think first; instead, our ideas come out as we talk. The person listening has to do the editing. I wouldn't think of as much as I do if I tried to be succinct. I verbalize most everything that's happening in my mind."

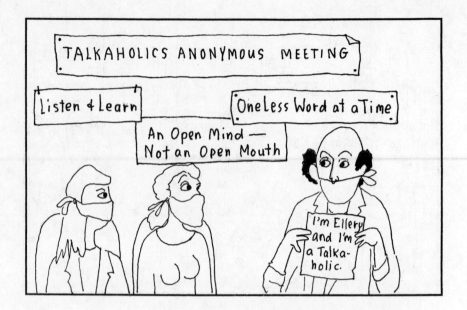

Larry works on trying not to be too self-centered. "*Awareness* has become one of the key words in my life since I got fired. When the chairman asked me to leave, I was crushed. Believing I was the smartest guy in the room and getting my ass kicked was good for me—it opened my eyes. Now I notice other people more. Teamwork is important, but I had not been looking around me to see what others were doing or needed."

The Wagele-Stabb Career Finder for Adventurers

Here are a few of the many possible ways for stretching your wings in new ways. Determining the results involves three easy steps: evaluating your strengths, selecting your dream careers from a table, and considering some practical concerns. The results are worth it! Follow the instructions below to identify your top strengths. You will then be asked to match them to career paths and to observe yourself, watching for which of them spark your greatest enthusiasm.

Try it once and see how easy it is. This test is engineered to coax your career preferences from the truest part of yourself. If you are uncertain about an answer, we suggest you stay with your first choice. Don't worry if you experience a little confusion; a certain amount frees you up to be all the more uninhibited in your choice. The key in steps 1 and 2 is *speed*.

Instructions for Using Career Tables

Step 1: My Strengths

First, read these five definitions. Rate them as they pertain to you and order your preferences in the box at the end.

Note: Any career type is capable of doing any job. The list of suggestions in the career table is not exhaustive, so we invite you to further investigate careers according to how well they use these five strengths.

Enthusiasm

To what degree do you infect others at work with your excitement?

LO 1 2 3 4 5 HI

Idealism

To what degree do you guide your work by noble concepts, meaningful principles, or artistic vision?   LO 1 2 3 4 5 HI

Seeking Challenges

How important is it to you to stretch yourself physically or mentally?   LO 1 2 3 4 5 HI

Social Networking

To what degree do you reach out to new people, stay informed by exchanging information, and keep in regular contact with many associates?   LO 1 2 3 4 5 HI

Synthesizing Information

Rank your ability to examine various forms of information and relate them to one another within a broad perspective.

LO 1 2 3 4 5 HI

Now rank your strengths in importance from A to E, with A being your strongest trait. Write them in below, as in the example.

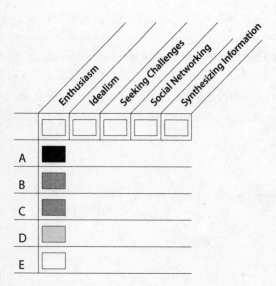

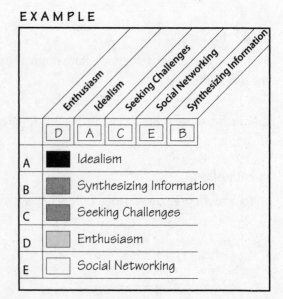

EXAMPLE

Step 2: My Favorite Career

Check the Career Tables below, starting with the ones that have the darkest-colored boxes (highest ratings) under your main strength. If you feel a special spark of excitement when you see one of the careers, write that one down. List up to four careers that most interest you:

Career _____

Career _____

Career _____

Career _____

Key: This chart shows the level at which each of the five strengths is used in each field (from the point of view of others who have held these jobs):

Exceptional	■
Significant	■
Somewhat	■
Minimum Requirement	□
Depends on Job	⁙

Business

Cell shading legend: □ = white, ░ = light gray, ▒ = medium gray, ▓ = dark gray, ■ = black

	Enthusiasm	Idealism	Seeking Challenges	Social Networking	Synthesizing Information
Accountant (independent CPA with private customers)	□	□	░	▒	░
Accounting staff (corporate accounting, budget analyst, etc.) # ®	□	□	▒	□	░
Administrative assistant (entry level) # ®	▒	□	□	░	░
Administrative executive secretary # ®	▒	□	░	░	░
Advertising agency consultant ↑ $	■	▒	■	▓	▒
Advertising specialist	■	▒	▒	■	▒
Auditor (e.g., CPA in large accounting firm conducting audits of other companies) #	□	□	░	░	▒
Brand manager	■	▒	■	▒	■
Business analyst (e.g., software implementation) $ # ®	□	□	▒	□	▒
Buyer (wholesale, retail)	□	□	░	▒	▒
CEO	■	▒	■	■	■
Customer support rep # ®	▒	░	□	░	░
Entrepreneur	■	▒	■	■	■
Finance & accounting executive $ ®	░	░	■	▒	■
Finance staff (corporate) # ®	□	□	▒	□	▒
Financial advisor ↑	▒	▒	▒	■	░
Financial analyst (equity research) ↑	▒	□	▒	■	■
Human resources manager	■	▒	░	■	▒
Investment banker/venture capitalist $	░	□	■	■	■
Management analyst ↑ $ # ®	░	□	▒	□	■
Management consultant $	▒	■	■	▒	■

Business (continued)

	Enthusiasm	Idealism	Seeking Challenges	Social Networking	Synthesizing Information
Marketing manager $	black	gray	gray	black	gray
Organizational psychology consultant (to human resources dept.) $	black	black	black	black	black
Product manager $ ®	black	gray	black	gray	gray
Project manager $ ®	gray	dotted	gray	gray	gray
Public relations specialist	black	light gray	gray	black	white
Real-estate broker or agent	black	light gray	gray	black	gray
Recruiter ®	black	light gray	gray	black	
Retail banker (teller, representative, etc.) #	light gray	white	light gray	black	
Sales executive $ ®	black	dotted	black	black	
Sales representative/business development manager # ®	black	dotted	gray	black	light gray
Small business owner	dotted	dotted	dotted	gray	black
Training & development manager $	black	gray	gray	black	gray

Construction & Manufacturing

	Enthusiasm	Idealism	Seeking Challenges	Social Networking	Synthesizing Information
Carpenter (general construction) #	light gray	white	light gray	dotted	white
General contractor	gray	white	gray	gray	black
Logistician (operations & materials coordinator) ↑	white	white	light gray	gray	gray

Education

	Enthusiasm	Idealism	Seeking Challenges	Social Networking	Synthesizing Information
English-as-a-second-language teacher	black	gray	light gray	light gray	gray
Principal	black	black	gray	light gray	gray
Professor	black	black	black	gray	black
Teacher (K–12 #) ®; (postsecondary) ↑	black	black	gray	light gray	gray

Government & Nonprofit

	Enthusiasm	Idealism	Seeking Challenges	Social Networking	Synthesizing Information
Consumer rights advocate	medium	black	medium	medium	medium
Detective (police or private) ↑	white	medium	medium	black	black
Environmental watch ecologist	light	medium	medium	medium	black
Executive director (nonprofit)	black	black	black	medium	medium
Program manager (nonprofit and govt.)	medium	black	medium	light	medium

Health Care

	Enthusiasm	Idealism	Seeking Challenges	Social Networking	Synthesizing Information
Counselor/social worker ↑ # ®	light	black	medium	light	medium
Doctor (especially emergency, ob-gyn, GP, orthopedics, physical medicine, rehabilitation, surgery) $	white	black	black	medium	black
Nurse ↑ # ®	light	black	medium	light	medium
Psychiatrist/psychologist ↑ $	light	black	medium	medium	black

Information Technology

	Enthusiasm	Idealism	Seeking Challenges	Social Networking	Synthesizing Information
Computer systems analyst ↑ $ ®	white	medium	medium	white	black
Database administrator ↑ $ ®	white	white	medium	white	medium
Desktop support/help desk rep	white	light	medium	light	medium
Information systems manager ↑ $	medium	medium	black	white	black
Information technology support engineer	white	medium	medium	light	medium
Network/systems administrator ↑ $ ®	white	white	medium	white	medium
Security expert ↑	white	medium	medium	white	medium
Software developer ↑ $ ®	white	medium	black	white	black
Technology executive $ ®	medium	light	black	black	black

Literature, Arts & Entertainment

	Enthusiasm	Idealism	Seeking Challenges	Social Networking	Synthesizing Information
Actor	black	black	black	dotted	black
Architect	light gray	black	black	black	black
Artisan/craftsperson	gray	white	gray	gray	light gray
Artist (painter, photographer, sculptor, etc.)	gray	black	black	light gray	black
Commercial artist (graphic designer, product designer, etc.)	dotted	gray	gray	light gray	light gray
Dancer	black	black	black	light gray	dotted
Director (plays, motion pictures, radio, TV)	black	black	black	gray	black
Editor (copy, books, newspaper)	dotted	black	black	light gray	black
Entertainer/comedian	black	dotted	black	light gray	dotted
Fashion designer	gray	dotted	black	gray	dotted
Illustrator, cartoonist	black	dotted	gray	dotted	dotted
Journalist (hard news)	white	black	black	black	black
Journalist (human interest)	black	black	black	black	gray
Journalist (opinion)	light gray	black	gray	black	gray
Managing editor $	black	black	black	gray	black
Musician (composer, conductor)	black	black	black	dotted	black
Musician (instrumentalist, vocalist)	gray	black	black	dotted	gray
Photographer (professional: ads, events, photojournalism, portraits, weddings)	black	white	gray	black	dotted
Talk show host	black	dotted	black	black	black
Travel writer	black	gray	gray	gray	gray
Writer (lyrics, nonfiction, novels, poems, scripts)	black	gray	black	light gray	black

Math, Engineering & Science in Industry

	Enthusiasm	Idealism	Seeking Challenges	Social Networking	Synthesizing Information
Mathematician	□	▨	■	□	■
Engineer					
Aerospace engineer $	□	▨	■	▨	■
Biomedical engineer ↑ $	□	▨	■	▨	■
Electrical engineer $ ®	□	▨	■	▨	■
Environmental engineer ↑ ®	□	▨	■	▨	■
Mechanical engineer ®	□	▨	■	▨	■
Product safety engineer	□	▨	■	▨	■
Scientist					
Biologist	□	▨	■	□	■
Chemist	□	▨	■	□	■
Environmental scientist ↑ ®	□	▨	■	□	■
Manager of research dept. (e.g., mentor young scientists and do PR for funding) $	▨	▨	■	▨	■
Materials scientist & engineer (e.g., nanotechnology)	□	▨	■	□	■
Physicist $	□	▨	■	□	■
Social scientist	▨	□	■	■	■

Service Industry

	Enthusiasm	Idealism	Seeking Challenges	Social Networking	Synthesizing Information
Bartender	▨	□	□	■	□
Chef	▨	■	▨	▨	▨
Gaming supervisor, investigator ↑ ®	▨	□	▨	▨	⋮
Hairstylist or barber	▨	■	▨	▨	▨

Service Industry (continued)

	Enthusiasm	Idealism	Seeking Challenges	Social Networking	Synthesizing Information
Hotel or bed-and-breakfast manager	light	light	light	gray	light
Interior designer	gray	black	light	light	light
Restaurant/banquet services staff #	light	light	white	light	white
Store or restaurant manager #	gray	light	gray	white	dotted
Tour leader	black	gray	light	black	gray
Travel agent	gray	light	light	black	gray

Spiritual Field

	Enthusiasm	Idealism	Seeking Challenges	Social Networking	Synthesizing Information
Human potential seminar leader	black	black	gray	black	light
Meditation or yoga teacher	white	white	white	light	light
Religious leader (chaplain, imam, pastor, priest, rabbi, etc.) ®	gray	black	gray	black	gray

Uniformed Professions

	Enthusiasm	Idealism	Seeking Challenges	Social Networking	Synthesizing Information
Astronaut	gray	gray	black	light	black
Commanding officer	black	black	gray	gray	gray
Diplomatic reception coordinator	gray	light	white	black	gray
Firefighter	gray	gray	black	black	white
Flight attendant	black	white	white	gray	
Military recruiter	black	light	light	black	black
Naval submarine officer	light	white	black	light	gray
Operations contingency planner	white	white	gray	white	black
Parachute instructor	black	white	gray	light	light
Pilot (airline, co-pilot, *Top Gun* fighter, flight engineer) $	gray	white	black	dotted	black

Uniformed Professions (continued)

	Enthusiasm	Idealism	Seeking Challenges	Social Networking	Synthesizing Information
Pilot (highway patrol) ↑	white	white	gray	dotted	gray
Special forces (and similar navy SEAL, etc.)	black	black	black	light gray	light gray

Other Fields

	Enthusiasm	Idealism	Seeking Challenges	Social Networking	Synthesizing Information
Air traffic controller $	white	white	black	white	black
Athlete	gray	dotted	black	gray	dotted
Athletic coach	black	black	gray	black	gray
Athletic events planner	black	light gray	dotted	gray	light gray
City planner	light gray	gray	gray	gray	black
Coach (career, executive, life)	black	gray	gray	gray	gray
Environmental science & protection technician ↑ ®	white	gray	light gray	white	gray
Explorer	black	black	black	dotted	dotted
Interpreter or translator ↑	white	light gray	gray	black	black
Inventor	gray	dotted	black	dotted	black
Lawyer (especially defense, civil rights) $	light gray	black	black	black	black
Maintenance & repair worker # ®	white	gray	white	light gray	white
Mechanic (airplane, car, motorboat, ocean liner)	white	gray	gray	light gray	dotted
Stay-at-home parent	black	black	gray	black	gray
Transportation manager	white	white	light gray	gray	gray

Step 3: Practical Considerations

After you've gone through the tables, note whether your favorite career fields match your needs for pay and security by checking for the following symbols in the Career Tables:

↑ = **Predicted Future Growth Area for Jobs**

$ = **High Pay**

= **Large Number of Present Openings**

® = **Recession-proof**

For more career ideas for the Adventurer,
see the recommended lists for the
Questioner and the Asserter.

CHAPTER EIGHT

The Asserter

Setting Clear Boundaries

I don't want to be a product of my environment. I want
my environment to be a product of me.

—Jack Nicholson's character in the movie *The Departed*

I F YOU ARE the eighth career type, you are primarily motivated by the desire to be *self-reliant* and *strong*. You are known for *decisiveness*, being *direct*, respecting *truth* and *justice*, and being *protective*. You not only defend yourself but also readily look after others who are weaker than you. Since most Asserters have strong *leadership* skills, you may often find yourself in the role as the boss—confident in your ability

to steer the ship in the direction you desire. Typical roles of an Asserter are police officer, plant manager, department head, litigating attorney, independent consultant, nursing administrator, union leader, and executive secretary. As an Asserter, you guard your department, clients, or business with all of your might.

You have a lust for life and enjoy what others might consider an *excess* of work, food, good times, friends, exercise, or other things you take pleasure in. Perhaps you have intimidated others unintentionally (Asserters often don't know their own strength). Perhaps you are so impatient, hotheaded, or formidable in negotiations that people of other personality types are afraid to go up against you. You know how to apply force to your and your organization's advantage. Some of you may be so *antiauthoritarian* in nature that you get in trouble with your bosses, which prevents you from rising as high as you might at your place of work.

Getting to Know Yourself

"Who has the power in this place or situation?" is frequently on an Asserter's mind. While you can put great energy into work, your focus on wanting to dominate can block out some of the more vulnerable voices. In making noise crashing around, you wouldn't want to drown out a song you have gestating in your heart. So when thinking of a career, it's important to look beyond an enforcer role to the softer person inside the armoring. For example, deeply affected by the tragedy in Cambodia, Bobby Muller, a U.S. Marine seriously wounded in Vietnam, decided to work for land-mine victims and all victims of war around the world. Outside Phnom Penh, Cambodia's capital, he established a prosthetic clinic, which now produces more than

I keep having this dream- that all the turtle shells disappear and the turtles need ME to take care of them.

140 prostheses and orthoses, and 30 wheelchairs each month. Muller co-founded the International Campaign to Ban Landmines, which received the Nobel Peace Prize.

You have the ability to live life to its fullest and to empower others. One of the choices to make along your career path is whether to head up your own enterprise or to work for someone else. Independence and being in charge are probably high on your list. Other preferences to assess in getting to know yourself are whether you are a visionary or like to do more practical, hands-on work and whether you are oriented to the thinking world or favor a career involving feelings and the world of people.

The career types before and after yours, called your wings, may influence your work style. If you lean toward the Adventurer, you tend to have quick energy while if you have a more developed Peacemaker wing, you are likely to be gentler and quietly strong.

Strengths Asserters Bring to the Workplace

Either through example, by your *self-assurance* and influence, or directly through calling the shots, you *lead*.

Enforcing Rules

As an Asserter, you may be the first person the boss thinks of to help with those difficult situations in which being direct and confident is essential, because you're a natural at laying down the law.

A junior high school principal's secretary and office manager, Evelyn, "kept on the staff's tails" all the time. If a teacher didn't follow the rules, she would say, "That's it, you're out. You're not going to get your supplies for the science department." If a teacher asked if he could be late, the principal would say, "Oh, okay." But Evelyn would say, "What? *Not* okay!" Everyone liked her, though. At her retirement the teachers gave her a gold medallion necklace, which they had affectionately inscribed "The Dragon Lady."

Sophia, who is raising four-year-old twins, models herself after a supportive mother bear. "It's my duty to set boundaries for them. It would be easier to just play along with their fantasies and enjoy them as children, but I have to keep the perspective that one day they will grow into adults. I'm so busy teaching them principles and laying the foundation for their lives. One of the key duties of a parent is to teach a child to live without you. If I don't show them the rules, I'm failing as a parent."

Famous Asserters

Rosie O'Donnell (born 1962) will stand up for her views with whatever it takes, no matter how shocking or outlandish she may appear to others, as a comedian, as a talk show host, and in her private life. She has appeared in movies (including *A League of Their Own* with Tom Hanks and Madonna, and *Sleepless in Seattle* as Meg Ryan's best friend). Her Emmy Award–winning daytime TV talk show was popular from 1996 to 2002 for her friendly attitude with her guests and interactions with the audience. In 2006 she became the co-host and moderator of the daytime women-oriented talk show *The View,* raising its ratings dramatically because of her strong opinions and eagerness to tackle serious news and controversial subjects.

O'Donnell is outspoken on gun control, on gay marriage, against the Iraq war, and on other issues. She contributed millions of dollars to set up a foundation for national standards for day care, funded by her memoir, *Find Me,* a *New York Times* bestseller, and she contributes generously to other charities and causes.

Mike Ditka, "Iron Mike" (born 1939), is the former coach of the Chicago Bears football team. Ditka is one of only two football figures to have won a Super Bowl as a player, assistant coach, and head coach. His code word is *ACE:* Attitude, Character, and Enthusiasm.

Jack Welch is the retired chair and CEO of General Electric. Three of the books about him are *At Any Cost, Straight from the Gut,* and *Winning.* During his tenure, GE increased its market capitalization by over $400 billion. He remains a highly regarded figure in business circles due to his innovative management strategies and leadership style.

More examples of famous Asserters: Indira Gandhi, Martin Luther King Jr., Sean Penn, Pablo Picasso.

(Please note: Figuring out the career type of famous people is guesswork. Some project public personas that are different from how they behave in private life.)

Leadership

Asserters want to make a strong impact on the world. Some excel in crises, some stand on soapboxes to build followings, some climb the corporate or military ladder to success, and some lead in quieter ways. Tessa thrives well in situations where you can't afford to mess up; the more critical the situation, the easier it is for her to stay clear and calm. Her belief in herself is so strong that the nurses under her follow automatically without asking a question. She is in charge of a unit of twenty-five high-risk labor and delivery mothers who have been drug users. In a crisis she moves into hyperdrive, controls the busy hospital traffic, and knows exactly what role each staff member is to perform.

Michelle Rhee is the chancellor (superintendent) of Washington, DC, schools. "I am a change agent, and change doesn't come without significant pushback and opposition," she says. She is a no-nonsense administrator. "People have to be held accountable for performing their tasks. Are they engaged in activities or outcomes? . . . The war is won in the classroom. It's all about leadership"*

Negotiation Skills

You can be relentless if you are negotiating contracts with vendors or customers to get the best terms. When your friends need help asking for a raise or setting up a deal, you are the one to call for advice and confidence before the bargaining starts. You are good at setting clear boundaries others might not have thought of. You will force all the parties to put their cards on the table rather than leave things unresolved.

Leading negotiations were some of Noah's shining moments. The best was a four-day talk with a leading oil conglomerate. His strategy was to present data to show that his firm had alternatives and to convince the conglomerate to grant most-favored pricing on a two-hundred-million-dollar purchase. "One trait I notice in other people is that they get nervous

---

*Harry Jaffe, "Can Michelle Rhee Save DC Schools?" Washingtonian.com, September 1, 2007, http://www.washingtonian.com/articles/people/5222.html.

when they are dealing with large sums of money. The amount doesn't fluster me whether it is two thousand or two hundred million. It's just about getting the best deal."

Protecting Others

Protecting others can be an expression of an Asserter's tough exterior and can promote cohesion in a group. Asserters look out for the weaker members who cannot look after themselves, generously pitching in to help them fight for justice, demand equal treatment at work, or raise money for causes such as helping abused children. Asserters often extend their personal boundaries to include their friends and family. Sophia loves her twin brother so much that if he fell in front of a train, she believes she would push him off the track and let herself get hit instead.

INDOMITABLE

One Asserter took action when she saw an elderly woman being taken advantage of: "I was mad to the bone when a clique of six tenants picked on people in our apartment complex. Six women, who called themselves the Tenants' Association, intimidated everyone with unfair rules and tried to force those they didn't like out of the complex. I especially felt sorry for an old lady they were trying to kick out for having a dog. Everyone else was afraid of the association, so I decided it was up to me to take them on. At the next meeting I stood up and said, 'I'd like to see the bylaws for this association.' They didn't have any. 'What the hell kind of association doesn't have bylaws? Were you voted into this office? What are you doing up there?' I said. 'We're volunteers,' they answered. 'What are you volunteering for—to cause trouble?' I asked, and told them off good. When I was finished, the sixty tenants who had been afraid to say anything started clapping. After that the clique was finished. People stopped being scared of them, and if they called a meeting no one went."

Standing Up for Justice

Asserters are so concerned about justice and truth that *in*justice and *un*truths can unleash huge amounts of energy for head-on fights. When something isn't right at work, they often can't sit still and allow it to go on but must do something to correct it. Phylece, a union member hopeful, expected that the entrance exam to join the electricians' union would be based on skill. Her head nearly exploded when she discovered the exam was based 80 percent on an oral interview meant to discriminate on the basis of physical appearance, race, and gender. She precipitated a class-action suit, after which the union was ordered to standardize the test questions and a board was put in place to oversee its fair administration.

What an Asserter Needs on the Job

Here are key things Asserters report they require to feel satisfied in their day-to-day work.

Autonomy

Asserters' first concern is often to make sure no one crosses their personal boundaries. More than wanting to dominate others, they don't allow anyone to dominate *them!* So they are often antiauthoritarians who present a tough persona that can ruffle people's feathers or present problems at work. Some rugged individualists do not work for anyone; not having a boss is almost as satisfying as having money to spend!

Asserters as their own bosses, however, sometimes complain of being too hard even on themselves. If they make a mistake, they can be unforgiving. Inadvertently hurting someone else becomes cause for beating oneself up. So they may choose to work for someone else who might be more lenient, as long as they aren't supervised too closely. They like to be left alone to do their work and, if necessary, have it inspected when the job is finished.

Being My Own Boss

If you decide to run your own show, you'd like to know some of the fields with the greatest opportunity for self-employment, according to the U.S. Bureau of Labor Statistics.

Here are some of the top fields for being self-employed that can be great professions for Asserters.

Career	Percent of those self-employed
Art director	53%
Athlete	31%
Carpet installer	54%
Child-care worker or nanny	43%
Chiropractor	59%
Construction manager	47%
Dentist	40%
Executive recruiter	32%
Farmer, rancher	99%
Hairstylist, cosmetologist	90%
Interior designer	32%
Lodging manager	50%
Massage therapist	70%
Personal financial advisor	38%
Podiatrist	44%
Private detective	34%
Real-estate broker or agent	59%
Landscaping service manager	35%

Challenge

Asserters push themselves to look for more responsibility and more pay, and to have more authority. Whether they are impatient and needing to be busy physically or wanting more mentally exciting projects to work on, challenge is a key to their happiness: "One boss I had knew how to handle me. He never put me with people below my level because he knew I needed stiff competition. Sometimes he'd set up my project as though it were a win-lose situation and I had to win. Feeling like my job was to outsmart everyone else really worked. He got my best ideas out of me that way, as well as my respect."

To Have My Energy Matched

Asserters dread being bored at work and hope to have intense and interesting work partners with whom to share occasional deep belly laughs. With people opposite them exerting a similar force, they don't feel they're operating in a void. They like to be met physically, intellectually, and emotionally, and they also have an aversion to people who are extremely mild or overly nice. From their perspective, they're normal and don't like being asked to reduce themselves to a quieter, calmer level. "We're accused of being 'too bad, too loud, too much, too fast, and too intense,' right? Why don't *you* raise yourself up?

You get louder and quicker and faster and raise *your* intensity!' What's comfortable for Asserters is to have others come up to meet us."

Clarissa believes you can't feel close to another person unless you have a good fight or at least an argument. "To me, if you won't fight with me, you don't love me. Since people do disagree, if you don't say so straight out and preferably with passion, it means you don't trust me with the real you. I can never trust what you are showing me and always wonder, 'What does she really think about the subject and about me?' After a fight, I always feel closer to the other person and reveal myself more trustingly."

Truth

Asserters will not stand for phoniness going on in the office. If their bosses don't know what they are talking about or the facts are incorrect, Asserters feel a terrible travesty is being perpetrated. People must say what they think instead of what they believe others want to hear. Truth and justice both rule Asserters' lives.

Who has not had an experience like the following? Once a group attending a conference in New York went sightseeing. Later at dinner Dick, from the conference, asked what they had seen. Every time Henry, an Asserter, started to answer his question, Dick would turn to someone else and change the subject. When Dick turned back, he would ask again what they had seen that day. Asserter Henry got tired of this and finally answered gruffly, "When I think you are ready to listen to the story, I'll tell you what we saw today." Everyone at the table went silent. It was an uncomfortable moment, but later everyone told Henry they had been trying get this point across to Dick for years.

is for justice. is for truth.

Asserters often keep the vulnerable person inside themselves hidden to all but their best friends and intimates. Expressing their soft side fulfills a deep need in Asserters and shows their true strength.

The Other Side of Being an Asserter

Here are some areas Asserters typically struggle with. As you manage your career, keep these themes in mind.

IT CAN BE HARD:

✓ to stay out of power struggles.

✓ to not show my irritation freely, but my annoyance can create a negative atmosphere at work.

✓ to have to depend on others when I'd rather be self-sufficient.

✓ to be seen so readily as a perpetrator.

✓ to work with the nonconfronting types.

I WORK ON:

✓ counting to ten before I act from anger.

✓ feeling okay about not always being met physically or in intensity.

✓ not being so worried about letting my vulnerable side show.

Coming On Too Strong

Asserters can feel they were merely walking and breathing and telling the truth in a situation when all of a sudden someone is astonished or feels hurt. A different career type, by contrast, might have used a velvet glove in the same situation. This difference between how Asserters experience themselves and how they are seen can be a major blind spot for them at work.

What different experiences the transmitter and transmittee had!

Leo learned that pushing his views in a heavy-handed way didn't work, so he tried to control his urge to tell people to shut up and do things his way. "I've gotten good in a corporate context, but I'm not so good at home when I let my guard down," he said. "When I know I'm right, I always seem to come on too strong."

Asserters get into trouble when they act on the belief that their boundaries have been crossed instead of double-checking first to see if it's true.

Excess

Three people were vying for the boss's job. Since they knew he would be retiring in a year, each started ordering the other two around as

though trying to knock them out of the race. One day the boss called them in one by one. "This is going too far," he said. "You're manager material, but there's room for only one guy at the top, and that's me. Either shape up or ship out. Whoever does his present job the best will take my place." After that they buckled down and tried to concentrate on their own jobs. It was unusual to have so many

Asserters all vying for the same job because they're a small percentage of the population.

Asserters are known for their lust for life and their gusto: "I ran twenty marathons and ran myself into the ground." "I climbed some of the tallest mountains in the Americas." "I'm almost fifty years old and I can't run anymore because I ruined my knees, but I still push myself on hundred-mile bike rides." All this from the same person! He sees himself as a hedonist, always wanting longer phone calls and visits, more good times, more food, and nothing second-rate.

Naïveté

Asserters' naïveté is tied in with their sense of idealism and wishing everyone would always tell the truth. For people who seem so tough, there's a kind of innocence about them—a denial that they tend to act as though they inhabit a dog-eat-dog world. They're often shocked when they find out people are afraid of them. Zubin told us, "Most of the time we're naive and innocent—except when we're being hedonists or getting even."

Being an Asserter brings out the hero in a person: "You're trying to be helpful. For example, you think you can go to New Orleans after the levees break and solve the whole problem. You think you know the answer better than anyone else. It's naive and stupid, like a little kid."

We can all learn from Asserters about how differently we come across compared to how we feel inside: "I may look like a bear to people when I'm just being a kid with an attitude—loud and excited. I have more energy than most, and it just pops out. I don't trust what other people are really thinking when we hit a snag [in our relationship] because people have dropped me as a friend without a word passing about why. I've had to live

HEY, BUDDY! I'm here to even the score!

"Yes, I get the job done, but sometimes I must admit I'm inappropriate about it, like the time I started working on the podium during a performance of Beethoven's Ninth Symphony. You should have seen the look the maestro gave me. That's the trouble with not always having the patience to hold back and wait for just the right moment."

alone a lot because of that. Yesterday an employee was upset because I had intimidated her. I had no idea I had done that and was close to tears trying to deal with my guilt over it."

Overt Anger

Most people in the office try to diffuse their anger or find indirect ways to express it. Though Asserters often get labeled as difficult, displaying anger openly helps maintain clear boundaries and honesty.

When Andy was younger, there was a big pricing snafu in one of the sales regions, and Andy's group was responsible for causing millions of dollars of loss. The supervisor of Andy's team, someone he had never liked, lined the team up, took off his hat, held it upside down, and said, "The next time there is a screwup like this I am going to take up a collection for the big boss." Andy immediately responded, "Why don't you put it in the urinal. We'll fill it up for you!" Andy was trying to put this man in his place, and the man was so shocked, he didn't even respond. He just walked out of the room. Andy had just committed a career-killing offense. "You just can't do things like that in corporate America," Andy said. "Now that I am older I might still think things like this to myself, but I've learned not to blurt them out."

Phylece said, "I go through life verbalizing critical comments and little irritations. These annoyances are small to me; I'm just processing and getting it all out and don't expect anyone to take care of these complaints. But others might experience them as huge. I should keep this in mind when I hear other people verbalizing things I don't understand, like their anxiety."

Revenge

Francine, in most ways, is a model citizen. She would never dream of trying to cheat someone else. Nevertheless, she will go overboard to get even with someone who tries to cheat her. Of course, Asserters, as with most types, can either be upstanding or belong to the criminal element of society. Some Asserters have been notorious, including King Henry VIII, Idi Amin, and Genghis Khan.

One day JeriLou woke up with foggy vision because she had a hangover. The only thing she could think of at the moment was to get back at whoever had done this to her (nobody). She looked around for something to take revenge on—and found her three pairs of glasses staring at her from her night table. Her binge on the previous night turned out to cost her a lot in terms of embarrassment and money.

The Wagele-Stabb Career Finder for Asserters

Here are a few of the many possible avenues in which you can use your talents in asserting leadership, determining the truth, and setting clear boundaries. Determining the results involves three easy steps: evaluating your strengths, selecting your dream careers from a table, and considering some practical concerns. The results are worth it! Follow the instructions below to identify your top strengths. You will then be asked to match them to career paths and to observe yourself, watching for which of them spark your greatest enthusiasm.

Try it once and see how easy it is. This test is engineered to coax your career preferences from the truest part of yourself. If you are uncertain about an answer, we suggest you stay with your first choice. Don't worry if you experience a little confusion; a certain amount frees you up to be all the more uninhibited in your choice. The key in steps 1 and 2 is *speed*.

Instructions for Using Career Tables

Step 1: My Strengths

First, read these five definitions. Rate them as they pertain to you and order your preferences in the box at the end.

Note: Any career type is capable of doing any job. The list of suggestions in the career table is not exhaustive, so we invite you to further investigate careers according to how well they use these five strengths.

Competitiveness

How strong is your desire to win, including the willingness to engage in conflict in order to do so?   LO 1 2 3 4 5 HI

Leadership

To what degree do you guide the group to decisions or make quick decisions yourself when that is called for?   LO 1 2 3 4 5 HI

Logical Thinking

How careful and methodical are you in determining facts?   LO 1 2 3 4 5 HI

Protectiveness

How strong is your drive to help and defend other people?   LO 1 2 3 4 5 HI

Self-Reliance

To what degree do you rely upon your own capabilities, judgments, and resources rather than on those of others?   LO 1 2 3 4 5 HI

Now rank your strengths in importance from A to E, with A being your strongest trait. Write them in below, as in the example.

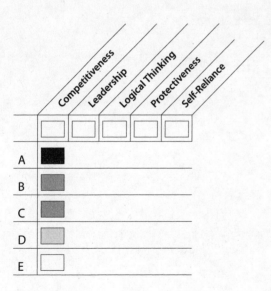

EXAMPLE

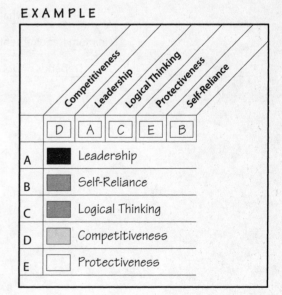

Step 2: My Favorite Career

Check the Career Tables below, starting with the ones that have the darkest-colored boxes (highest ratings) under your main strength. If you feel a special spark of excitement when you see one of the careers, write that one down. List up to four careers that most interest you:

Career _____

Career _____

Career _____

Career _____

Key: This chart shows the level at which each of the five strengths is used in each field (from the point of view of others who have held these jobs):

Exceptional	■
Significant	■
Somewhat	■
Minimum Requirement	□
Depends on Job	⠿

Business

Business	Competitiveness	Leadership	Logical Thinking	Protectiveness	Self-Reliance
Accountant (independent CPA with private customers)	light	light	black	light	medium
Accounting staff (corporate accounting, budget analyst, etc.) # ®	light	white	black	light	white
Administrative assistant (entry level) # ®	white	white	light	light	white
Administrative executive secretary # ®	light	light	medium	light	light
Advertising specialist	medium	white	light	white	white
Auditor (e.g., CPA in large accounting firm conducting audits of other companies) #	light	light	black	black	light
Brand manager	black	medium	medium	light	light
Business analyst (e.g., software implementation) $ # ®	light	white	medium	white	white
Buyer (wholesale, retail)	black	white	medium	light	white
CEO	black	black	black	medium	medium
Compensation and benefits manager	light	light	medium	light	white
Convention planner	medium	medium	light	white	white
Customer support rep # ®	white	white	light	medium	white
Entrepreneur	black	black	black	dotted	dotted
Finance & accounting executive $ ®	black	black	black	black	light
Finance staff (corporate) # ®	light	white	medium	white	white
Financial advisor ↑	light	light	medium	medium	dotted
Human resources manager	light	black	medium	black	light
Investment banker/venture capitalist $	black	dotted	black	light	white
Management analyst ↑ $ # ®	medium	white	black	white	white
Management consultant $	black	dotted	black	dotted	light

235

Business (continued)

	Competitiveness	Leadership	Logical Thinking	Protectiveness	Self-Reliance
Marketing manager $	■	▒	▒	░	□
Product manager $ ®	▒	▒	▒	░	░
Project manager $ ®	░	▒	▒	▒	░
Public relations specialist	▒	░	░	□	□
Real-estate appraiser					
Real-estate broker or agent	░	□	■	□	▒
Recruiter (especially executive recruiter) ®	■	░	▒	▒	⣿
Retail banker (teller, representative, etc.) #	░	░	░	░	░
Sales executive $ ®	■	■	░	░	░
Sales representative/business development manager # ®	■	▒	░	░	░
Small business owner	■	■	⣿	▒	■
Tax preparer	□	□	░	░	▒
Training & development manager $	░	▒	░	░	░

Construction & Manufacturing

	Competitiveness	Leadership	Logical Thinking	Protectiveness	Self-Reliance
Carpet installer	▒	□	░	□	▒
Construction manager	▒	■	▒	▒	▒
First-line supervisor of operations #	■	■	░	▒	▒
Plant manager	■	▒	▒	▒	░
Union leader	■	■	░	■	▒

	Competitiveness	Leadership	Logical Thinking	Protectiveness	Self-Reliance
Education					
Principal	▨	■	▨	■	▨
Professor	■	▨	■	░	■
Superintendent	■	■	▨	▨	░
Teacher (K–12 #) ®; (postsecondary) ↑	░	■	⁘	■	▨
Government & Nonprofit					
Administrative services manager	░	▨	▨	░	▨
Civil service office worker	□	░	░	░	░
Detective (police or private) ↑	▨	░	▨	▨	■
Executive director (nonprofit)	▨	■	▨	▨	▨
Government contracts administrator ®	▨	■	▨	░	▨
Government property inspector	░	▨	■	▨	■
Government service executive $	■	■	▨	▨	▨
Investigator (child support and missing persons)	░	░	▨	■	░
Politician (city council member, governor, mayor, representative, senator)	■	■	■	▨	▨
Program manager (nonprofit and govt.)	░	■	▨	░	░
Social & human services assistant ↑ ®	□	□	░	■	□
Treasurer or comptroller $	▨	■	■	▨	■
Treasury or office of the comptroller staff	░	■	▨	░	▨

Health Care

	Competitiveness	Leadership	Logical Thinking	Protectiveness	Self-Reliance
Chiropractor ↑	light gray	white	gray	black	black
Counselor/social worker ↑ # ®	white	dotted	gray	black	gray
Doctor (especially emergency, orthopedics, surgery) $	black	black	black	black	black
Health services manager	light gray	medium gray	light gray	light gray	light gray
Nurse ↑ # ®	light gray	dotted	gray	black	gray
Psychiatrist/psychologist ↑ $	light gray	dotted	black	black	black
Veterinarian ↑ ®	light gray	dotted	black	black	black

Information Technology

	Competitiveness	Leadership	Logical Thinking	Protectiveness	Self-Reliance
Computer systems analyst ↑ $ ®	white	white	black	white	light gray
Database administrator ↑ $ ®	light gray	white	gray	white	light gray
Desktop support/help desk rep	white	white	white	light gray	gray
Information systems manager ↑ $	light gray	medium gray	black	light gray	light gray
Information technology support engineer	white	white	gray	light gray	gray
Network/systems administrator ↑ $ ®	light gray	white	gray	white	light gray
Security expert ↑	white	white	gray	white	light gray
Software developer ↑ $ ®	light gray	white	black	white	light gray
Technology executive $ ®	black	black	gray	gray	white
Testing/quality assurance specialist ®	light gray	white	gray	light gray	gray

Literature, Arts & Entertainment

	Competitiveness	Leadership	Logical Thinking	Protectiveness	Self-Reliance
Actor	gray	white	light gray	white	gray
Agent (for artists, performers, athletes)	black	gray	black	black	gray

Literature, Arts & Entertainment (continued)

	Competitiveness	Leadership	Logical Thinking	Protectiveness	Self-Reliance
Art director	light gray	medium gray	medium gray	white	medium gray
Artist (painter, photographer, sculptor, etc.)	light gray	white	light gray	white	black
Director (film, theater)	light gray	black	black	medium gray	black
Journalist (hard news)	black	medium gray	black	medium gray	black
Journalist (human interest)	medium gray	light gray	medium gray	medium gray	medium gray
Journalist (opinion)	medium gray	light gray	black	dotted	medium gray
Managing editor $	light gray	black	black	medium gray	medium gray
Musician (composer, instrumentalist, vocalist)	dotted	white	medium gray	white	black
Musician (conductor)	black	black	medium gray	light gray	medium gray
Writer (lyrics, nonfiction, novels, poems, scripts)	light gray	light gray	dotted	white	black

Math, Engineering & Science in Industry

	Competitiveness	Leadership	Logical Thinking	Protectiveness	Self-Reliance
Mathematician	dotted	dotted	black	white	medium gray
Engineer					
Aerospace engineer $	medium gray	dotted	black	white	light gray
Biomedical engineer ↑ $	medium gray	dotted	black	white	light gray
Computer hardware engineer $	medium gray	dotted	black	white	light gray
Electrical engineer $ ®	medium gray	white	black	white	light gray
Environmental engineer ↑ ®	light gray	dotted	black	light gray	light gray
Mechanical engineer ®	light gray	white	black	white	medium gray
Nuclear engineer $	medium gray	white	black	white	medium gray
Petroleum engineer $	medium gray	white	black	white	medium gray
Product safety engineer	white	dotted	black	light gray	medium gray

Math, Engineering & Science in Industry (continued)

	Competitiveness	Leadership	Logical Thinking	Protectiveness	Self-Reliance
Scientist					
Atmospheric scientist $	light gray	dotted	black	white	gray
Biologist	gray	white	black	white	gray
Chemist	gray	white	black	white	gray
Environmental scientist ↑ ®	gray	white	black	white	gray
Epidemiologist	gray	dotted	black	gray	gray
Manager of research dept. (e.g., mentor young scientists and do PR for funding) $	gray	black	black	gray	gray
Materials scientist & engineer (e.g., nanotechnology)	light gray	dotted	black	white	gray
Physicist $	light gray	dotted	black	white	gray
Social scientist	light gray	dotted	black	white	gray

Service Industry

	Competitiveness	Leadership	Logical Thinking	Protectiveness	Self-Reliance
Bartender	white	white	white	light gray	gray
Bodyguard	light gray	gray	white	black	black
Bouncer	gray	gray	white	black	black
Chef	gray	black	gray	white	gray
Child-care worker or nanny #	white	black	gray	gray	gray
Gaming supervisor, investigator ↑ ®	gray	black	gray	gray	gray
Hairstylist or barber	gray	white	white	light gray	black
Hotel or bed-and-breakfast manager	light gray	black	white	gray	gray
Insurance adjuster	white	white	gray	white	black

	Competitiveness	Leadership	Logical Thinking	Protectiveness	Self-Reliance
Service Industry (continued)					
Interior designer	▦	☐	☐	☐	■
Landscaping service manager ↑	▨	▦	☐	☐	■
Massage therapist ®	☐	☐	☐	☐	▦
Restaurant or bakery staff #	☐	☐	☐	☐	▨
Store or restaurant manager #	▦	■	▨	▦	▨
Spiritual Field					
Meditation or yoga teacher	☐	☐	☐	☐	▨
Religious leader (chaplain, imam, pastor, priest, rabbi, etc.) ®	▦	■	▦	■	▨
Uniformed Professions					
Combat team leader	▦	■	▨	■	▦
Commanding officer	■	■	▦	■	■
Infantry officer	▦	■	▨	■	▦
Ship captain	▦	■	▦	■	■
Contract negotiator	■	▦	■	▨	⊡
Drill instructor	▦	■	▨	▦	▨
Firefighter (e.g., aviation firefighter)	▨	▦	▨	■	▨
Flight attendant	☐	▨	☐	▦	▦
Foreign military advisor (Green Beret)	▦	▦	▦	▦	▨
General or admiral	■	■	▦	■	▦
Mercenary	▦	▨	☐	▦	■
Pilot (airline, co-pilot, *Top Gun* fighter, flight engineer) $	▨	⊡	■	▦	⊡

Shading legend: □ = empty · ▦ = dotted · ░ = light · ▒ = medium · ■ = dark

Uniformed Professions (continued)

	Competitiveness	Leadership	Logical Thinking	Protectiveness	Self-Reliance
Pilot (highway patrol) ↑	□	▦	▒	▒	▦
Police officer	▒	■	▒	■	▒
Police sergeant	▒	▒	▒	■	░
Transportation dispatcher	□	░	▒	□	□

Other Fields

	Competitiveness	Leadership	Logical Thinking	Protectiveness	Self-Reliance
Air traffic controller $	□	■	■	■	■
Animal trainer ↑	▒	▒	□	▒	■
Athlete	■	▦	▦	▦	▒
Athletic coach	■	■	▒	▒	▒
Athletic events planner	░	▒	▒	□	▒
Coach (career, executive, life)	▒	▒	▒	▒	▒
Environmental science & protection technician ↑ ®	□	░	▒	░	▒
Farmer, rancher #	▒	▒	░	■	■
Inventor	▦	▦	▦	▦	■
Judge $	▒	■	■	□	▒
Lawyer (especially corporate attorney, personal injury) $	■	▒	■	▒	▒
Maintenance & repair worker # ®	□	□	□	□	░
Mechanic (airplane, car, motorboat, ocean liner)	□	□	▒	□	░
Stay-at-home parent	▦	■	▒	■	▒
Storage and distribution manager	▒	▒	▒	□	□

Other Fields (continued)	Competitiveness	Leadership	Logical Thinking	Protectiveness	Self-Reliance
Transportation inspector	□	□	■	□	▨
Transportation manager	■	▨	■	▨	■

Step 3: Practical Considerations

After you've gone through the tables, note whether your favorite career fields match your needs for pay and security by checking for the following symbols in the Career Tables:

↑ = **Predicted Future Growth Area for Jobs**

$ = **High Pay**

= **Large Number of Present Openings**

® = **Recession-proof**

For more career ideas for the Asserter,
see the recommended lists for the
Adventurer and the Peace Seeker.

CHAPTER NINE

The Peace Seeker

Maintaining Inner Calm

I F YOU ARE the ninth career type, you have a sense of *ease* about you, you *see all sides* of an issue, and you value *harmonious* work relationships. You try to remain *cheerful* and *good-natured* with co-workers, families, and friends and maintain a pleasant and stable environment. You are a good *team player* and meld well with varied personalities, so co-workers are comfortable confiding in you with their problems and concerns—information you can draw on to gently nudge the team to cohesion.

Introverted Peace Seekers have a quiet presence while extraverted Peace Seekers tend to fill the room with their outgoing personalities. Careers range from fields where Peace Seekers bring comfort, well-being, or information to others to fields where they are critical players in politics or corporate America. Typical roles are as sales account manager, family practice physician, psychologist, journalist, librarian, government worker, resort manager, and social scientist. They sometimes have trouble figuring out their career type because they may identify with all nine!

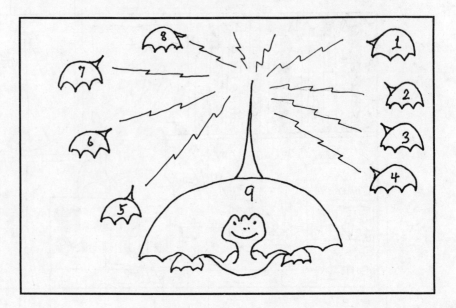

Getting to Know Yourself

Deep within you is an ocean of bliss—a oneness.

—David Lynch, writer/director/producer

As Peace Seekers, you feel the connection to all humankind, all beings, or all matter. You might easily be called universalists. Nigel said, "One of the most fundamental questions in my search for truth is to try to apprehend, or at least draw nearer to, the 'felt experience' of other beings. Anything else seems like delusion." This appreciation of life, your calming effect, and your abilities to be fair and to enjoy small things draw people to you.

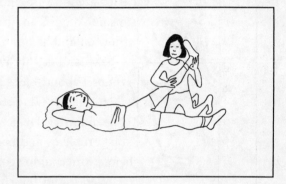

Your desire to feel connected and to avoid conflict can be overwhelming, so you join the flow when with others. If you had a separate desire before, it is likely to be forgotten. Once alone again, you feel angry with yourself for losing touch with your original agenda. You may think, "What happened to my true self? Now I wish I had pushed for my own needs, for at the time I almost forgot who I was!"

Peace Seekers are known for having well-developed physical instinct— a body intelligence. Kirsten applies kinesthetic intuition when she works with clients suffering from ailments from sports injuries to strokes. She nurtures others in physical therapy, a job where you have to be strong and feel comfortable with closeness, such as putting your arms around stroke victims and lifting them. She uses her knowledge of anatomy, physiology, and neuroscience to assist patients by creating exercises that strengthen muscles or relieve chronic pain.

The types next to yours, called your wings, often influence your personality. If you lean toward the Asserter, you may have an antiauthoritarian streak mixed in with your peace-seeking nature. If you have a more developed Perfectionist wing, you are likely to be rather controlled or fastidious.

Strengths Peace Seekers Bring to the Workplace

Peace Seekers often stand out for their *empathy* and *sensitivity* and for being *supportive* of *human dignity*.

Adaptability

You are appreciated by co-workers for being flexible. You often receive spirit awards for being good sports and remaining unruffled. Duncan works in a pressure cooker in one of the fanciest restaurants in New York City. It's a good thing he's so relaxed because sometimes the kitchen runs into a crisis and he has to improvise, or one of the chefs doesn't show up and he has to do double duty. "Everybody around me can be tense, but I always keep my cool and adapt. What is there to be upset about? Life goes on."

James was a software engineer in the early days of the Internet industry. He needed to think creatively when solving technology problems and building tools online that had never been built before. You couldn't go by the book, for the book hadn't been written yet. Working in the chaotic environment of a startup company, he had to be adaptable. The engineers who joined the company later and built on top of James's systems followed the rules and patterns he had created. The chief information officer complimented him using a military analogy: "With today's starting engineers it's like bringing in the infantry. They don't have to be as flexible when they wield these big systems. But you were like a commando working in the streets with the locals; you were yourself in a foreign place having to work with what you found."

Peace Seekers as leaders are usually humble and can change course when it's called for. Perhaps the most famous Peace Seeker, the Dalai Lama, is quick to admit when he is wrong—a rare quality in world leaders.

Broad Perspective

As Peace Seekers, you see the big picture and are among the most considerate of all the career types. When you travel the halls at work, in the neighborhood, or in the world, you try to put yourselves in others' shoes in order to understand their perspectives.

Wendy Hopkins, who recently retired as director of alumni relations at Williams College, was widely respected for her long career working with twenty-five thousand alumni and alumnae ranging from their early twenties to their nineties. Her constituents lived all over the globe and were involved in thousands of professional and personal pursuits, from African dance to homeschooling. One co-worker described Wendy as "the glue that holds the organizational structure together." Wendy helped add more inclusive language to the association's vision statement so that the group fully represents all its constituents. She was a reassuring presence, calm and unflappable, and a good listener who welcomed all voices to the table.*

Listening

When speaking with clients, most people rehearse in their heads what *they* want to say. As Peace Seekers, however, you want to hear out everyone and give each person a chance to participate. Your listening skills are career assets that earn trust and put people at ease.

Being a friend of Dave's is satisfying because he lets them know he fully receives their messages. "I'm mostly interested in subtlety of tone, whether having a feeling about the underlying emotional stance of someone's e-mail or hearing subtle nuances in music."

When Jerry worked for a corporate communications company, he would be assigned to the challenging or "jerky" clients, whom he was usually able to transform into happy customers. He's having the same success in his current government position. "Some rude and demanding city residents send questions to our department and copy the board of supervisors on the e-mails, as though they are trying to get us in trouble," Jerry said.

---

*Kate Lombardi, "All in the Family," *Williams Alumni Review,* January 2008.

"I make a point of paying attention to their concerns rather than blowing them off, though I must say blowing them off is tempting."

Openness

Your sense of wonder imbues you with an appreciation of humankind, nature, technology, and the feelings that works of art produce. You pass your appreciative attitude along to friends and co-workers. David has been opening himself up to his friend's music, adopting it as his own, translating it to guitar—improving it and interpreting it—for twenty years. He takes a piece that his friend has composed for himself to sing and first absorbs it. Then he produces it the way his friend would produce it if he could play guitar. "George Martin did this for the Beatles as their producer. He was a big part of their sound because of his receptivity." David adds, "Peace Seekers understand at a body level. Our openness has a spiritual kind of sensuality about it—seeing new and interesting colors rather than judging what's good and what's bad. We have an accepting mind-set that sees an interesting kaleidoscope of flavors coming from that person, whether we like the individual flavors or not."

Famous Peace Seekers

Audrey Hepburn (1929–1993), one of the greatest film actresses, grew up in the Netherlands during the Nazi occupation and gave ballet performances to raise funds for the Dutch resistance. Her experiences of hunger led her to become heavily involved in UNICEF. After the war she won an Academy Award for *Roman Holiday*. Other films include *Breakfast at Tiffany's* and *My Fair Lady*. Her fashion styles continue to be popular, though she did not place importance on them. She preferred casual, comfortable clothes.

Carl Gustav Jung (1875–1961), a psychiatrist, studied anthropology, comparative religion, philosophy, and archaeology and sought universals in human nature. Major contributions included personality typology and research on archetypes—the images of hero, king, queen, lover, and warrior, for example. His study of types led to the Myers-Briggs Typology System (MBTI).

Jerry Garcia (1942–1995) was lead guitarist, vocalist, and principal songwriter of the psychedelic rock band the Grateful Dead, part of the alternative scene in the Bay Area, California. His guitar playing melded elements from bluegrass, Celtic, and jazz. Garcia was noted for his "soulful extended guitar improvisations," harmonic bridges, and never playing a song the same way twice.

More examples of famous Peace Seekers: Grace Kelly, Garrison Keillor, Abraham Lincoln, and Ringo Starr.

(Please note: Figuring out the career type of famous people is guesswork. Some project public personas that are different from how they behave in private life.)

Patience

You spend whatever time it takes to manifest your inner vision and to live in the present seeking peace; you give people and situations time to improve rather than hurrying the process. Your employees flourish because they feel supported, you tolerate their quirks, and they don't feel criticized. When you're the worker bee, your managers appreciate your endurance and lack of complaints when the going gets tough. Your patient stance provides a sense of stability.

Just as Nigel sprinkles his conversation with, "It's no big deal," Kevin often uses his favorite expression, "It is what it is," and is accepting when there are difficulties in a project.

Flora goes with the flow. "If a decision has to be made by another department," she says, "the end result and speed of resolution are out of your hands. It's less stressful to be patient with how quickly we get an answer (which is usually much too slow) and to accept the outcome." As auditor, Flora has written a letter informing the employees what they can do when their salaries are garnered for back taxes—whom to call, which agency gives employee assistance in taxes, how to get more time to file or to pay child support, and so on. "I'm patient when employees ask me about these things, realizing they sometimes need to hear the answer two or three times."

What a Peace Seeker Needs on the Job

Here are key things Peace Seekers report they require to feel satisfied in their day-to-day work.

Comfort

Physical and emotional well-being for you means staying on an even keel, as if coasting along smoothly on a bike. What brings comfort varies widely among Peace Seekers. If you're an introvert, you might select an office where you can close your door. If food comforts you, you make

sure you have ample liquid and snacks. You make business trips easier by booking familiar hotels, scheduling ample breathing room, or choosing a plane with individual in-seat movie screens.

Dave says he's selfish about adjusting his chair, the lighting, his clothes, and the temperature. "While I'd rather not create conflicts about who's running the guitar store, if the healthiness of the situation is at stake I take action."

For Sophie, comfort is being yourself and not having to worry about your demeanor. "In the sales department at the corporate headquarters, the employees are fashion oriented. When I'm not seeing a customer, I like to wear clothes that aren't too tight or ostentatious; overdressing brings too much attention to myself. I like not having to act a way that is outside my normal behavior."

Fair Is Fair Is Fair Is Fair

Almost nothing inspires your mediating abilities more than wanting to shine a light on something unfair going on. If there's a disagreement among your employees, you'll go out of your way to restore balance. You might encourage the odd person out to speak in a meeting, tactfully approach the quiet person to ask her for her opinion, or carefully apply the company policy to make sure no one receives unfair advantages. When certain vendors ask for favors, you think through the ramifications and make sure you don't give anyone preferential treatment.

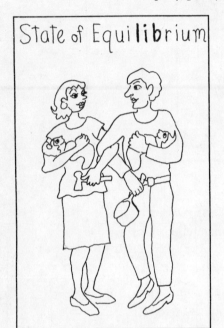

State of Equilibrium

Peace Seekers sometimes resort to stubbornness in order not to actively engage in conflict, but in Nick's case being stubborn was a good thing. The university didn't pay him what it owed him, so he went up the administration from level to level to level until he finally got what he wanted. He was stubborn on his own behalf.

Just the Right Amount of Distractions

As Peace Seekers, some of you wish you could tune out the little pieces of information you catch as they float by because they feel like too much chatter and clutter. Others welcome some of this static. In any case, focusing isn't always easy for a Peace Seeker. Your ideal work situation gives you the flexibility to turn the volume of this noise up or down to just the right level. This may mean being allowed to wear noise-blocking headphones, having your own office, or sharing your office with just the right amount of people, dogs, and goldfish.

In grad school Jerry would roam around with his backpack on, searching for the perfect setup for studying. It couldn't be too comfortable. If he tried writing papers in quiet libraries, he would think about other things or get drowsy. He discovered his ideal spot was the busiest part of a bright café with lots of action going on—where there was the optimum amount of distraction for him to focus.

It's hard for Jason to work at home, even though his job would allow it, because it's too chaotic there with the TV and music going and three other people in a small space. "I have a hard time tuning things out soundwise or visually, but my messy desk doesn't bother me. I feel I can keep track of a lot of things at the same time that way, but if it's irrelevant junk it can distract me, so I try to do some straightening from time to time."

Conflict Avoidance

While other career types might crave challenges, feeling loved by their co-workers, being the special one in their unit, or being the most in control, what Peace Seekers tend to want most is for their working conditions to be pleasant: calm and serene.

Jason avoided going into academia, though he loves the intellectual stimulation there, because he finds that world too territorial. He appreciates the foundation where he works now for the shared social values. Tommy, an anthropology professor, also prefers an environment that is not too territorial. However, he doesn't enjoy talking nicely to avoid conflict if being nice comes from a lack of courage to confront others. When conducting certain research interviews, by contrast, "overnice, sweet-talking, and being superpolite are good if you wish to elicit open responses from others." When he had to grade students' papers, he had to offer criticism, but he didn't want the students to feel bad, so it took time to gracefully inform them how to improve.

An aldercation is when you go away and spend a couple of weeks under the drees.

The least favorite part of Sophie's account management job is when her team reviews cases that are contentious. "The big honchos pick at your strategy, asking, 'Where did you come up with your numbers, and how do you predict membership growth?' Fortunately, right now I'm just there to support. The senior account manager's neck—not mine—is on the line, but it still makes me nervous. If I become a senior account manager, *I'm* going to have to deal with that. For harmonious working conditions, I'll have to change my career."

To Be Connected

Many Peace Seekers desire a sense of connectedness to others through their work. Group-oriented James feels much more at home at Amazon

.com compared to the too-large corporate culture of his previous employer. He explains, "Jeff Bezos, the CEO, has coined the term *the two-pizza team* for his vision of breaking up the company into teams so small they can be fed with two pizzas. These tight-knit teams can move fast, focus on a specific feature, and pursue goals without being held up by red tape."

Team conference calls are the high point in Sophie's week and where she finds the strongest sense of belonging. Brainstorming with her fellow account managers about the best ways to serve particular corporate clients, Sophie jumps at the role of the team scribe, jotting down notes and later distributing the talking points. "There's nothing better than putting in time and energy on working well *together*. When the team review goes well, I am delighted."

While James and Sophie like to bond with the whole team, Amy prefers one-on-one connections. Amy and her husband run a business together. She is "attached at the hip" to her husband. If she could, she would prefer to talk to him every minute of the day—at work, going home on the train, taking a shower, you name it. They're like two pages in a book.

The Other Side of Being a Peace Seeker

As you contemplate your own career, keep in mind these areas where Peace Seekers typically struggle.

IT CAN BE HARD:

✓ to find myself doing comforting activities when I should be doing more essential tasks.

✓ to say no. I will do almost anything to avoid discord.

✓ to show my anger or even to know when I am angry.

I WORK ON:

✓ facing important decisions, even if they are disturbing.

✓ taking clear positions, even at the risk of angering someone.

✓ prioritizing my time rather than treating everything as equally important.

Inertia

Inertia means keeping going if you're in motion or staying put if you're at rest. Some Peace Seekers can hardly get out of their working mode long enough to turn off their computers and BlackBerries—even on weekends or vacation—while others have trouble getting started and are accused of being lazy.

Peace Seekers often stay in jobs they don't like longer than they wish they had. They did not listen to what their instincts were telling them. Sonja has been reporting in for the past four years to a job where she couldn't achieve her long-term goals. The main attraction was playing Ping-Pong during the breaks. Thankfully, she just realized she's been wasting her time like Rip Van Winkle, who woke up to find that twenty years of his life were gone. Now she's going to look for a more challenging job with a better future.

Losing Touch with What I Want

While you may be making things easier for your co-workers by going along with them because you're not aware of what you truly want, saying "whatever *you* want" might get on your co-workers' nerves.

Some Peace Seekers accept jobs that do not use their abilities, which often leads to resentment. Another version of not being in touch with what you want is to become busy with the needs of people around you instead of fulfilling your own career. Sometimes Ghana would fool himself that he was being productive when he was engaged in distracting activity instead of making appointments and running experiments. He would be listening to others' problems because his colleagues appreciated him for that. "I finally realized I'd be better off concentrating on getting ahead, my exercise, my spiritual practice, and my own being."

Debbie drifted in her first two years of college without a clear sense of her strengths. Then a professor, who was impressed with her in a business speaking class, recommended that she consider acting. When she appeared in her first play, a comedy, the audience reacted excitedly to her performance. "But my self-esteem was so low that when I came backstage and the cast laughed and cheered, I thought they were making fun of me. Only later did I realize they thought I had done a good job. When I look

back, the universe seemed to be screaming, 'You matter.' I have been acting ever since."

Jerry has volunteered for years as a yoga meditation leader. "From
meditation I've become comfortable with focusing inside myself rather
than getting swayed by what's outside. It has helped me find my own positive internal voice. When meditating, I'm in this place where nothing else
matters—not other ideas, not other people—just me."

Not Standing Up for Myself

Peace Seekers, who value harmony, are often tempted to adapt too much
to others. Remember that some positions are worth not backing down on,
even if you have to get involved in a dispute. Standing up for themselves
can be difficult for Peace Seekers.

In the last few years David has tried to detach from his usual role as
mediator. "It's not always the best thing to insist on such an easy flow," he
says. "Sometimes overlooking or denying problems leads to fading away,
like beaming to somewhere on *Star Trek*. Or like when an abused child
goes to some other place in her imagination to escape the reality of the
present. When the guy who runs the guitar store is stressed and looking
for problems, I turn on my gentleness with him. His constant static-y anxiety in my environment is tickling some of my own anxiety, so I soothe his
in order to help myself be calm. I'm not really agreeing with him as much
as I'm *looking as though* I'm agreeing with him. But when something is
wrong I need to call it out instead of sweeping it under the rug."

Peace Seekers can often state their true opinions and are assertive in
one specific area of their lives. David doesn't like to confront, but he can
be surprisingly outspoken where music is concerned: "It's a safe subject for
me. I'm highly opinionated about music."

Procrastination

Difficulty prioritizing is often a major element in the habit of procrastination. You can get so caught up in details or feel so comfortable gliding
along that you lose track of time. Or you might put off confronting a

problem, hoping that you will become resolute enough to pull the trigger. In other cases you might just forget. You *meant* to go back to complete your degree, but you didn't look up the admissions requirements online because you were always busy playing in the band with your friends.

David is spread in a lot of different directions. "Priorities are a problem. Every item on the list is of equal value, so it's hard to pick one. Each one says, 'Pay attention to me now!' so I don't pay attention to any of them."

For some, procrastination consists of redoing experiments and trying to get them right, or spending hours rewriting papers and having a hard time finishing them. Then you think if you take a break it will give you a new perspective, and it often does, but taking a break may spur more procrastination. "Jason's band has been mixing a CD for over a year. We always have new ideas. The scary thing is, the longer your break, the more perspective you get."

Jerry had already walked in the graduation ceremony for his MA diploma at the Massachusetts Institute of Technology but hadn't finished his thesis, so his fiancée postponed their wedding. "She didn't want to marry me until I had completed my degree. Up until that point I was my typical optimistic self about making deadlines—I procrastinated as usual. I thought I could just throw it together, but my advisor rejected my submission. 'This would be okay as a term paper, but it's supposed to be a thesis.' My second challenge was when I met my fiancée for a romantic getaway in Hawaii on my way home from doing research for the thesis in India. To lighten my suitcase, I had mailed all my interviews [from India] to my home address. Well, they never arrived. So my fiancée helped me piece everything back together from memory. Thank goodness I was engaged to a smart woman in a PhD program who knows how to write these things. If it weren't for her, I would still be working on that thesis."

Jason's boss thinks he should be able to wrap up a report quickly and neatly, but Jason wants to look deeper and deeper into the data to understand it more thoroughly. "I keep writing and have to edit out all the redundancy. I get curious about the details and never reach the point where it's done. Meanwhile, I'm generating hundreds of pages of material. I'll have lots of little stories, but I can't put all three hundred of them in the paper. I need a collaborator who's a finisher."

The Wagele-Stabb Career Finder for Peace Seekers

Here are a few of the many possible avenues for maintaining inner calm while pursuing a rewarding career. Determining the results involves three easy steps: evaluating your strengths, selecting your dream careers from a table, and considering some practical concerns. The results are worth it! Follow the instructions below to identify your top strengths. You will then be asked to match them to career paths and to observe yourself, watching for which of them spark your greatest enthusiasm.

Try it once and see how easy it is. This test is engineered to coax your career preferences from the truest part of yourself. If you are uncertain about an answer, we suggest you stay with your first choice. Don't worry if you experience a little confusion; a certain amount frees you up to be all the more uninhibited in your choice. The key in steps 1 and 2 is *speed*.

Instructions for Using Career Tables

Step 1: My Strengths

First, read these five definitions. Rate them as they pertain to you and order your preferences in the box at the end.

Note: Any career type is capable of doing any job. The list of suggestions in the career table is not exhaustive, so we invite you to further investigate careers according to how well they use these five strengths.

Capacity to Repeat

Rate your tolerance for doing one thing over and over and your ability to deliver consistency.

LO 1 2 3 4 5 HI

Empathy

How well do you listen in order to understand and experience the feelings or attitudes of another person?

LO 1 2 3 4 5 HI

Mediating

Rate your ability to help differing parties negotiate or to see one another's point of view.

LO   1   2   3   4   5   HI

Synthesizing Information

Rank your ability to research and examine various forms of information and relate them to one another within a broader perspective.

LO   1   2   3   4   5   HI

Teamwork

How well do you cooperate with the group, acting with others in the interest of a common cause?

LO   1   2   3   4   5   HI

Now rank your strengths in importance from A to E, with A being your strongest trait. Write them in below, as in the example.

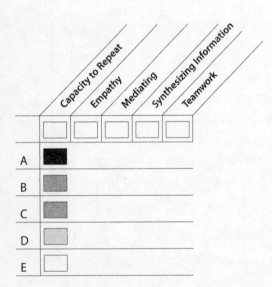

EXAMPLE

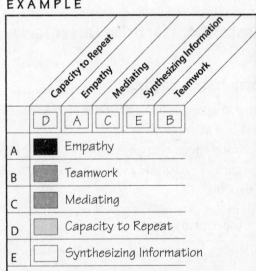

Step 2: My Favorite Career

Check the Career Tables below, starting with the ones that have the darkest-colored boxes (highest ratings) under your main strength. If you feel a special spark of excitement when you see one of the careers, write that one down. List up to four careers that most interest you:

Career _____

Career _____

Career _____

Career _____

Key: This chart shows the level at which each of the five strengths is used in each field (from the point of view of others who have held these jobs):

Exceptional	⬛
Significant	⬛
Somewhat	⬛
Minimum Requirement	☐
Depends on Job	⠿

Business

	Capacity to Repeat	Empathy	Mediating	Synthesizing Information	Teamwork
Accountant (independent CPA with private customers)	■	▦	□	▦	▦
Accounting staff (corporate accounting, budget analyst, etc.) # ®	■	□	□	▦	▦
Actuary ↑	■	□	□	■	▦
Administrative assistant (entry level) # ®	■	▦	▦	▦	▦
Administrative executive secretary # ®	■	▦	▦	▦	■
Advertising specialist	▦	▦	▦	▦	▦
Auditor (e.g., CPA in large accounting firm conducting audits of other companies) #	■	□	□	□	□
Banker (especially community development)	▦	■	▦	▦	■
Business analyst (e.g., software implementation) $ # ®	▦	□	□	▦	▦
Buyer (wholesale, retail)	▦	□	□	▦	□
CEO	░	□	▦	■	■
Compliance officer (e.g., brokerage, health care) $	■	□	▦	▦	▦
Customer support rep # ® _	■	▦	▦	▦	▦
Economist	▦	□	▦	■	□
Entrepreneur	⋯	⋯	⋯	■	⋯
Finance & accounting executive $ ®	▦	▦	▦	■	■
Finance staff (corporate) # ®	■	▦	□	▦	■
Financial advisor ↑	▦	▦	□	▦	▦
Human resources specialist _	▦	■	■	▦	■
Investment banker/venture capitalist $	□	▦	▦	■	▦
Management analyst ↑ $ # ®	░	▦	□	■	■

Business (continued)

	Capacity to Repeat	Empathy	Mediating	Synthesizing Information	Teamwork
Management consultant $	white	light	medium	black	medium
Marketing manager $	light	medium	light	medium	medium
Market research specialist	light	medium	light	black	light
Organizational psychology consultant (to human resources dept.) $	medium	black	black	black	black
Product manager $ ®	white	medium	light	medium	medium
Project manager $ ®	light	medium	medium	light	black
Real-estate broker or agent	medium	medium	medium	medium	light
Recruiter ®	black	medium	medium	medium	medium
Relationship manager	black	black	black	light	black
Retail banker (teller, representative, etc.) #	black	medium	light	light	black
Sales/business development representative # ®	light	medium	medium	light	medium
Sales executive $ ®	light	medium	medium	medium	black
Small business owner	dotted	dotted	dotted	black	dotted
Tax preparer	black	light	white	medium	white
Training & development manager $	medium	black	medium	medium	light
Web designer (graphics, user interface) $	white	medium	light	medium	medium

Construction & Manufacturing

	Capacity to Repeat	Empathy	Mediating	Synthesizing Information	Teamwork
Building inspector ↑	medium	white	light	medium	white
Carpenter (and related building skills) #	black	white	white	white	dotted
Construction manager	medium	white	light	medium	black
First-line supervisor of operations #	medium	white	light	medium	black

	Capacity to Repeat	Empathy	Mediating	Synthesizing Information	Teamwork
Construction & Manufacturing (continued)					
Logistician (operations & materials coordinator) ↑	▒		░	▒	▒
Plant manager	▒		░	▒	█
Education					
Counselor	░	█	█	▒	⠿
Education administrator ↑	▒	░	▒	▒	▒
Educational researcher	░	▒		█	▒
Professor	▒	░	░	█	░
Teacher (K–12 #) ®; (postsecondary) ↑	⠿	█	▒	▒	░
Government & Nonprofit					
Administrative services manager	░		░	▒	▒
City planner	░		░	█	▒
Civil service office worker	█		░	▒	▒
Court reporter ↑	█		░	░	░
Executive director (nonprofit)	▒		▒	░	░
Government contracts administrator ®	▒		░	█	░
Government executive $	░		░	█	█
Politician (city council member, governor, mayor, representative, senator)	▒	░	░	▒	█
Program coordinator (nonprofit and govt.)	▒		░	░	█
Social & human services assistant ↑ ®	█	█	▒		█
Treasurer or comptroller $	▒		░	█	
Treasury or office of the comptroller staff	▒		░	█	▒

Health Care

	Capacity to Repeat	Empathy	Mediating	Synthesizing Information	Teamwork
Chiropractor ↑	░	▒	□	▒	□
Counselor/social worker ↑ # ®	□	█	▒	▒	⋮⋮
Dental hygienist ↑ ®	█	▒	□	▒	□
Dentist $	▒	█	□	░	▒
Doctor (especially anesthesia, GP, ob-gyn, pediatrics, public health) $	░	█	□	█	⋮⋮
Health services manager	░	░	░	█	█
Hospice worker	░	█	□	□	⋮⋮
Laboratory technician ↑	█	□	□	▒	□
Massage therapist, physical therapist	▒	▒	□	▒	□
Nurse ↑ # ®	█	█	▒	▒	▒
Personal and home care aide ↑ #	█	█	▒	▒	▒
Pharmacist $ ®	█	□	□	█	▒
Pharmacy technician ↑	█	▒	▒	▒	▒
Physical therapist ↑ ®	█	█	▒	▒	▒
Psychiatrist/psychologist (especially marriage counselor) ↑ $	░	█	█	█	▒
Veterinarian ↑ ®	▒	█	□	█	

Information Technology

	Capacity to Repeat	Empathy	Mediating	Synthesizing Information	Teamwork
Computer systems analyst ↑ $ ®	▒	□	░	█	░
Database administrator ↑ $ ®	▒	□	░	▒	░
Desktop support/help desk rep	█	░	█	▒	█
Information systems manager ↑ $	░	░	▒	█	█

Information Technology (continued)

	Capacity to Repeat	Empathy	Mediating	Synthesizing Information	Teamwork
Information technology support engineer	light gray	light gray	black	dark gray	medium gray
Network/systems administrator ↑ $ ®	white	white	light gray	medium gray	light gray
Security expert ↑	medium gray	white	light gray	medium gray	light gray
Software developer ↑ $ ®	medium gray	light gray	light gray	black	light gray
Technology executive $ ®	white	light gray	medium gray	black	black
Testing/quality assurance specialist ®	medium gray	white	light gray	light gray	light gray

Literature, Arts & Entertainment

	Capacity to Repeat	Empathy	Mediating	Synthesizing Information	Teamwork
Actor	black	black	light gray	black	black
Agent (for artists and performers)	medium gray	light gray	black	medium gray	black
Architect	light gray	black	black	black	black
Art director (marketing dept. or independent studio) $	medium gray	medium gray	medium gray	light gray	medium gray
Artisan/craftsperson	medium gray	white	white	light gray	dotted
Artist (painter, photographer, sculptor, etc.)	white	medium gray	white	black	white
Commercial artist (graphic designer, product designer, etc.)	light gray	light gray	white	light gray	medium gray
Copywriter (ads, brochures, Web sites)	dotted	light gray	white	medium gray	dotted
Critic (books, movies, music, theater, food, etc.)	medium gray	light gray	white	black	white
Director (plays, motion pictures, radio, TV)	dotted	medium gray	medium gray	black	black
Editor (copy, books, newspaper)	black	black	black	black	black
Film editor	dotted	light gray	black	black	black
Illustrator, cartoonist	light gray	light gray	white	dotted	dotted
Journalist (hard news)	white	medium gray	light gray	black	white
Journalist (human interest)	white	black	medium gray	medium gray	white

	Capacity to Repeat	Empathy	Mediating	Synthesizing Information	Teamwork
Literature, Arts & Entertainment (continued)					
Journalist (opinion)		▒	░	▒	
Multimedia artist or animator ↑	░	░		█	⋯
Musician (any medium, e.g., bluegrass or classical)	█	░	⋯	█	⋯
Photographer (professional: ads, events, photojournalism, portraits, weddings)	▒	░		⋯	⋯
Technical writer ↑	⋯			█	⋯
Writer (lyrics, nonfiction, novels, poems, scripts)		▒		█	⋯
Math, Engineering & Science in Industry					
Mathematician				█	
Engineer					
Aerospace engineer $	▒		⋯	█	░
Biomedical engineer ↑ $	▒		⋯	█	▒
Electrical engineer $ ®	▒			█	░
Environmental engineer ↑ ®	▒		⋯	█	░
Mechanical engineer ®	▒			█	░
Product safety engineer	▒	░	⋯	█	░
Scientist					
Atmospheric scientist $	▒			█	⋯
Biologist	▒			█	▒
Chemist	▒			█	▒
Environmental scientist ↑ ®	▒			▒	▒
Epidemiologist	▒			█	⋯

Math, Engineering & Science in Industry (continued)

	Capacity to Repeat	Empathy	Mediating	Synthesizing Information	Teamwork
Manager of research dept. (e.g., mentor young scientists and do PR for funding) $	▓	▓	▓	■	▓
Materials scientist & engineer (e.g., nanotechnology)	▓	□	□	■	⦂
Physicist $	▓	□	□	■	⦂
Social scientist	■	▓	░	■	░

Service Industry

	Capacity to Repeat	Empathy	Mediating	Synthesizing Information	Teamwork
Bartender	▓	░	□	□	⦂
Chef	■	░	░	▓	░
Child-care worker or nanny #	■	■	░	▓	▓
Gaming supervisor, investigator ↑ ®	■	░	□	⦂	▓
Hairstylist or barber	▓	░	░	░	▓
Hotel or bed-and-breakfast manager	▓	□	░	░	⦂
Massage therapist ®	■	■	□	░	░
Personal organizer	■	░	░	▓	■
Restaurant, banquet, or bakery staff #	▓	░	□	□	▓
Skin care specialist ↑	■	▓	□	░	□
Store or restaurant manager #	▓	░	░	▓	⦂
Trainer (athletic, fitness, personal) ↑	■	░	░	▓	■
Travel agent	▓	░	□	▓	░

Spiritual Field

	Capacity to Repeat	Empathy	Mediating	Synthesizing Information	Teamwork
Funeral home director	▓	■	▓	▓	▓
Meditation or yoga teacher	■	░	□	░	⦂

	Capacity to Repeat	Empathy	Mediating	Synthesizing Information	Teamwork
Spiritual Field (continued)					
Monk, nun, yogi	■	░	⦂	⦂	⦂
Religious leader (chaplain, imam, pastor, priest, rabbi, etc.) ®	■	■	■	▒	▒
Uniformed Professions					
Astronaut	■	□	□	■	▒
Chief of staff	□	░	■	■	░
Commanding officer	░	▒	▒	▒	■
Crew member (boat, helicopter, multiengine air, ship, etc.)	■	□	□	□	▒
Equal-opportunity specialist	□	■	▒	■	□
Flight attendant	■	□	▒	□	■
Joint service or international staff member	░	□	■	□	□
Pilot (airline, co-pilot, *Top Gun* fighter, flight engineer) $	■	□	□	■	▒
Pilot (highway patrol) ↑	■	□	□	▒	□
Police officer	▒	░	■	▒	▒
Support services noncommissioned officer (supply, transportation, etc.)	▒	□	░	□	■
Team coordinator (e.g., combat logistics planning)	▒	□	░	▒	■
Other Fields					
Air traffic controller $	■	□	□	■	■
Animal trainer ↑	■	■	□	░	□
Athlete	■	□	□	⦂	⦂
Athletic coach	▒	░	▒	▒	■

Other Fields (continued)

	Capacity to Repeat	Empathy	Mediating	Synthesizing Information	Teamwork
Coach (career, executive, life)	gray	black	light gray	gray	black
Environmental science & protection technician ↑ ®	dark gray	light gray	white	gray	gray
Interpreter or translator ↑	light gray	black	black	black	gray
Inventor	dotted	dotted	white	black	dotted
Judge $	light gray	white	black	black	dotted
Lawyer (especially mediation) $	light gray	light gray	black	black	black
Librarian	black	white	white	gray	white
Maintenance & repair worker # ®	black	white	white	white	dotted
Mechanic (airplane, car, motorboat, ocean liner)	black	white	white	dotted	dotted
Paralegal ↑	black	white	white	gray	gray
Stay-at-home parent	black	black	gray	gray	black
Surveyor ↑	black	white	gray	gray	light gray
Transportation inspector	black	white	light gray	gray	dotted

Step 3: Practical Considerations

After you've gone through the tables, note whether your favorite career fields match your needs for pay and security by checking for the following symbols in the Career Tables:

↑ = **Predicted Future Growth Area for Jobs**

$ = **High Pay**

\# = **Large Number of Present Openings**

® = **Recession-proof**

For more career ideas for the Peace Seeker,
see the recommended lists for the
Asserter and the Perfectionist.

CHAPTER TEN

Fundamentals to Look for in Your Work Situation

Now that you have a sense of your career type, let's evaluate your current situation. If you're already well into your career, reflect on what you like and dislike about your current and previous roles. If you are a student considering your first career track, think about the teachers, role models, and acquaintances you admire the most and why. If you are bringing one career to a close and looking to reinvent your career, what would you like to do that you haven't done yet?

Do you need to make some minor changes to your current situation, or do you need to go out and find a new job altogether?

To get you started, in this chapter we highlight a few examples of people with the same career type as yours who describe which specifics of their jobs worked particularly well for them. Next we ask you to fill out a Job Fit Worksheet to clarify what is most important for *your* satisfaction based on your career type. Then we ask you to rate your general requirements, such as compensation and work hours. From there you'll build your top ten priorities for a career that suits you.

The three common elements people look for in a job are the *income* it will provide, the opportunity to work on their interests or *passions,* and their *affiliation* with other people.

I. Situations That Work for Perfectionists

In this section, you begin to zero in on your unique preferences. For Perfectionists, what counts is the opportunity to carry out their ideals, which can come in many forms. Some are interested in making details perfect. Others care about being organized or organizing their work environment.

Here are some examples of real careers that worked for other Perfectionists.

Speech Pathologist

Following her passion and making improvements.

Julie gives children the attention and expertise they need and loves to see progress. She works with difficult cases, such as children born with birth defects or who have slow development. Being introverted, she finds that the one-to-one relationship with clients in a quiet atmosphere suits her temperament. After working in a private speech therapy office in a large city, she moved to a small town to work in a Head Start program. She demands precision of herself at work and does art in the natural environment in her wooded home setting after work.

Chartered Accountant

Working for income and attending to details.

R.W. changes the world one individual at a time by teaching others. After he became a certified public accountant, he worked in client education. The accounting aspect of the work suited his interest in paying attention to details. Many years later R.W. assumed a managerial position in a large accounting firm.

Project Manager at a Nonprofit

Affiliating and using organizational skills.

Originally Mark got off on the wrong track, thinking he wanted to become a massage therapist, and he attended an expensive holistic institute that involved a thousand hours of training. "School was great and the fellow students I practiced on were young, attractive, and athletic. But once I had to work with real clients, I found I wasn't comfortable doing hands-on body-to-body work." Now Mark is a project manager for a nonprofit, where he loves making a difference by supporting its mission. He works extremely long hours, making the most of his strong organizational skills, and has had many promotions.

Now let's take a look at jobs you have held to identify which of them fit your personality the best. You can do this same exercise looking to the future rather than the past, if you prefer, or if you don't have a lot of job experience. In the Job Fit Worksheet below, rate how each job meets each of the five requirements, then total the points in each column. Which job scored highest? This exercise is designed to help you identify your own requirements for career satisfaction. At the end of this chapter on page 305 we'll help you prioritize them.

Job Fit Worksheet #1: Perfectionist

Complete this worksheet to compare three jobs you have held or are thinking of pursuing. Rate each one from 1 (low) to 5 (high), then add up the totals.

	Job Title 1: _____	Job Title 2: _____	Job Title 3: _____
To what degree can I carry out my *ideals* . . .	. . . in job #1? 1 2 3 4 5	. . . in job #2? 1 2 3 4 5	. . . in job #3? 1 2 3 4 5
How much am I supported in my quest to *improve* things . . .	. . . in job #1? 1 2 3 4 5	. . . in job #2? 1 2 3 4 5	. . . in job #3? 1 2 3 4 5
How *hardworking* are the colleagues and managers . . .	. . . in job #1? 1 2 3 4 5	. . . in job #2? 1 2 3 4 5	. . . in job #3? 1 2 3 4 5
How much *order* and *neatness* exist . . .	. . . in job #1? 1 2 3 4 5	. . . in job #2? 1 2 3 4 5	. . . in job #3? 1 2 3 4 5
To what degree are the *standards* clear . . .	. . . in job #1? 1 2 3 4 5	. . . in job #2? 1 2 3 4 5	. . . in job #3? 1 2 3 4 5

TOTALS

2. Situations That Work for Helpers

In this section you begin to zero in on your unique preferences. For some Helpers, what counts is the opportunity to be needed and appreciated, perhaps by helping someone else shine. Some like to offer care and advice. Others want to be an essential hub for the spokes of an organization.

Here are some examples of real careers that worked for other Helpers.

Independent Writing Consultant

Affiliating and helping others become successful.

Clare was impressed at career day in high school when a journalist spoke, but it was not until much later that she realized she could become a writer too. First she authored a large resource book while working for a business that helped kids develop confidence in their academics skills. Then at a software firm she helped marketing directors express promotional content more eloquently. After building up a solid résumé of writing, she became an independent consultant. Her task now is to listen to her clients, write what she thinks they want to say, and then double-check with them to make sure she has captured it to their liking.

Chief of Staff

Working for income and serving as an integral part of the organization.

Charles considered several career paths, including foreign service and nonprofit work. Deciding he could make the biggest impact as a major donor, he pursued a career in investment banking. After achieving financial success, he entered public service and helped congressional candidates raise campaign funds. Then he helped Homeland Security by coordinating the deployment of six thousand National Guard troops in Operation

Jump Start and improved information flow between the department, the White House, and Congress. Charles became the department's chief of staff, the trusted right-hand man to the top boss, and helped competing departments work successfully together.

Psychotherapist

Following his passion and counseling others in relationships.

Going to a psychotherapist himself inspired Peter to follow a career in therapy. The field was a perfect fit because it combines intellectual challenge with the opportunity to interview clients, encourage them, and watch them grow. After working in the inner city with a clientele of chronic addicts, he now runs his own psychotherapy practice working with adults on careers and relationships. Peter takes pleasure working in a field where he can feel genuine love and compassion for his clients.

Now let's take a look at jobs you have held to identify which of them best fit your personality. You can do this same exercise looking to the future rather than the past if you prefer or if you don't already have a lot of job experience. In the Job Fit Worksheet below, rate how each job meets each of the five requirements, then total the points in each column. Which job scored highest and why? This exercise is designed to help you identify your own requirements for career satisfaction. At the end of this chapter on page 305 we'll help you prioritize them.

Job Fit Worksheet #2: Helper

Complete this worksheet to compare three jobs you have held or are thinking of pursuing. Rate each one from 1 (low) to 5 (high), then add up the totals.

	Job Title 1: _____	Job Title 2: _____	Job Title 3: _____
How much do I *make a difference* in other people's lives...	... in job #1? 1 2 3 4 5	... in job #2? 1 2 3 4 5	... in job #3? 1 2 3 4 5
How much is my contribution *appreciated*...	... in job #1? 1 2 3 4 5	... in job #2? 1 2 3 4 5	... in job #3? 1 2 3 4 5
How well can I *match the needs* of the company...	... in job #1? 1 2 3 4 5	... in job #2? 1 2 3 4 5	... in job #3? 1 2 3 4 5
Does the company treat employees with *care*...	... in job #1? 1 2 3 4 5	... in job #2? 1 2 3 4 5	... in job #3? 1 2 3 4 5
How *feel-good* and *attractive* is the environment...	... in job #1? 1 2 3 4 5	... in job #2? 1 2 3 4 5	... in job #3? 1 2 3 4 5
TOTALS			

3. Situations That Work for Achievers

In this section you begin to zero in on your unique preferences. For some Achievers, what counts is the opportunity for advancement or how this job will further their reputation. Others are interested in making things work better. Still others care most about the material rewards.

Here are some examples of real careers that worked for other Achievers.

Chief of Radiology

Affiliating and being a respected leader.

Others influenced Richard to follow what they considered appropriate paths for him. With encouragement from his parents and the help of a college professor, he pursued medicine and ended up at a hospital that emphasized affordable health care. For fifteen years he was the chief of radiology. Early on he wanted to change the world and the system. But by the end he realized he could make just as meaningful an impact by simply assisting an individual woman who came to him with a suspicious lump in her breast and needed to make a decision about what to do. He became a healer as opposed to just a diagnostician.

Executive Coach

Working for income and increasing efficiency.

In the course of her career, Mandy has gone from a college residence hall leader to forging a reputation for success in the cutting-edge field of executive coaching for CEOs of Fortune 500 corporations. Her first big contract was with Apple Computers. She then spent years working with companies from Sun Microsystems to Hewlett Packard to Intel. She gets to know people within the context of the corporate culture and then helps them find more effective ways to work together.

From Chief Operating Officer to Professor

Following her passion and driving to achieve.

Ginger earned both a BA and an MA in modern thought and literature in four years at Stanford University and then took a stint in business. She started as an assistant director of a learning center for kids that was hiring top college grads to become the company's future leaders. Ginger developed a new service for them, which became a cornerstone of the national corporation's revenue model. The company acquired a high school tutoring business, and when she was twenty-five she became its chief operating officer. This wasn't her life's calling, however. After winning a poetry contest and giving a big poetry reading, she pursued a PhD in comparative literature. Now she combines her management experience and literary passion as a tenured professor of a university's center for new media.

Now let's take a look at jobs you have held to identify which of them best fit your personality. You can do this same exercise looking to the future rather than the past, if you prefer or if you don't already have a lot of job experience. In the Job Fit Worksheet on the next page, rate how well each job meets each of the five requirements, then total the points in each column. Which job scored highest and why? This exercise is designed to help you identify your own requirements for career satisfaction. At the end of this chapter on page 305 we'll help you prioritize them.

Job Fit Worksheet #3: Achiever

Complete this worksheet to compare three jobs you have held or are thinking of pursuing. Rate each one from 1 (low) to 5 (high), then add up the totals.

	Job Title 1: _____	Job Title 2: _____	Job Title 3: _____
How much *opportunity for advancement* exists ...	... in job #1? 1 2 3 4 5	... in job #2? 1 2 3 4 5	... in job #3? 1 2 3 4 5
Is there *plenty to do* ...	... in job #1? 1 2 3 4 5	... in job #2? 1 2 3 4 5	... in job #3? 1 2 3 4 5
How much can my *reputation* be augmented ...	... in job #1? 1 2 3 4 5	... in job #2? 1 2 3 4 5	... in job #3? 1 2 3 4 5
How much *prestige* is there ...	... in job #1? 1 2 3 4 5	... in job #2? 1 2 3 4 5	... in job #3? 1 2 3 4 5
How great are the potential *rewards* (material or other) ...	... in job #1? 1 2 3 4 5	... in job #2? 1 2 3 4 5	... in job #3? 1 2 3 4 5
TOTALS			

4. Situations That Work for Romantics

In this section you begin to zero in on your unique preferences. For some Romantics, what counts is compassion for one's fellow humans. For others, their own creativity, meaningful work, or putting a high value on beauty are the most important.

Here are some examples of real careers that worked for other Romantics.

Lawyer Who Found Meaning in Volunteering

Working for income and contributing compassion.

Ron wouldn't have picked law naturally, but his insistent parents groomed him from early childhood for this field. The long hours of studying necessary to get into the best schools, then through law school and to pass the bar exam forced him to soft-pedal his compassionate nature. In middle age he was enjoying a stylish lifestyle as a lawyer but needed to add more meaning to his life. He became a Buddhist and volunteered at a Zen hospice many hours a week. Forming relationships with the dying was a way to develop and practice compassion, which he did very creatively. This included activities that were unusual for hospice workers, such as taking the dying on interesting outings.

Office Worker to Counselor

Affiliating and following a meaningful profession.

Sylvia was skilled at working with payroll and other office jobs because her grandfather had trained her to do the bookkeeping for his shop. After college she worked in the city tax collector's office for ten years but longed to do something else. Sometimes, when things didn't go well at work, she'd feel very sensitive and start crying. Working in a large impersonal office was hard for her because it was hard to get close to people there. Finally, she became a psychotherapist and developed a respected practice. Although she was good at office work, it was only after understanding herself and her emotional needs that she realized a different career would be more rewarding.

Pioneering Minister

Following her passion and creating beauty.

When Kate was in high school, her father pushed her to be the next great woman scientist, but it was her interest in spirituality that ultimately made her a female pioneer—at a time when ministers were almost all males. After seminary she spent twenty-six years as an ordained head of a church, expressing both spirituality and originality. Her inspiring services included lovely liturgical music, dance, lighting, and banners as well as interesting sermons. Instead of reading the same Christmas story over and over, Kate focused on a detail of a parable that would help her parishioners understand it in a new way. They would say, "Wow, I've never thought of that. Your sermon touched me and really made me think."

Now let's take a look at jobs you have held to identify which of them best fit your personality. You can do this same exercise looking to the future rather than the past, if you prefer, or if you don't already have a lot of job experience. In the Job Fit Worksheet below, rate how well each job meets each of the five requirements, then total the points in each column. Which job scored highest and why? This exercise is designed to help you identify your own requirements for career satisfaction. At the end of this chapter on page 305 we'll help you prioritize them.

Job Fit Worksheet #4: Romantic

Complete this worksheet to compare three jobs you have held or are thinking of pursuing. Rate each one from 1 (low) to 5 (high), then add up the totals.

	Job Title 1: _____	Job Title 2: _____	Job Title 3: _____
How much freedom do I have for expressing my *individuality* . . .	. . . in job #1? 1 2 3 4 5	. . . in job #2? 1 2 3 4 5	. . . in job #3? 1 2 3 4 5
How well does the *setting* and *atmosphere* fit me . . .	. . . in job #1? 1 2 3 4 5	. . . in job #2? 1 2 3 4 5	. . . in job #3? 1 2 3 4 5
How *authentic* is communication . . .	. . . in job #1? 1 2 3 4 5	. . . in job #2? 1 2 3 4 5	. . . in job #3? 1 2 3 4 5
How *creative* can I be . . .	. . . in job #1? 1 2 3 4 5	. . . in job #2? 1 2 3 4 5	. . . in job #3? 1 2 3 4 5
How much *alone time* do I have . . .	. . . in job #1? 1 2 3 4 5	. . . in job #2? 1 2 3 4 5	. . . in job #3? 1 2 3 4 5
TOTALS			

5. Situations That Work for Observers

In this section you begin to zero in on your unique preferences. For some Observers, what counts is the opportunity to share their knowledge. Others focus on studying and working on important issues. Others are interested in the level of independence the job affords.

Here are some examples of real careers that worked for other Observers.

Internet Search Engine Expert

Working for income and sharing knowledge.

Diana is an expert on Internet search engine optimization (SEO), but this didn't always seem possible. Many of her relatives had worked only for the phone company, and no one had gone to college. Her first attempt at college was unsuccessful. Then she began reading voraciously and realized that she wanted to study philosophy. She completed her PhD, but few jobs were available. Luckily, as a student employee, she fell into a documentary film project that had an Internet component, and she figured out how to apply the knowledge she had gained about how humans think in an Internet career. She worked for Internet start-ups, and now she's an independent Internet marketing strategy consultant, has written a book about how people make sense of their universe with use of the Internet, and has created SEO kits to market to small businesses.

Psychologist and "Green Technology" Practitioner

Following his passion and focusing on important issues.

In 1968, after finishing a degree in anthropology, while fishing on a causeway in Biscayne Bay looking at the Miami skyline, John had the realization that civilization as we know it cannot endure. He traveled around Mexico, Oregon, Hawaii, and the Ozarks and finally settled in Minnesota. There he studied energy; ran the first low-income weatherization program in Minnesota; developed, installed, and found dealers for a solar hot air panel; and was active in the Minnesota renewable energy scene. He lived off the grid for thirty years in Minnesota in a house he built in the woods. He practiced as a licensed psychologist until 2003, when he was diagnosed with lung cancer and given a few weeks to live. He survived, touched many students' lives campaigning in schools against smoking, and now is back working vigorously on renewable energy projects.

Artist and Teacher

Affiliating and retaining his independence.

Gus majored in art in college and had talent as a painter but not the temperament to promote himself. He got a junior high school teaching job for two years, which was difficult because the kids had not chosen to be in art class. He then tried working on a PhD and landscaping, then came back to teaching and realized he needed to do it in a way that would suit his personality. He wanted to develop relationships with the children instead of being a disciplinarian. His interest in the civil rights movement helped him connect with the African American students especially. Because he did so well with discipline problems, he was able to get a special education class in a new high school, where he could work individually with students, which he preferred. His classroom was located away from the hubbub on the far end of the school property.

Now let's take a look at jobs you have held to identify which of them best fit your personality. You can do this same exercise looking to the future rather than the past, if you prefer, or if you don't already have a lot of job experience. In the Job Fit Worksheet below, rate how well each job meets each of the five requirements, then total the points in each column. Which job scored highest and why? This exercise is designed to help you identify your own requirements for career satisfaction. At the end of this chapter on page 305 we'll help you prioritize them.

Job Fit Worksheet #5: Observer

Complete this worksheet to compare three jobs you have held or are thinking of pursuing. Rate each one from 1 (low) to 5 (high), then add up the totals.

	Job Title 1: _____	Job Title 2: _____	Job Title 3: _____
How much *time alone* do I have . . .	. . . in job #1? 1 2 3 4 5	. . . in job #2? 1 2 3 4 5	. . . in job #3? 1 2 3 4 5
How *quiet* is the environment . . .	. . . in job #1? 1 2 3 4 5	. . . in job #2? 1 2 3 4 5	. . . in job #3? 1 2 3 4 5
How much *independence* am I afforded . . .	. . . in job #1? 1 2 3 4 5	. . . in job #2? 1 2 3 4 5	. . . in job #3? 1 2 3 4 5
How *interesting* is the work . . .	. . . in job #1? 1 2 3 4 5	. . . in job #2? 1 2 3 4 5	. . . in job #3? 1 2 3 4 5
To what degree is my *expertise* respected in . . .	. . . in job #1? 1 2 3 4 5	. . . in job #2? 1 2 3 4 5	. . . in job #3? 1 2 3 4 5
TOTALS			

6. Situations That Work for Questioners

In this section you begin to zero in on your unique preferences. For some Questioners, what counts are opportunities to make a difference by fighting for a cause. Some like to prove their loyalty and compassion. Many like intellectual stimulation. Some are most concerned about financial security or working for a boss they trust.

Here are some examples of real careers that worked for other Questioners.

Handling the Tough Kids

Following her passion and expressing loyalty.

Arlette's career path didn't look like it would end up where it has. After college, she studied in France on a Fulbright scholarship, then came back to New York to pursue acting and get a graduate degree in French literature. After getting married and having two children, she became interested in social welfare and worked one-on-one with kids with extremely serious emotional problems. She student taught in East Harlem and got a special education credential. When she substituted in high schools and in difficult fourth- to sixth-grade classes, a principal heard about how well she worked with children and created a job for her as a reading specialist working with difficult children. Children respond to her enthusiastically because of her humor, compassion, and loyalty to them.

Attorney Standing Up for Civil Rights

Affiliating and fighting for causes.

Ouklemedao worked to foster developing governments in Ethiopia and Palau after law school. Then he joined a nonprofit called the Consumers Union, where he discovered a discrepancy between what the group sought to accomplish as a civil rights organization and how it was treating its own lower-level employees. The group's terminology was an example of the problem. There were "the professional staff" (the lawyers) and "the nonprofessional staff" (the workers, who were all women of color). People acted surprised if a nonprofessional came up with a good idea. Even though he was seen as a troublemaker stirring things up, Ouklemedao pushed for and held a series of meetings to help employees resolve problems in the workplace together.

Accounting to E-commerce

Working for income and gaining knowledge.

Hailey joined a startup after college, learned accounting on the fly with her college textbooks, and got an accounting degree in her off hours. Three years later her company had millions in revenue and employed over a hundred people, and she was fulfilling the role of company comptroller. Accounting wasn't stimulating enough, however, and her hard work wasn't yielding the rewards she expected. She then got an MBA and chose a traditional path at the Clorox Company in order to best obtain classical brand management experience. At such a large corporation she didn't like having to go through seven layers of bosses to get decisions made. She realized start-ups were better environments for her to use her strong problem-solving skills. Once Hailey moved to a product marketing position at a more entrepreneurial online photo company, she was pleased with her career choices.

Now let's take a look at jobs you have held to identify which of them best fit your personality. You can do this same exercise looking to the future rather than the past, if you prefer, or if you don't already have a lot of job experience. In the Job Fit Worksheet below, rate how well each job meets each of the five requirements, then total the points in each column. Which job scored highest and why? This exercise is designed to help you identify your own requirements for career satisfaction. At the end of this chapter on page 305 we'll help you prioritize them.

Job Fit Worksheet #6: Questioner

Complete this worksheet to compare three jobs you have held or are thinking of pursuing. Rate each one from 1 (low) to 5 (high), then add up the totals.

	Job Title 1: _____	Job Title 2: _____	Job Title 3: _____
How *secure* do I *feel* in the physical and political environment . . .	. . . in job #1? 1 2 3 4 5	. . . in job #2? 1 2 3 4 5	. . . in job #3? 1 2 3 4 5
How *challenging* will the work be . . .	. . . in job #1? 1 2 3 4 5	. . . in job #2? 1 2 3 4 5	. . . in job #3? 1 2 3 4 5
How much *financial and job security* can I achieve . . .	. . . in job #1? 1 2 3 4 5	. . . in job #2? 1 2 3 4 5	. . . in job #3? 1 2 3 4 5
How much do I *trust* and respect the boss and co-workers . . .	. . . in job #1? 1 2 3 4 5	. . . in job #2? 1 2 3 4 5	. . . in job #3? 1 2 3 4 5
How loyal do I feel to the *cause* or company's mission . . .	. . . in job #1? 1 2 3 4 5	. . . in job #2? 1 2 3 4 5	. . . in job #3? 1 2 3 4 5
TOTALS			

7. Situations That Work for Adventurers

In this section you begin to zero in on your unique preferences. For some Adventurers, what counts is variety in the job. Others are interested in the social networking. Still others care about adventure and trying new activities.

Here are some examples of real careers that worked for other Adventurers.

Naval Officer

Affiliating and having constant variety.

The navy was an ideal career field for Jonas, partly because all jobs were limited to a two-year tour of duty. He made friends all over the world, and fulfilling his duties as an officer gave him a sense of belonging. Every year he would put in a preference card for his next assignment. What fun he had, always thinking about the next possibilities! When he would start a new job he was already thinking about the one after that. "Being a chief engineer on a cruiser was a thrill a minute. I enjoyed problem-solving for crises, such as equipment casualties and water shortages."

Financial Advisor

Working for income and developing social networks.

Parker's mother groomed her to become an artist like herself. Though Parker was talented, she realized a career in art didn't suit her lively temperament and was not her true calling. She was interested in entrepreneurship, so she pursued an MBA, then jumped from a teen magazine to a hedge fund and six years ago became a financial advisor. Because she is paid a percentage of her clients' assets every year, the more social networking she does, the more quality clients she gains and the fewer hours she'll have to put in over time. Parker is motivated to commit for the long haul and receives the structure she needs from this plan. She expects to eventually live off the annuity stream and have more free time for her kids and other pursuits.

Desktop Support in Antarctica

Following her passion and trying new things.

Antarctica represented adventure, beauty, challenge, and community to Adrienne, all in one. She was so eager to work for the science station that they created the first computer help desk position for her, even though she knew nothing about computer networking. The search-and-rescue team took her to ride on a snowmobile over the ice, visit ice caves, watch seals, and ride a helicopter to see orcas. In two seasons she gained enough tech support and system administrator skills to qualify her to became a project manager at a software company in the United States. This adventure suited her perfectly and launched her stimulating career in technology.

Now let's take a look at jobs you have held to identify which of them best fit your personality. You can do this same exercise looking to the future rather than the past, if you prefer, or if you don't already have a lot of job experience. In the Job Fit Worksheet below, rate how well each job meets each of the five requirements, then total the points in each column. Which job scored highest and why? This exercise is designed to help you identify your own requirements for career satisfaction. At the end of this chapter on page 305 we'll help you prioritize them.

Job Fit Worksheet #7: Adventurer

Complete this worksheet to compare three jobs you have held or are thinking of pursuing. Rate each one from 1 (low) to 5 (high), then add up the totals.

	Job Title 1: _____	Job Title 2: _____	Job Title 3: _____
Do I find the work *fascinating* . . .	. . . in job #1? 1 2 3 4 5	. . . in job #2? 1 2 3 4 5	. . . in job #3? 1 2 3 4 5
How much *flexibility* do I have . . .	. . . in job #1? 1 2 3 4 5	. . . in job #2? 1 2 3 4 5	. . . in job #3? 1 2 3 4 5
How many *possibilities* can I explore . . .	. . . in job #1? 1 2 3 4 5	. . . in job #2? 1 2 3 4 5	. . . in job #3? 1 2 3 4 5
Is there plenty of *variety* . . .	. . . in job #1? 1 2 3 4 5	. . . in job #2? 1 2 3 4 5	. . . in job #3? 1 2 3 4 5
Am I appreciated for *networking* . . .	. . . in job #1? 1 2 3 4 5	. . . in job #2? 1 2 3 4 5	. . . in job #3? 1 2 3 4 5
TOTALS			

8. Situations That Work for Asserters

In this section you begin to zero in on your unique preferences. For some Asserters, what counts is doing things their own way. For others, it's important to have a challenging job, take control of a situation, or lead.

Here are some examples of real careers that worked for other Asserters.

Tile Setter

Following her passion and being independent.

Phylece is a self-employed licensed ceramic and stone tile contractor. Because she is a night owl and cannot adjust to morning hours, she works from eleven in the morning to seven at night. Being in control of her work enables her to accept the jobs she wants, do all the work herself so she can maintain her high standards for quality, and take time off whenever she wants to go to the beach, get a haircut, or go to a political event. She has thought of working for another company but is not willing to get up unreasonably early, work by their production standards, or abide by their rules.

Oil Executive to Renewable Fuels Entrepreneur

Working for income and enjoying challenge.

After the Peace Corps, Noah desired a career that would give him high pay, so he ended up at a major oil company. His positions included pricing analysis, inside sales, market research, environmental engineering, and business unit management. He wanted challenge and to be a big fish in a small pond. "After twenty-five years, I worked under someone whom I fought with practically daily for a year. That was ridiculous, so I quit." Now he manages an alternative renewable fuels business and is his own boss. He makes his own schedule, is highly paid, and works from home.

Computer Programmer to Healer

Affiliating and sharing his expertise.

Computer programming fit Greg's brain perfectly. He solved big problems for businesspeople. The field was fun and well paid. If another person was in charge, he or she had to be competent, though. "By age forty, I needed to calm myself with an exercise plan, tai chi. With practice I could feel some kind of energy coming out of my palms. When my wife was gravely ill, including anemia and low adrenals, and not getting better, I tried something her acupuncturist showed me. I placed my palms on her adrenals every morning. Her health improved." After that Greg become an energy-work healing practitioner. Fixing physical difficulties is similar to debugging software, so he's still using his problem-solving skills, but helping people with their personal difficulties appeals to his heart and is more rewarding.

Now let's take a look at jobs you have held to identify which of them best fit your personality. You can do this same exercise looking to the future rather than the past, if you prefer, or if you don't already have a lot of job experience. In the Job Fit Worksheet below, rate how each job meets each of the five requirements, then total the points in each column. Which job scored highest and why? This exercise is designed to help you identify your own requirements for career satisfaction. At the end of this chapter on page 305 we'll help you prioritize them.

Job Fit Worksheet #8: Asserter

Complete this worksheet to compare three jobs you have held or are thinking of pursuing. Rate each one from 1 (low) to 5 (high), then add up the totals.

	Job Title 1:	Job Title 2:	Job Title 3:
How much *independence* do I have ...	... in job #1? 1 2 3 4 5	... in job #2? 1 2 3 4 5	... in job #3? 1 2 3 4 5
How much *control* do I have ...	... in job #1? 1 2 3 4 5	... in job #2? 1 2 3 4 5	... in job #3? 1 2 3 4 5
How much acceptance for my *direct* style ...	... in job #1? 1 2 3 4 5	... in job #2? 1 2 3 4 5	... in job #3? 1 2 3 4 5
How much am I *challenged* ...	... in job #1? 1 2 3 4 5	... in job #2? 1 2 3 4 5	... in job #3? 1 2 3 4 5
How much *room for advancement* is there ...	... in job #1? 1 2 3 4 5	... in job #2? 1 2 3 4 5	... in job #3? 1 2 3 4 5
TOTALS			

9. Situations That Work for Peace Seekers

In this section you begin to zero in on your unique preferences. For some Peace Seekers, what counts is a breadth of interesting material to consider. Others concentrate on comfort. Still others care about the level of balance between their life and their work.

Here are some examples of real careers that worked for other Peace Seekers.

Educational Researcher

Following his passion and considering a breadth of material.

When Jason learned that with a social studies major he could actually get paid to study, designing technologies for education, he pursued a PhD

in instructional design. Jason makes K–12 curriculum models. He created a role for himself in which he is both a computer technician working independently and a collaborator within think tanks. Because he is an extravert, the social aspect of a think tank gives him energy, but it also involves competition. He's become successful by showing that he can work by himself and get things done independently while intermittently providing leadership in groups when he is needed.

Writer and Attendant for the Disabled

Affiliating and having a comfortable work life.

Nick considers his real career to be writing; he has written a novel and is finishing up a screenplay. For income, however, he has worked as a civil servant and as a personal aide. "I have a long time frame. I'm willing to defer my writing career because I'm usually happy doing what I'm doing at the moment, whatever that may be. My career is whatever is happening right now. When I took a job in civil service I didn't need to feel committed to the profession. This job as an aide is comfortable enough. It doesn't give me my life purpose. I'm making a living while writing my novel on the side. Meanwhile, I enjoy the personal attendant work and making others happy."

President of a Manufacturing Firm

Working for profit and keeping life balanced.

Paul is one of the mellowest guys you could know. Though he surfs, he doesn't fit the stereotype of a slacker. He inherited a manufacturing business from his father and expanded it through acquiring companies in the same product niche. He developed his compassionate management style when he supervised men in mines and applied it later to the family business. He has a gentle demeanor and treats owners and employees well. When he purchases a firm, he puts in place a team and an incentive plan that includes favorable conditions for his new employees and improves profitability in the first eighteen months. Then he becomes a hands-off manager in order to maintain a balanced lifestyle for himself and his family.

Now let's take a look at jobs you have held to identify which of them best fit your personality and why. You can do this same exercise looking to the future rather than the past, if you prefer, or if you don't already have a lot of job experience. In the Job Fit Worksheet on the next page, rate how well each job meets each of the five requirements, then total the points in each column. Which job scored highest and why? This exercise is designed to help you identify your own requirements for career satisfaction. At the end of this chapter on page 305 we'll help you prioritize them.

Job Fit Worksheet #9: Peace Seeker

Complete this worksheet to compare three jobs you have held or are thinking of pursuing. Rate each one from 1 (low) to 5 (high), then add up the totals.

	Job Title 1: _____	Job Title 2: _____	Job Title 3: _____
How *humanitarian* are the principles ...	... in job #1? 1 2 3 4 5	... in job #2? 1 2 3 4 5	... in job #3? 1 2 3 4 5
How *comfortable* is my work space ...	... in job #1? 1 2 3 4 5	... in job #2? 1 2 3 4 5	... in job #3? 1 2 3 4 5
How *fair* is the management ...	... in job #1? 1 2 3 4 5	... in job #2? 1 2 3 4 5	... in job #3? 1 2 3 4 5
How reasonable are the *work hours* ...	... in job #1? 1 2 3 4 5	... in job #2? 1 2 3 4 5	... in job #3? 1 2 3 4 5
How *conflict-free* is the environment...	... in job #1? 1 2 3 4 5	... in job #2? 1 2 3 4 5	... in job #3? 1 2 3 4 5
TOTALS			

My General Job Necessities

You've considered certain job factors that best fit your career type needs. What about other requirements such as pay and benefits? Review this list of general job necessities, and weigh the importance of each category from 1 (low) to 5 (high).

1. What level of *compensation* is acceptable to you, including base salary or hourly rate, bonuses, retainers, commissions, stock options, pension plan, 401(k) matching, housing allowance, car allowance, and so on? How high is your tolerance for risk? For example, how important is the security of your compensation over many years as compared to your comfort with unpredictability?

   Weight importance 1 2 3 4 5

2. How important are the *hours* and *benefits* package: how many hours a week you work, at what time, and which days? Think about such benefits as health insurance, vacation, tuition assistance, sabbaticals, gym access, or any other services offered.

   Weight importance 1 2 3 4 5

3. What are your *commuting* and *work-from-home* requirements? Figure out how far you are willing to travel to work and how much time you are willing to take to commute. How many days a month are you willing or able to take business trips? What is your maximum budget for tolls, parking, fuel, and public transportation? How many days a week do you need to, or are you available to, work from home, if that is asked of you?

   Weight importance 1 2 3 4 5

4. Think about how important *career advancement* is for you at this stage of your career. Some factors to consider are new skills learned, increase in job title, or the opportunity to manage more people and larger budgets. Will you be satisfied with the job itself,

or will you be happier if you can see a clear path for advancement? Would you like to take the experience from this job and use it for opportunities in other firms? Do you want this job in order to make beneficial contacts? For long-term career advancement, do you require personal PR in the form of publications, speaking engagements, newspaper quotes, and increased presence of your name on the Internet?

Weight importance   1   2   3   4   5

5. Think about how you will fit with the work *culture*: how you will fit with the boss, the size of the work team, the overall company culture, the industry, or the mission.

Weight importance   1   2   3   4   5

Putting It All Together

Now create your priority list for your ideal work situation. In the table below, we have prefilled general job necessities 1 to 5 for you. To add the specific needs of your career type, refer to the Job Fit Worksheet for your type earlier in this chapter. Write down the needs from that list in column A, items 6 to 10.

The last step is to look at the list in column A and reprioritize needs 1 to 10 in column B. This is necessary, as you may find that some general needs rank higher in importance for you than type-specific needs, and vice versa.

Column A: Enter Needs from My Job Fit Worksheet	Column B: Enter My Reprioritized Needs List
1. Compensation	1. _____
2. Hours & Benefits	2. _____
3. Location	3. _____
4. Advancement	4. _____
5. Culture	5. _____
6. _____	6. _____
7. _____	7. _____
8. _____	8. _____
9. _____	9. _____
10. _____	10. _____

You've identified how you weigh ten factors in your career satisfaction. Now what? Before leaping out of your current job, make sure there's no way to improve it. Sometimes people get antsy and want to leave their situation, only to regret it later. Believe us, this happens quite often. But that doesn't mean you should be unhappy at work. You shouldn't! Career counseling (including this book) can help you stay in your present employment, just as couples' counseling can improve a marriage. Perhaps at the next performance review you can talk with your boss about how you might adjust your job responsibilities or some of the many other factors that we've discussed so far. If you're self-employed, what factors in your work situation are within your own control to change? If you are just out of school or it's time for you to pursue a new job, the next chapter guides you through the successful steps of a job hunt tailored to your career type and to you as an individual.

CHAPTER ELEVEN

Job-Hunting Guide

So you've decided to start a job search. This guide is for any job-hunting situation that involves *researching* openings, writing a *résumé, interviewing,* or *negotiating* a job offer. We supply information here for a variety of purposes—from the traditional corporate job hunt to applying for a loan to start your own business. If you are applying for a position in a uniformed profession, the salary and title specifics may be nonnegotiable and may not be required, but our fundamental interview guidelines will still apply. If you are an independent artist, musician, or writer or are running your own enterprise with your own funding, read this chapter for suggestions on how to shape your personal brand and how to negotiate for payment for your work.

Identifying Your Job Objectives

Romantics & Introspecting

Romantics can help you reflect on the strengths that make you unique and what elements might be missing in your present career that you can add to your list of needs.

The first step of a successful job hunt is to develop clear job objectives. Then you can create a plan to market yourself to potential employers. You are your own best product to sell! The foundation of your plan will be the list of strengths you bring to the job and the list of needs you expect the job to fulfill from your career type chapter. A solid plan includes identifying clearly who will be interested in paying you for your work, where the best opportunities are, and how you compare to your competition.

Let's review your strengths and needs and then identify your most suitable job objectives.

Your Strengths

Review your work in the Career Finder section for your type, and rewrite your personal ranking of your best strengths. If you are not sure of your career type, select the set of five strengths (based on the nine possible sets) that fits you best at this stage in your life.

My Strengths List:
(prioritized)

A. _____

B. _____

C. _____

D. _____

E. _____

Right: a sample prioritized list of strengths completed by a Perfectionist.

Sample of prioritized strengths:

Courteousness	Logical Thinking	Making Improv...	Metic...

	D	A	C	E	
A	■	improving things
B	▨	responsibility
C	▨	logical thinking
D	▨	courteousness
E	□	meticulousness

Below, write your favorite four careers that use these strengths (found in the Career Finder *or* from your own experience and research), and circle any of the following symbols that apply:

↑ = **Predicted Future Growth Area for Jobs**

$ = **High Pay**

= **Large Number of Present Openings**

® = **Recession-proof**

Career _____ ↑ $ # ®

Career _____ ↑ $ # ®

Career _____ ↑ $ # ®

Career _____ ↑ $ # ®

Your Needs

Now rewrite your reprioritized needs list from the one you created in chapter 10 on page 305:

1._____

2._____

3._____

4._____

5._____

6._____

7._____

8._____

9._____

10._____

Your Job Objectives

Select two jobs that fit well with your strengths and needs lists (to the best of your knowledge prior to further research). You will be creating one full plan for each job objective. This means two different résumés, cover letters, series of interviews, and so on. You may be interested in Job Objective #1 but are not having success in that area. However, a similar Job Objective #2 may also interest you, and you may discover you can get many more interviews and job offers in that field. As you can imagine, *more* than two objectives will require too much work to execute effectively. Nonetheless, most candidates do need *two* for maximum flexibility in the job market. For simplicity of this book we will walk you through the steps for one job objective, but plan on repeating the same steps for the second one.

My Objectives:

1. _____

2. _____

Three Case Studies

As we walk you through the job-hunting process, we'll introduce you to three people at different stages of their careers. In order not to be repetitive, we're including Troy only for his résumé, cover letter, and job negotiation. Here are all three individuals' job objectives:

Romantic career type Lindsay just graduated from college.

Lindsay recently graduated and is looking for a full-time job. As a Romantic career type, she has identified the strengths she enjoys using most: *ability to discern* (her enjoyment of thinking about things) and *sense of meaning.* She was a philosophy and literature major in college and had tried a couple internships in publishing, finding the field a good fit for her. Now she needs more experience working her way up to becoming an editor. She is hoping for an editorial assistant job. Her second choice is to find a paying internship that will lead her to the right paid position. Here are her priorities:

Job Objective #1: Editorial Assistant

Job Objective #2: Managing Editorial Paid Intern

Adventurer career type Julia has over ten years of experience in the job market.

Julia has been working as a business analyst for e-commerce companies. As an Adventurer career type, she has identified that the strengths she most enjoys using are *seeking challenges* and *synthesizing information*. She likes e-commerce, but her business analyst role is too detail oriented and repetitive. She has experience working with product managers and marketers, and she is knowledgeable enough about their work to parlay her résumé into those roles for a lateral career shift. She is equally interested in both fields, but she doesn't know where she will have more luck on the job market, so she identifies two goals and will create one plan for each job field:

Job Objective #1: Product Manager

Job Objective #2: Online Marketer

Peace Seeker career type Troy is seeking his third career.

Troy, after a first career as an air force mechanic and a second in information technology, has most recently been doing office administration at a nonprofit organization he believes in. He enjoys the friendly atmosphere at his workplace, but after a dip in his investment account, he needs to earn a higher income to reach his retirement goals. He has identified that the strengths he most enjoys using are *synthesizing information* and *teamwork*. Since the pay scale is higher for technology jobs, he would like to return to that arena, but he'll have to brush up on his tech skills and changes in the field. He also likes the idea of a high-paid customer support job that uses his technology knowledge, so he has identified these goals:

Job Objective #1: Support Engineer

Job Objective #2: System Administrator

Writing Your Résumé

The title of this section could be "Writing and Rewriting and Rewriting Your Résumé." You will create a starter résumé and cover letter, but expect to edit them each time you apply for a job, customizing your materials to fit the specifics of that job. If you are not the perfect candidate, find ways to address your weaknesses and show how your other skills and attributes compensate for them. Do not try to reuse the same résumé for each job objective. Put the most important skills and experience—most likely a different set each time—front and center for each job. The posted descriptions of the jobs you apply for will determine which elements you highlight.

Analyzing Job Descriptions

Ideally for your Job Objective #1, many sample job descriptions will be available online. Do a search for your ideal job title on a few of the following Web sites:

- Monster.com
- Yahoo! HotJobs
- Craigslist
- LinkedIn
- Indeed.com

Also visit Salary.com for researching typical job responsibilities and salaries.

If your job objective is so rare that it is not posted on major job sites, you'll need to get creative. Go to the "Jobs" or "Careers" section of a potential employer's Web site (usually found in the footer of their home page) or the Web site of a specialty executive recruiter in your field. Or ask for copies of job descriptions from knowledgeable people in that field.

Collect about five different job descriptions, and create a list of the key skills and experiences required for those jobs. Make note of the exact terms used, and reuse them on your own résumé.

Sample Job Descriptions

Here's one of the postings that Lindsay, the recent college graduate Romantic, found on Craigslist:

Job Description: Editorial Assistant

The Editorial Assistant position provides an excellent introduction to online publishing. You will gain in-depth knowledge of the editorial and production process with cutting-edge technologies. You are encouraged to develop, hone, and refine your editorial skills as well as your project management and communication skills.

Specific Responsibilities:
- Check editorial changes/do comparison proofreads
- Perform quality control of digital textbooks by comparing to original PDFs
- Check accuracy of metadata for digital textbooks
- Ensure the editorial changes from proofreaders and reviewers are implemented correctly

- Check XML-rendered online assignments against manuscripts
- Coordinate and track projects
- Work with publishers and production contractors to coordinate the creation of digital textbooks
- Work with publishers and other Aplia team members to coordinate the creation of demos for all new products
- Update/maintain bug-tracking database
- Update/maintain key pieces of documentation; create new documentation as needed
- Assemble and maintain online "courses" (our format for presenting homework products)
- Assemble and check completed courses
- Update courses on a weekly basis to make new assignments available to sales reps and professors
- Maintain courses and user accounts on our development site

Additional Projects
- Processing invoices in a timely manner
- Maintaining and managing department resources, including books, files from publishers, and reviewer, freelancer, and author contact data
- Answering occasional customer support queries

Requirements
- Bachelor's degree in related field
- At least 1 year experience in editorial capacity
- Excellent knowledge of grammar and command of the English language
- Must be proficient in Microsoft Word and Excel

Preferred Qualifications
- Familiarity with CMS
- Experience with HTML and XML

In the meantime Julia, the business analyst Adventurer, found this appealing job posting on the LinkedIn Web site:

Job Description: Product Manager

- Understand and lead the analysis of the competitive environment, customers, and product metrics to determine the right feature set to drive engagement and usage on LinkedIn.
- Drive global product requirements definition, product planning, and product design (including writing PRDs) of new product features and enhancements.
- Develop a comprehensive product & marketing road map to deliver on the business goals for LinkedIn in upcoming year & beyond.
- Work with the product development team and other cross-functional team members to bring features live to the site.
- Clearly communicate product benefits to our users and internal stakeholders.

Requirements

- Must be passionate about the Internet, emerging Web technologies, and community building with a demonstrated track record of visionary execution.
- At least 5 years' experience in a product management or equivalent role, preferably in building Web products, with a demonstrated ability to drive product planning, development, and launch.
- The ideal candidate would have a keen understanding of the most recent trends around consumer Web usage and direct hands-on experience with social networking.
- The candidate must be able to manage and lead across highly cross-functional teams.
- Must have excellent oral and written communication skills and be able to interact and understand technical subjects/emerging technologies and their relevance to the marketplace.
- Must be able to interact with diverse groups of technical and nontechnical people.
- Must be able to communicate effectively to senior executives internally and externally.

After Lindsay and Julia had each collected five job descriptions, they created tables listing key requirements and matching them to examples from their own experience. They put the most common requirements in the table with the most important ones first.

Lindsay's Table for Her Job Description

Job Requirements	Lindsay's Experience (Planning notes to herself)
Proofreading, copyediting, and quality control	I worked for four months as an editorial intern at the *Paris Review*, a prestigious literary magazine, and for McSweeney's, one of the most innovative publishing companies in America. I also recently completed UC Berkeley's Introduction to Copyediting course, and I now work as a freelance editor. Résumé bullets: • Copyedited Dave Eggers's forthcoming book, *Zeitoun*, in entirety under a tight deadline. • Read and screened hundreds of manuscripts weekly as a key team member in a quarterly issue of the *Paris Review*.
Coordinating and tracking projects	I was the photo editor of my high school yearbook, which required a great deal of organization and coordination with the other editorial staff. Résumé bullets: • Photographed and developed photos for entire yearbook in darkroom and designed layout for pictures for school yearbook. • Managed staff of four student photographers.

| Creativity | I earned a bachelor's degree in literature and philosophy, which taught me how to read, write, and think. Studying literature and philosophy also gave me the academic background needed to be an excellent writer. |

Résumé bullets:

- Awarded honors in both majors.

- Wrote *In Bloom*, a collection of short stories, as senior thesis.

| Customer support | I had an administrative role at the *Paris Review* that required me to interact with different types of people in the publishing world, from important editors and publishers to writers and poets. I also interacted with clients as a cashier and barista at La Boulange, a café in San Francisco. |

Résumé bullet:

- Acted as liaison between authors, publishers, and the *Paris Review* in administrative role.

| Processing invoices in a timely manner | In my free time I help out with the invoices for my friend's sole proprietorship, Oliver Gardens. Also, writing for my college newspaper required me to meet strict deadlines and to write and research in a timely manner. |

Résumé bullet:

- Wrote weekly articles under deadline for college newspaper, the *Forum*.

Julia's Table for Her Job Description

Job Requirements	Julia's Experience (Planning notes to herself)
Understanding customer needs	In my previous positions as a business analyst, I was a little more behind the scenes than a product manager would be. Nonetheless, here are some relevant experiences I can highlight and possibly rewrite later to show off better. Résumé bullets: • Met with business and cross-functional teams to define requirements on portal enhancements. • Wrote use case documents. • Worked with user experience team for optimal Web design and content.
Product requirements definition (PRD)	I mostly wrote business requirements documents (BRDs), which are similar, and I can sometimes substitute terms in my marketing materials.
Product & marketing road map	Since I was a business analyst before and not really a product manager, this wasn't my responsibility, but at one job I did draft one. Résumé bullet: • Made recommendations on future product feature sets and drafted product road map for future releases.
Communication with stakeholders	Most of my jobs have required communication skills. Résumé bullets: • Collaborated with third-party vendors and internal IT to resolve production support issues. • Brainstormed weekly with company's special task group, the innovation team, for out-of-box thinking.

- Collaborated with cross-functional teams to investigate and analyze deficiencies, impacts, risks.

- Presented deliverables to executive management and conducted training to end users.

Metrics	I haven't been officially in charge of metrics, but I have worked with data.

Résumé bullet:

- Analyzed user segmentation data and produced adoption trending reports.

My Table for My Job Description

Do the same exercise here based on the five job descriptions you collected. For more copies of this form, download it from *www.careerwithinyou.com*.

Job Requirements	My Experience

Matching Jobs to Career Types

Once you've carefully analyzed the job posting based on what the employer is looking for, do this second exercise to look for a potential match between the role and your career type. Here are the matches Lindsay and Julia identified:

Lindsay's Matching Career Strengths

Job Requirements	Lindsay's Corresponding Strengths as a Romantic
• Perform quality control of digital textbooks by comparing to original PDFs	Aesthetic sense
• Work with publishers and other Aplia team members to coordinate the creation of demos	Imagination
• Check editorial changes/ do comparison proofreads • Ensure the editorial changes from proofreaders and reviewers are implemented correctly • Excellent knowledge of grammar and command of the English language	Ability to discern
• You are encouraged to develop, hone, and refine your ... communication skills • Assemble and maintain online "courses"	Sense of meaning

Julia's Matching Career Strengths

Julia noticed that the technology mentioned in her job description was for social networking online, and she was able to read between the lines in the product manager postings to uncover other potential matches to her personality.

Job Requirements	Julia's Corresponding Strengths as an Adventurer
• Must be passionate . . . with a demonstrated track record of visionary execution	Enthusiasm (and some Idealism)
• Must be able to manage and lead across highly cross-functional teams	Synthesizing information
• Must have excellent oral and written communication skills and be able to interact and understand technical subjects/emerging technologies and their relevance to the marketplace	
• Must be able to interact with diverse groups of technical and nontechnical people	
• Must be able to communicate effectively to senior executives internally and externally	
• Must be passionate about community building	Social networking
• The ideal candidate would have experience with social networking.	
• Building Web products, with a demonstrated ability to drive product planning, development, and launch . . .	Seeking challenges

- Keen understanding of the most recent
  trends around consumer Web usage . . .

- Able to interact and understand
  technical subjects/emerging
  technologies and their relevance
  to the marketplace.

While this is not always possible with standard job postings, see if you can read between the lines to uncover potential matches with your own personality:

Job Requirements   **My Corresponding Strengths**

Creating a Starter Résumé

There are two types of résumés: the chronological and the functional. It's usually best to use the chronological résumé format, listing all your positions from most to least recent. If you have little or no work experience or are making a drastic career change, create a functional résumé with your experience (work, school, or volunteer) organized by relevant skill categories. In your chronological résumé, account for all gaps of time. The rule of thumb for length is to show one page for every ten years you have worked. Never fudge information for recruiters. Interviewers are likely to notice discrepancies and disqualify you immediately from the candidate pool. Recent graduates should feature their education at the top of the résumé while more seasoned candidates should feature their education at the bottom. See sample formats on pages 329–334.

Under each description of your past positions, provide bullet points addressing the requirements you've found in job descriptions in the desired field. Start each one with action verbs, and include specific metrics, qualifiers, and examples of what you accomplished. When possible, use the same terminology and order of prioritization that appears in the job posting. Change these bullet points with slightly different terminology and varying order of appearance when you customize your résumé for each job.

You'll get the best results by not assuming that interviewers will automatically translate your experience into their terms. Do the work for them in your résumé and cover letter. In Lindsay's case the employer uses the phrase "Assemble and maintain online courses," so she will repeat *assemble, maintain,* and *online* somewhere in her résumé. Another job posting might require her to "create and manage Web content," so for that résumé she'll change *assemble* to *create, maintain* to *manage,* and *online* to *Web.* She'll also reorder her bullet points. This job description mentions proofreading first, so she'll list her proofreading first under her internship. Another employer might prioritize that task lower in the description, so she'll move the order of the bullet point down accordingly.

For examples of how to write your bullet points, see those above that Lindsay and Julia wrote for their job descriptions, as well as examples for all nine career types in the "Type-Specific Strengths: Samples," below. Then see finished products in the sample résumés provided.

In the last line of your résumé, add some of your personal interests. Pick likely conversation starters for interviews or interesting subjects that will make your résumé stand out. At the same time, pick interests that are not controversial and don't scare away the interviewers or raise any red flags about your candidacy. Here's what Julia added to her résumé:

Interests: Enjoy mountain biking, traveling in Asia, and
playing Beatles songs on my guitar.

The most important element of your résumé will be the executive summary at the top. Add this last. You will alter this advertisement for yourself somewhat for each job interview. After you have finished writing all the bullet points under each position, write a summary of your top skills that will fill the main requirements for the job. Be sure to also highlight one of your most impressive accomplishments in your executive summary. See the résumés of Lindsay, Julia, and Troy on pages 329–334 for examples.

Before your résumé is ready for distribution, spell-check it and ask a friend to review grammar and vocabulary choices several times. Since mistakes in your résumé can be grounds for immediate disqualification, it has to be perfect. Many interviewers assume that if you cannot create a mistake-free résumé, you will be sloppy or make mistakes on the job.

If you don't feel confident writing your starter résumé, consider hiring one of the résumé services listed on major job sites. Their copywriters can help put extra pizzazz into its wording and make you stand out from other candidates.

POINTER

Perfectionists & Polishing Your Résumé

Perfectionists can help you organize your résumé, look for mistakes in spelling and grammar, and express logically what you want.

Type-Specific Strengths: Samples

You may wish to use synonyms for your strengths or other related terms that fit better in the context of your job application. Keep in mind how your strengths are useful for this job, then write down an overall message you'd like to provide the employer about who you are. Are you someone with high standards and a strong sense of responsibility? Are you someone who resourcefully meets a customer's needs? Work some of the descriptors of your intangible qualities into the bullet points of your résumé. Then to make each bullet point strong, be as specific as possible about tangible results of work you have done in the past.

Write your bullet points loosely in the form of feature-benefit statements. While a feature in your résumé might be "flawless security work," what does that tangibly result in for the employer? The benefit might be "48 months without security compromises." Another feature might be "delivered new product" with the benefit of "retained 95% of the customers." Bullet points on résumés should be written in the past tense for past jobs. The order of the feature (what you did) and the benefit (what the result was) doesn't matter as long as you include both. Here are creative ways nine different people we discussed earlier in this book conveyed a message about their career type within traditional résumé bullet points:

Career Type	Job Objective	Career Strength and Related Résumé Terms	Overall Message for Employer
1. Perfectionist Jake	Director of Security	Meticulousness: Flawless, Uncompromised Standards, Disciplined	High Standards and Responsibility

Jake's résumé bullet:
• Strove to keep security program flawless so that private information remained uncompromised for 48 consecutive months (to present date).

2. Helper Darlene	Human Resources Consultant	Resourcefulness: Helpful, Creative, Knowledgeable	Knowledge, Resources to Meet Company Needs

Darlene's résumé bullet:
• Served as valuable resource for company employee wellness initiative with stress relief programs, satisfaction surveys, and helpful reports showing impact to the bottom line.

Career Type	Job Objective	Career Strength and Related Résumé Terms	Overall Message for Employer
3. Achiever Priscilla	Vice President of Business Development	Public Relations Skills: Polished Presentations, Reputation, Delivers Sales Results	Winning Image for the Company

Priscilla's résumé bullet:

- Earned top reputation for winning sales presentation approach resulting in $45 billion in deals to date.

Career Type	Job Objective	Career Strength and Related Résumé Terms	Overall Message for Employer
4. Romantic Adria	Bank Loan for Starting Own Ice Cream Shop	Aesthetic Sense: Attractive Designs, Fashionable, Stylish	Hip, Trendsetting Flair

Adria's résumé bullet:

- Created ten unique flavors based on latest training in organic ingredients at culinary institute, which generated loyal following of ice cream enthusiasts in Seattle and database of 1700 repeat customers.

Career Type	Job Objective	Career Strength and Related Résumé Terms	Overall Message for Employer
5. Observer Diana	Search Engine Optimization Contract	Complex Thinking: Highly Trained, Multifaceted Analytics, Expert Knowledge	Expert in Complex Analysis

Diana's résumé bullet:

- Examined thousands of industry online searches and broke down multifaceted click-through data to identify optimal Web marketing strategy; communicated intricate results clearly to senior executives, and helped client gain funding for $500K project.

Career Type	Job Objective	Career Strength and Related Résumé Terms	Overall Message for Employer
6. Questioner Jennifer	User Design Consultant	Exactness: Careful, Scrutinize, Detailed	Reliable Scrutiny of Details

Jennifer's résumé bullet:

- Preserved the bank's brand standards, vigilantly scrutinizing over 100 submissions per quarter by outside vendors for 6 departments.

Career Type	Job Objective	Career Strength and Related Résumé Terms	Overall Message for Employer
7. Adventurer Julia	Product Manager	Multidisciplinary thinking: Multitalented, Ability to Multitask, Fast-paced	Versatile Thinker in Fast-paced Technology Sector

Julia's résumé bullet:

- Retained 95% of users by delivering timely product enhancements amid rapidly changing competitive environment, relying on multidisciplinary thinking in product management skills, and leading cross-functional team of technical and nontechnical staff.

Career Type	Job Objective	Career Strength and Related Résumé Terms	Overall Message for Employer
8. Asserter Sophia	New Corporate Client for Executive Search	Clarifying: Leader in Finding the Right Candidates, Strong Negotiator, Adept at Navigating Restrictions	Leader in Human Resources Negotiations

Sophia's résumé bullet:

- Collaborated with client, transforming frustrating tasks of negotiating boundaries and restrictions to a satisfying experience of finding more possibilities within the executive search.

Career Type	Job Objective	Career Strength and Related Résumé Terms	Overall Message for Employer
9. Peace Seeker Troy	Software Support Engineer	Synthesizing Information: Broad Perspective, Research	Extensive Research on Broad Array of Information

Troy's résumé bullet:

- Received top customer engagement ratings for listening to the customer and effectively assimilating information about 10 different network services.

Things Career Types Are Unlikely To Do

Sample Résumés

On the following pages are sample résumés for Lindsay and Julia with the key skill requirements in boxes and career strengths highlighted in gray shading. (*Note: Do not use boxes or highlighting in your actual résumé.*)

Lindsay Quella

2000 21st Street San Francisco, CA 99999 / LQuella@email.com 917.555.5555

SUMMARY

Skilled proofreading assistant, with strong discernment for quality control and aesthetics, seeking **Editorial Assistant** position. Experience coordinating and tracking projects for yearbook staff.

EDUCATION

UC Berkeley Extension, San Francisco, CA   *Fall 2008*
- Editorial Workshop I: Introduction to Copyediting

Claremont McKenna College, Bachelor of Arts in Literature and Philosophy   *December 2007*
- Dual major GPA 3.7 / 4.0, Cumulative GPA 3.4 / 4.0; awarded honors in both majors.
- Wrote *In Bloom,* a collection of creative writing for senior thesis
- Junior year study abroad at University of Nantes, France

EXPERIENCE

Freelance Editor, San Francisco, CA   *April 2009–Present*
- Prepared for book launch, performing quality control of Web site and checking accuracy of metadata.
- Copyedited Dave Eggers's forthcoming book, *Zeitoun,* in entirety under tight deadline.
- Read, edited, and wrote sections of a manuscript to be published by HarperCollins in January 2010.

McSweeney's, *Editorial Intern,* San Francisco, CA   *Fall 2008–Spring 2009*
- Researched, copyedited, and fact-checked for McSweeney's, *The Believer,* and 826 Valencia.
- Read and reviewed unsolicited manuscripts.

The Paris Review, *Editorial Intern,* New York, NY   *Spring 2008*
- Copyedited literature submissions for publication and fact-checked authors for *Paris Review* interviews.
- Provided customer support, acting as compassionate liaison between authors, publishers, and the *Review*.
- Wrote reader's reports on *Review* submissions and other published fiction in national literary magazines.
- Read and screened hundreds of weekly manuscripts in a timely manner.

Medo Organization, *ESL Instructor and Program Coordinator,* Soloy, Panama   *Summer 2007*
- Assembled courses for and implemented sustainable ESL program.
- Taught English to both indigenous and nonindigenous Panamanians.
- Received funding award through McKenna International grant.

La Perverie School, *Assistant English Teacher,* Nantes, France   *Fall 2006*
- Created lesson plans and developed projects for high school English classes.
- Taught middle-school history and high school English classes.

SKILLS AND INTERESTS

- Microsoft Excel, PowerPoint, and Word   •   Advanced French   •   Certified advanced scuba diver
- Yearbook Photography Editor   •   Invoicing for Oliver Gardens   •   Newspaper writer

Julia Yu

100 Monument Ave, Indianapolis, IN 99999, juliayu@email.com, (317) 555-5555

**Executive
Summary**

Enthusiastic senior business analyst with 10 years of information management experience seeking a product management challenge where I can lead the vision for the product road map. Avid customer of social networking tools with a personal network of 300+ professionals on LinkedIn. Retained 95% of Anthem online customers through major product changes and improved E*TRADE sales turnaround time by 14%.

Work Experience

2007–present **Anthem Insurance**   Indianapolis, IN
An independent health plan with 6.2 million members and $15B in operating revenue

Sr. Business Analyst / Product Manager, eBusiness Department (3/2009–present)
- Retained 95% of users by delivering timely product enhancements in rapidly changing competitive environment, relying on versatility in product management skills and leading cross-functional team of technical and nontechnical staff.
- Identified customer needs, wrote use case documents and worked with user experience team for optimal Web design and content.
- Wrote business & product requirements documents (BRDs & PRDs) and business cases.
- Collaborated with third-party vendors and internal IT to resolve production support issues.
- Analyzed user segmentation metrics and produced adoption trending reports.

Business Analyst, Sales Department (8/2007–2/2009)
- Met with business and cross-functional teams to define customer requirements for portal enhancements. Developed use cases based on three key customer segments.
- Wrote business requirements documents (BRDs), produced engaging PowerPoint presentation and received high recognition for presentation to sales management.
- Made recommendations for product features and drafted product road map for future releases.
- Brainstormed weekly with company's innovation team to generate outside-the-box thinking.
- Collaborated with cross-functional teams to investigate project deficiencies, impacts and risks.

2004–2007 **E*TRADE Financial**   Chicago, IL
A global provider of financial services to retail, corporate and institutional customers

Business Analyst
- Reengineered sales operations processes incorporating Salesforce.com to improve sales turnaround time from 7 weeks to 6 weeks.
- Proposed client-specific solutions for road map of mission-critical enterprise applications.
- Wrote request for proposal (RFP) and request for information.

2002–2004 **Accenture (formerly Anderson Consulting)**   Chicago, IL
A global management consulting, technology services and outsourcing company

Analyst Lead
- Supported consulting needs of corporate customers: Lucent Supply Chain Management and Allstate Insurance Risk Management Systems.
- Managed scope, priorities, time line and resources on team project assignments.
- Wrote business and technical requirements (BRDs and TRDs) for product enhancements.
- Provided production support and performed end-to-end testing: unit testing, functional testing, regression testing and integration testing.
- Presented deliverables to executive management and conducted training for end users.

Education **Kansas State University,** Manhattan, Kansas, **BA** 2002, *Management Information Systems.*
Scholarship recipient based on National Merit Scholar achievement

Interests Enjoy mountain biking, traveling in Asia and playing Beatles songs on my guitar.

Here is a sample technical résumé for Troy, the Peace Seeker, with his career strengths highlighted in gray shading. *(Note: Do not present your actual résumé with any highlighting around the text.)* Troy has twenty years of experience in the air force and five years of experience in training. However, Troy focuses the majority of his résumé on the recent six years that are most relevant for the technical support engineer job for which he is applying. Since the most important requirement for the job is knowledge of specific systems and computer programming languages, he lists those first in a "Technical Proficiencies" section.

Troy White

3000 Mandela Parkway   **Telephone** (510) 555-5555
Emeryville, CA 99999   **E-mail** twhite@email.com

OBJECTIVE
To obtain an employee position as a Technical Support Engineer at Xinet.

QUALIFICATIONS SUMMARY
Six years of experience as a technical support professional with over four in UNIX system administration. Strong team player, adapting well to fast-paced environments demanding strong technical, troubleshooting, and interpersonal skills. Broad research and troubleshooting abilities. Patient and comfortable working with individuals at all levels. Resourceful in completing projects and able to multitask effectively. Outstanding listening and communication skills.

TECHNICAL PROFICIENCIES
Platforms: UNIX (Solaris 2.3–Solaris 2.10, Debian and Red Hat Linux), Windows 95–Windows XP, limited experience with Windows 2000 servers.

Networking services: TCP/IP, DHCP, VPN, DNS, NIS, NFS. Limited experience with Samba and Apache, in addition to some experience with Active Directory. Knowledge of Internet routing, including OSPF, ROUTD, and RIP.

Mail Services: Solid understanding of Internet mail, including mail transfer agents (MTAs) such as Postfix and mail protocols such SMTP, POP3, and IMAP.

Networking: Ethernet, FDDI, and token ring.

Programming: Solid Bash shell scripting, Korn shell scripting, and Perl programming; limited experience with C, PHP, and MySQL.

Hardware: PCs (Dell, Gateway, Toshiba, Compaq) and Sun SPARC stations.

EXPERIENCE
Sun Microsystems, Menlo Park, CA   Oct. 2009 –Present
Support Engineer (Contract via Teva Systems)
- Received top customer engagement ratings for listening to the customer and effectively assimilating information for about 10 different network services.

Tech Foundation, Emeryville, CA   Aug. 2007–Sept. 2009
Back Office Administrator
- Provided Tier II technical support for our customer facing product support team.
- Installed and configured Linux servers running Debian Linux with a standard LAMP install using Drupal as the Content Management System.
- Empathically supported customer service staff in answering inquiries regarding systems, product support, and registration issues.
- Served as primary backup for several back office positions (AP, fulfillment, reporting).
- Conducted user acceptance testing of New CRM and operations software.
- Wrote 40-page training document detailing use of systems for front office personnel.
- Provided internal technical support to staff to include removing and fighting malware.

SUN Microsystems, Menlo Park, CA   Feb. 2006–July 2007
UNIX System Administrator (Contract via SES Consulting)
- Provided technical support to end users in a UNIX environment running Solaris 2.5–2.7.
- Installed Sun workstations for new employees.
- Set up new user accounts and managed most directory services with NIS/YP.
- Helped users with all day-to-day technical problems, achieving high accuracy marks for repetition of tasks.
- Installed new software on Sun workstations and aided users in new software installs.
- Provided phone support for remote user problems throughout the country.

Network Appliance, Santa Clara, CA   May 2004–Jan. 2006
UNIX System Administrator (Contract via Cyber Tech Consulting)
- Served on team responsible for the installation, management, and monitoring of over 40 Solaris, Linux, and Windows systems and associated hardware/software, providing internal services to Network Appliance employees worldwide.
- Wrote several shell scripts in Perl and Bash to monitor system activity and automate routine tasks.
- Installed and configured servers and attached and configured Network Appliance filers for hot swappable disk management and built-in RAID configuration.
- Installed and supported PCs running Windows 98–Windows XP, helping users with all technical problems ranging from e-mail to printing.
- Installed UNIX client machines for programmers making sure all network file systems were available and any necessary packages were customized for a particular programmer's needs.

Board of Trade Clearing Corporation, Chicago, IL   Aug. 2003–Mar. 2004
Technical Support Staff
- Helped users install modem software and troubleshoot any network connectivity issues.
- Maintained Netscape Web servers and installed minirouters for ISDN use.

Ford Aerospace & Communications Corp., Detroit, MI   Mar. 1998–May 2003
Engineering Safety Training Consultant
- Launched award-winning safety training program and trained hundreds of engineers.

United States Air Force
Noncommissioned Officer   Jan. 1978–Dec. 1997
- Served in multiple leadership roles around the world managing teams of technicians, and received recognition for mediating abilities.

Education

University of Phoenix, Troy, MI   Graduated May 2003
Bachelor of Science in Information Technology–Information Technology Support

Interests
- Love cooking comfort food, watching NASCAR, and discussing movies with movie fans.

Getting the Word Out

Now that your starter résumé is complete, you're ready to go public with your first marketing campaign. You'll soon be gathering feedback on how you compare to the competition and how to best position yourself to potential customers (that is, a hiring team) once you're out there giving your elevator speech (below), sending out your cover letter, posting your résumé online, and talking to recruiters. Plan to make small forays into the job market at first so you can go back and fine-tune your marketing materials. You'll become increasingly effective at your job hunt each time you get the word out.

Your Elevator Speech

Your elevator speech is a two- to three-sentence advertisement about yourself that is so short you could tell it to someone while riding in an elevator. Since you have only three minutes to give your pitch, you need to immediately say the most important points about what you do and what you

offer. You will use your elevator speech over and over again in interviews, networking conversations, cover letters, e-mails, and the executive summary of your résumé. Start with what you write as the executive summary of your cover letter. Make sure it addresses what the employer is looking for as well as highlights at least one of the strengths of your career type. Edit it as needed to sound natural, as though you are saying it at a cocktail party when someone asks you, "What do you do?" Practice your pitch on friends, and ask for feedback.

As you use your elevator speech you will get a sense of the response and how you compare to others looking for similar jobs. Keep revising it as necessary until it really grabs people and opens doors for you.

Here is a sample elevator speech:

I work on a retainer basis with both pharmaceutical and biotech companies to assist in the recruitment of senior-level executives. My competitors will juggle your project around among a number of staff people, but when you retain me, you get me, a leader in the field. I meet all my candidates myself, I interface with you, the client, and I conduct all the mechanics of the search. I personally protect your interests, down to clarifying the final details in your salary negotiation.

—Sophia Brown, an Asserter

Networking

Beyond submitting standard job applications, make networking a large component of your job search. According to the U.S. Bureau of Labor Statistics, 70 percent of all jobs are found through networking. Many hidden opportunities exist that are never advertised online. Other jobs *are* posted for the public, but candidates within the hiring manager's circle of acquaintances and connections on LinkedIn get their foot in the door first. So why not ensure one of those acquaintances is *you?* Start out by talking to friends and family, and expand your circle from there. The ultimate goal is for your contacts to put you in touch with hiring managers.

POINTER

Adventurers & Networking

Adventurers can help you with this step of the job-hunting process by attending events with you and showing you how to reach out and find contacts in your field.

Your Friends and Family

Give your elevator speech (over e-mail, the phone, or in person) to your friends and family, and ask them if they have acquaintances, former co-workers, or distant contacts related to your desired field they can tell about you. Follow up on leads, and keep notes (or, better yet, a spreadsheet) of whom you talk to, when, what you talked about, and the contact e-mail and phone numbers.

Your Former Co-workers and Classmates

Once your closest contacts are keeping a lookout for you, selectively contact former co-workers or classmates. Ask for feedback and tips, and alert them to watch out for relevant job postings. If you see a job posting at a company at which they work, ask your contacts to forward your cover letter and résumé for you directly to the hiring manager. Many companies will reward your colleagues with a referral bonus if you get hired, so you are also helping them out by not going through the staffing department.

Distant Connections

Reach out to people who don't know you but either are already doing the job you want or are in the same field. You'll encounter many people who are happy to talk to you through a friendly e-mail or a polite cold call. While you might at first hesitate to reach out to strangers, statistics show that distant connections produce higher results than friends and family.* Give it a try. You'll uncover exceptional opportunities out there. Some ways to find more networking opportunities are:

- Searching for individuals at particular companies using social networking Web sites and asking a friend of a friend you are linked to online to introduce you to this person.

- Receiving recommendations from friends and colleagues about individuals to reach out to.

- Doing a Google search on a company or topic and sending a friendly letter to an individual mentioned in an article.

Industry, Alumni/ae, and Special-Interest Events

During your job hunt attend events where (1) you will meet individuals in your field of interest or (2) you will reconnect with friends and colleagues who would be happy to help you. Give your elevator speech to as many people as possible. Collect business cards or contact information, and over time reconnect with key contacts in your spreadsheet you haven't spoken to for a while. Here are suggestions for events:

- High school or college reunion

- Family reunion or wedding

- Holiday party

- Fund-raiser

---

*Malcolm Gladwell, *The Tipping Point: How Little Things Can Make a Big Difference* (New York: Little Brown, 2000), pp. 53–54.

- Lecture

- Group sporting event

- Jewelry or cookware party

- Church, synagogue, or mosque event

- Industry convention

- Product focus group

- Nature walk or city guided tour

- Job-hunting support group meeting

- Career resource center workshop

- Toastmasters meeting

- Parents' day at your children's school

- Political or charity volunteers' meeting

Hiring Managers

Ideally your networking efforts will lead to informational interviews with hiring managers in your field of choice. Be encouraged to know that you can network with a hiring manager even though there are no open positions to fill at the time or there is a hiring freeze. Don't let this stop you from making industry contacts. Kindly let the hiring manager know you are simply interested in a friendly informational interview (explained below) to learn more about the organization. Thanks to the groundwork you set, when the requirement to hire someone arises later, the manager will remember you positively from your meeting and can fast-track you for a formal interview when the timing is right.

Informational Interviews

A good way to uncover opportunities is to request an open-ended meeting with an individual at an organization where you'd like to work. When you make it clear you would like an informational interview, the pressure is off for both of you because you are not asking for a job. Be respectful of the other person's time, and ask for only thirty minutes. If this is not possible, then ask for fifteen minutes to speak over the phone. The purpose of the meeting is to become acquainted and to learn more about the organization. Have a few questions prepared ahead of time. In this meeting you will gather information that will help you hone your job-hunting plan and materials. You can also practice giving your elevator speech. In many cases at the end of the meeting the other person will give you helpful advice and possible leads for jobs. Sometimes you will even be invited back to interview for an actual job opening. In any case, be sure to follow up the next day with a thank-you note to reinforce that you will be remembered.

Internships: Another Way to Break In

Internships are a great opportunity to learn the skills you need to break into a career. A good internship allows you to learn the ins and outs of a trade by a hands-on method. Many are unpaid, which can be a burden if you don't have the luxury to work for free, while some include a small stipend. Having an internship not only shows on your résumé that you took initiative in your area of interest and developed necessary skills, but an internship also opens up a network of people who can help you later on in a search for a full-time job. In some industries, publishing, for example, unpaid internships are practically a rite of passage. Not surprisingly, other industries that generally tend to be more lucrative, such as finance, often offer well-paid internships. The ideal internship is one where the company you are working for hires interns with the intention of offering a full-time job in the future. Companies almost always prefer hiring from within, and a good way to get your foot in the door with your ideal job's company is to be an intern first.

Your Cover Letter

Each time you request an informational interview or apply for a job, attach a cover letter. Paste it into the body of the e-mail and attach it in a word-processing document. This letter will allow you to present a version of your elevator speech to the recruiter and the employer. Here is a sample cover letter from Troy, the Peace Seeker whose Job Objective #1 was to leave the nonprofit world for a higher-paid position as a support engineer.

Dear Xinet hiring manager,

I am that rare technology professional who enjoys the process of communication. Whether it be listening, speaking, or expressing concepts in writing, my greatest skills lie in hearing out customers and making the complex digestible. I believe these skills, along with my diverse technology work experience, make me uniquely qualified for the Technical Support Engineer position recently posted on Craigslist.

My most relevant experience for a career at Xinet is in the field of Unix system administration, where I've worked with a number of the technologies you mention, from Unix and Windows to MySQL and Apache. After working at the Board of Trade Clearing Corporation, Sun Microsystems, and Network Appliance (see résumé attached), I took a few years away from system administration at the nonprofit Tech Foundation. My purpose was to dedicate a few years to giving back to the community by providing technical support and discounted software to other nonprofits and charities. With that goal accomplished, I recently took a three-month contract with Sun Microsystems as a technical support engineer. My current goal is to find a long-term employee position in a similar role.

My résumé provides a complete list of the technologies I have worked with. What it doesn't fully mention are the important intangibles I possess: my ability to learn quickly, my strong sense of customer service, and my enjoyment researching and playing with new technologies.

I have included a writing sample for your review along with this résumé and cover letter.

If my qualifications fit with what your company is looking for in a candidate, I welcome an opportunity to speak further with you.

Sincerely,
Troy White

POINTER

Helpers & Writing Cover Letters

Helpers can assist you by perceiving what the employer is really looking for, picking up unspoken requirements the employer may have, and showing you how to craft charming and diplomatic cover letters.

Online Job Sites

Unless you are targeting a niche field, many of the jobs you seek can be found on Craigslist, Indeed.com, LinkedIn, Monster.com, and Yahoo! Hot-Jobs. Scan these sites on a daily or weekly basis, doing an advanced search for the key words, title, or geography you seek. It can also be helpful to subscribe to a Rich Site Summary (RSS) feed such as Google Reader. This way all the postings are delivered to one place. In many cases, a new job posting prompts many applications within the first day or two, so submit your job application immediately. (And, of course, rely on networking at the companies with job postings to increase your chances for a hiring manager to put your application toward the top of the candidate list.)

Keep your online profile updated on LinkedIn so your résumé is immediately available to those from whom you are requesting informational interviews. In some cases recruiters will seek you out based on who you are linked to on this site. Keep building your list of connections with people you trust and respect. In some cases individuals with more connections rise to the top of recruiters' searches. However, do not link with strangers or individuals whose reputations you are not familiar with.

Put together a schedule for posting your résumé on Monster.com and Yahoo! HotJobs: Have both of your résumés ready, one for each job objective. Post résumé #1 on Monster.com and Yahoo! HotJobs during the first week. After a couple weeks take down résumé #1 and post résumé #2. After a couple more weeks take down #2 again and repost #1. The more recently you have uploaded your résumé, the higher it will appear on the recruiter's search results. If your résumé has been posted for a long time, it may not even make the results, whereas after you upload it, recruiters receive alerts about your credentials and may call you within twenty-four hours.

Alternate between two résumés because early in your job hunt you don't know which one will bring more success.

Headhunters, Recruiters, and Employment Agencies

Types of recruiters vary. Some are in-house employees working for the human resources department. Their style is noticeably different from that of external recruiters. Some in-house recruiters focus on outreach to attractive candidates, selling you on the merits of the company; others focus on protecting the company and the hiring manager's time by following best practices, policies, and legal guidelines of hiring. Your job with most in-house recruiters is to impress them, and it is likely you will not experience much pressure from them to take a particular job.

Retained Recruiters vs. Contingency Recruiters

External recruiters are outside consultants hired by employers to actively search for great candidates. These recruiters find you through your online résumé, news articles that mention you, or referrals from people who know you. Retained recruiters receive compensation whether or not the employer hires you, which means you will notice less pressure to take the job they are seeking to fill. Retained firms search to fill upper-management positions or jobs that require hard-to-find skills.

Contingency recruiters get paid only if the employer hires you, so while they are also looking for the best-fitting candidate, you will notice more pressure to take the job. Contingency recruiters need to work on volume, placing as many people as possible per month in order to make enough to pay their own bills. You'll have to remain clear about your boundaries and what you need, or you could get pushed into a situation that isn't right for you.

One of the benefits external recruiters offer is that they can coach you on how to put your best foot forward when you meet with the employer. So do take advantage of extra information and resources the external recruiters provide. Be careful when it comes time to negotiate your own compensation. The external recruiter will be getting a cut, and some job hunters have reported they lost job opportunities because their recruiter was too aggressive on their behalf regarding the salary.

Help recruiters whenever you can, and refer them to other potential candidates. They will remember you were helpful and may call you next time for just the right job.

Employment Agencies

Agencies also vary in terms of how they get paid and to what degree they are representing your interests as compared to the employer's interests. Ask these questions up front to understand how each one operates. Some employment agencies will offer you training classes, career coaching, and extra career-enrichment resources.

Contracting and Temporary Work

If you have the time to take a short-term assignment, it can get your foot in the door of an organization you wouldn't normally get to interview with. You will meet people on your contract assignment and expand your network. Also, when higher-ups in the organization see you in action, they might consider offering you a permanent position.

Preparing for Interviews

You can never be too prepared for an interview, whether it is informational or for a specific job opening. Do your homework in advance by looking up the company online, reading articles about its constituents or competitors, and perusing biographical information about the person who will be interviewing you. Interviewers might ask you what you think of their products and services, so gather your thoughts about what you read and observe. Be prepared to make suggestions from your fresh set of eyes and to ask insightful questions. If you know people who have worked for this organization, call them in advance and ask for context and tips.

Review the job description again for clarity about the requirements of the organization. Review your elevator speech and résumé again, matching your experience against those requirements. Skilled interviewers will use a technique called behavioral interviewing, where they will inquire about specific examples of your experience. They will ask you questions such as, "Tell me about a time you solved a complex puzzle," or "Tell me about a time you dealt with an angry customer." Quiz yourself on the key

POINTER

Achievers & Successful Interviewing

Achievers can help you present yourself well, give you feedback when you polish up your elevator speech, do mock interviews with you, and advise you on how to dress for winning the job.

requirements of the job by stating examples of actual accomplishments you made and situations you handled.

In your answers, speak to the *situation*, the *action*, and the *result*. For example, you could say, "The *situation* was that the customer was angry because his system had been down for four hours and he was on hold for twenty minutes. The *action* I took was to hear the customer out, help him file a formal complaint, and then help escalate his problem to the top priority. The *result* was that we saved a high-value customer, and he later wrote a letter to my boss expressing thanks for superior service."

Here are common questions you can expect in the interview and advice as to how to handle them:

- *"Tell me a little bit about you."* Give your elevator speech. This advice may sound obvious, but many interviewees are unprepared for this. Most people either say too little or talk too long about the wrong things. Interviewees allow the interviewer to drive the direction of the conversation so that they never get to hit on the most important points about why they are right for the job. You get around all these problems by delivering your well-rehearsed pitch within the first three minutes.

- *"Walk me through your résumé."* Start with the job that is most relevant to the position you are interviewing for. Be careful not to get bogged down on small details. Stay with the most important ones. (Warning: A common mistake is to immediately start off on the wrong foot when the interviewer asks this of you first instead of "Tell me about you." Take charge of the situation by sneaking in your elevator speech while you are both staring at your résumé.)

- *"Tell me about a time when . . ."* Describe a relevant situation, action, and result.

- *"What are your weaknesses?"* Have something prepared ahead of time. Give a weakness that can be turned around into a strength, such as, "I can be a perfectionist about my work, but sometimes I need to do a better job delegating." Then turn it around to show what a hard worker you are.

- *"Do you have any questions for me?"* Don't say no. Have some questions made up ahead of time that show you did your research on the organization. Then before you say good-bye, ask the interviewer, "What are the next steps?"

If you haven't interviewed for a while, do a mock interview with a friend for practice. If you have an interview coming up for a dream job, schedule another interview first to get some of the kinks out of your presentation.

Ideally, all interviews are two-way streets where the employer gets to ask questions to see if you're the person needed for the job and you get to ask questions to see if the group is the one you want to work for. Unfortunately, the conversation tends to be one-way at first, but you still need to interview the organization and get to the bottom of the ten items in your list of prioritized needs. If you ask too many of these questions in the first interview, you could sound presumptuous or demanding. In the first interview, focus on selling the employer on your candidacy, but listen closely for any clues. After the interview make some notes for yourself on what you noticed about this job situation. Ask more questions on the second or third interview, keeping in mind that most of your questions will be answered during the negotiation process after you receive an offer. Rather than getting too excited about an offer and accepting it quickly, be sure to fully vet the employer to make sure this is the right situation for you.

Making Decisions Using Your Job Fit Worksheets

You're close to receiving an offer from one organization. There may be another firm you are talking to at the same time. Which one would be better for you? Do you need to stall the first one? In chapter 10 you identified the fundamentals you're looking for in a job. Now it's time to fill out a Complete Job Fit Worksheet, not only to choose the next appropriate company and role, but also to prepare for negotiating your job offer. Compare two jobs you are thinking of accepting. In chapter 10 you'll find questions 1 to 5 in the Job Fit Worksheet for your career type and the full description of questions 6 to 10 under My General Job Necessities on page 303. Weigh the importance of each category from 1 (low) to 5 (high). Rate each job opportunity from 1 (low) to 5 (high). Then multiply the weight times your rating, and add up the totals to determine the best situation for you.

For more copies of worksheets,
see the downloadable forms on our Web site:
www.careerwithinyou.com

POINTER

Questioners & Identifying What to Watch Out For

Questioners can help you make careful decisions about job security, financial planning, a retirement fund, and short- and long-term career risks you might not have considered.

Complete Job Fit Worksheet

	Job Title 1: _____	Job Title 2: _____
1. _____ Priority 1–10: _____ **Weight importance 1 2 3 4 5**	. . . in job #1? 1 2 3 4 5 **Weight × Rating = ____**	. . . in job #2? 1 2 3 4 5 **Weight × Rating = ____**
2. _____ Priority 1–10: _____ **Weight importance 1 2 3 4 5**	. . . in job #1? 1 2 3 4 5 **Weight × Rating = ____**	. . . in job #2? 1 2 3 4 5 **Weight × Rating = ____**
3. _____ Priority 1–10: _____ **Weight importance 1 2 3 4 5**	. . . in job #1? 1 2 3 4 5 **Weight × Rating = ____**	. . . in job #2? 1 2 3 4 5 **Weight × Rating = ____**
4. _____ Priority 1–10: _____ **Weight importance 1 2 3 4 5**	. . . in job #1? 1 2 3 4 5 **Weight × Rating = ____**	. . . in job #2? 1 2 3 4 5 **Weight × Rating = ____**
5. _____ Priority 1–10: _____ **Weight importance 1 2 3 4 5**	. . . in job #1? 1 2 3 4 5 **Weight × Rating = ____**	. . . in job #2? 1 2 3 4 5 **Weight × Rating = ____**

	Job Title 1: _____	Job Title 2: _____
6. How well will I be compensated? Priority 1–10: _____ **Weight importance 1 2 3 4 5**	. . . in job #1? 1 2 3 4 5 **Weight × Rating = ____**	. . . in job #2? 1 2 3 4 5 **Weight × Rating = ____**
7. How strong is the hours and benefits package? Priority 1–10: _____ **Weight importance 1 2 3 4 5**	. . . in job #1? 1 2 3 4 5 **Weight × Rating = ____**	. . . in job #2? 1 2 3 4 5 **Weight × Rating = ____**
8. How well does the location suit my commuting or work-from-home requirements? Priority 1–10: _____ **Weight importance 1 2 3 4 5**	. . . in job #1? 1 2 3 4 5 **Weight × Rating = ____**	. . . in job #2? 1 2 3 4 5 **Weight × Rating = ____**
9. How will this position help my career advancement? Priority 1–10: _____ **Weight importance 1 2 3 4 5**	. . . in job #1? 1 2 3 4 5 **Weight × Rating = ____**	. . . in job #2? 1 2 3 4 5 **Weight × Rating = ____**
10. How comfortable is the workplace culture for me? Priority 1–10: _____ **Weight importance 1 2 3 4 5**	. . . in job #1? 1 2 3 4 5 **Weight × Rating = ____**	. . . in job #2? 1 2 3 4 5 **Weight × Rating = ____**
TOTALS		

Closing the Deal: Negotiations

You rarely have more negotiating power than the day before you accept a job offer. Don't wait until after you accepted the job to go after a pay raise, ask for time off, or request the privilege to work from home. If you anticipate important needs in the first eighteen months from the day you take the job, ask for these things now. At the same time, approach the negotiations with flexibility, and don't scare away the employer by being overly demanding during the negotiation. If employers experience you as presumptuous, they might change their minds about making you an offer. Most people, however, report that they don't negotiate enough on their own behalf. Don't sell yourself short.

What's negotiable varies from organization to organization. One job may have an inflexible pay rate while another job may allow considerable wiggle room. One company may have strict titles while another might make up customized titles for each employee. One employer may require you to be in the office during strict work hours while another employer may not care if you telecommute five days a week. Your objective is twofold: to create a list of your own priorities and to find out which items are negotiable for this organization.

For guidance, use the job fit worksheet for general needs on page 305 to create your personal list of priorities. Then talk to the hiring manager,

POINTER

Asserters & Negotiating

After you are clear about your priorities, Asserters can advise you on the offer negotiation by giving you confidence and encouraging you to push for what you want.

Be polite... ...but not TOO polite.

recruiter, or human resources manager to find out which items are negotiable. Read about Troy's negotiation to learn how you might conduct your own.

Troy's Negotiation List

To show you all that is involved in conducting your own negotiation, we will walk you through Troy's story. When it's time for your negotiation, insert your own name and customize your lists.

First, Troy read through the examples of potential negotiation items in the list below and put a check mark (✓) next to the items that were relevant to him:

Compensation	Hours, Location & Benefits	Advancement Items
Base salary ✓	Work days	Title
Hourly rate	Weekly work hours ✓	Training ✓
Annual bonus ✓	Health insurance	Length of time until promotion
Signing bonus ✓	Vacation ✓	Clear deliverables required for promotion
Retainer	Specific vacation days needed ✓	
Commission	Unpaid time off	Clear deliverables required for pay raise
Stock options	Sabbatical	
Pension plan	Work from home ✓	Reporting structure
401(k) matching	% of time in business travel	Direct reports
Housing allowance	Gym membership	Scope of responsibilities
Car allowance	Concierge services	Registration for major conventions
Other:	Tuition assistance	Other:
	Other:	

When Troy received a job offer over the phone, he told the manager he was pleased to hear the news and asked if he could set up some time to go over the details of the offer. This was a polite way to signal to the hiring manager that he would like to negotiate some of the points. It also allowed time for both parties to prepare and do some research prior to this important conversation. Before their phone appointment, Troy prepared a priority list. The hiring manager also checked some facts, including how high his boss would allow him to go on the salary negotiation. The next day Troy spent thirty minutes on the phone with the hiring manager talking through the nine items outlined on the next page. Troy learned that some of these items were nonnegotiable, but he also uncovered some options that he did not know were available. While he was not able to take specific vacation days in the first six months, he learned he could take unpaid time off to attend his brother's wedding. He also found out that after five years of service, all employees were eligible for a one-month paid sabbatical.

Take a blank sheet of paper, and create two columns to keep track of your priorities and what you learn about the areas where the organization is flexible.

My Priority List	Company's Ability to Negotiate

My Priority List

Base salary

Health insurance

Training

Vacation

Weekly work hours

Work from home

Annual bonus

Signing bonus

Specific vacation days needed

Company's Ability to Negotiate

Negotiable Items:

Base salary: pay ranges by $20K (not revealed to the candidate but manager had flexibility)

Training: manager has a large training budget and can even pay Troy's predecessor to come back on the weekends to train him

Signing bonus: manager's discretion from $0 to $20K (range not revealed to candidate)

Unpaid time off: available anytime per approval by manager

Nonnegotiable Items:

Health insurance: all employees have access to the same health plan choices

Work from home: employees cannot work from home on a regular basis, only on special occasions

Weekly work hours: strict work hours of operation—all must arrive by 8:15 a.m.

Vacation: set vacation benefit policy for all employees based on seniority

Annual bonus: same payout scale applies to all employees

Specific vacation days needed: company policy says no vacation days until after six months

Sabbatical: all employees eligible after five years

Over the phone with the employer, Troy methodically went through his list, starting with the first item, the base salary. He asked for $5,000 more per year. The manager said he would check on that and get back to him. (Even though he had received verbal permission from his boss to go higher, the manager also had to fill out special request forms and get the increase approved by the vice president of human resources.) Troy continued down the list, making specific requests. The manager said he'd see what he could do and called Troy back two days later to make improvements to the offer.

When you are done following the same steps Troy did, you should have a list that looks something like this:

Improvements to Troy's Original Job Offer

- *Base salary.* Increased by $2,000 from original offer.

- *Training.* Manager agreed to pay Troy's predecessor to come back to train him. He also agreed to send Troy to a training week in Atlanta, Georgia, including registration, hotel, and expenses.

- *Signing bonus.* A $5,000 bonus to be paid thirty days after Troy's first day of employment.

- *Unpaid time off.* Troy could take two days off for a four-day weekend to attend his brother's wedding. (Paid vacation days were not possible due to strict company policy about vacation accruals.)

Like Troy, you may manage a relatively painless negotiation process before you accept your position. Identify your priorities, take the time to talk them through with the hiring manager, calmly explain your needs, and make matter-of-fact requests. Allow the hiring manager time to check on company policy to see whether or not the initial offer can be improved.

Realizing the Career Within You

Be sure to follow through on each stage of your job-hunting process. Seek help if part of it seems difficult, and try to make an adventure out of it. Step by step you'll get closer to landing the job that you'll look forward to performing every day. By this point you've determined your career type as well as your particular combination of career strengths and needs. You now know yourself better in many ways. We wish you all the best as you meet the career within you and bring it to full fruition.

Reading-Group Questions and Discussion Topics

1. Which of the nine career types do you recognize in people you have worked with?

2. Do you see yourself in more than one career type? How do you alter your personality and work style for different bosses, co-workers, or clients?

3. Which cartoons did you laugh at the most? Which cartoons hit a chord for you or remind you of someone you know?

4. Which characters in the book inspired you? Can the strength of another type help you with something your own type is weak in?

5. What parts of your personality led you to your present career? For example, the Questioner side of Mary Dawn, concerned about caring for people at risk of illness and disease, influenced her to become a nurse. The Observer side of her loved the analytical interpretation of lab values, so she later pursued scientific research with the field of nursing.

6. According to Enneagram theory, each career type has a tendency to lean at times toward two other particular types besides its wings. Do you notice yourself behaving more like one of these types that are connected to yours when you are unusually stressed or relaxed?

a. The Perfectionist tends toward the Adventurer and the Romantic.

b. The Helper tends toward the Asserter and the Romantic.

c. The Achiever tends toward the Questioner and the Peace Seeker.

d. The Romantic tends toward the Helper and the Perfectionist.

e. The Observer tends toward the Adventurer and the Asserter.

f. The Questioner tends toward the Achiever and the Peace Seeker.

g. The Adventurer tends toward the Perfectionist and the Observer.

h. The Asserter tends toward the Observer and the Helper.

i. The Peace Seeker tends toward the Questioner and the Achiever.

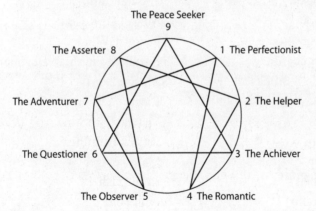

7. The nine personality types are sometimes organized according to three types of intelligence: emotional intelligence, mental intelligence, and body intelligence. What differences in point of view do you notice between the "heart" types (leaning on their emotional intelligence—Helpers, Achievers, Romantics), "head" types (leaning on their mental intelligence—Observers, Questioners, Adventurers), and the "body" types (leaning on their gut instinct—Asserters, Peace Seekers, Perfectionists)?

Acknowledgments

We'd like to extend a special thanks to the following exceptional people who contributed in many generous ways to our book:

Thomas Alexander

Karla Anderson

Eivor Atkinson

Scott Benbow

Karlyn Berg

Jennifer Borchardt

David Lincoln Brooks

Michael Brown

Joyce Burks

Robin Burns

Lila Caffrey

Jim Campbell

Shirley Caputo

Tiffany Caputo

Dionne Chambers

Jacqueline Chen

Elaine Chernoff

Tom Clark

Findlay Cockrell

Karen Costarella

Nicolina Costarella

Mary Beth Crenna

Kelsey Crowe

Damon Danielson

Tessa deCarlo

Abigail De Kosnik

Penny deWind

Elizabeth Phythian Dorfman

Allison Don

Richard Dorsay

Melissa Dworkin

Patrick Fanning

Mani Feniger

Knute Fisher

Fran Foltz

Dori Giller

Jaki Girdner

Harriet Glaser

Manny Glaser

David Gray

Bronwyn Harris

Jason Hengels

Mary Dawn Hennessey

Bertina Hou

Yuri Iwaoka-Scott
Julia Sefkow Kaplan
Nancy Kesselring
Dale Knutsen
Ari Krawitz
Steve Kresge
Chris Kung
Harriet Whitman Lee
Pamela Lund
Carolyna Marks
Karen McArdle
Tom McClure
Jeffrey McKay
Helen Meyer
Olga Milosavljevic
Karen Mockrin
Pat Newmann
Carol Olson
Kirby Olson
Athena Papadakos
Craig Paullin
John Pennington
Farrah Plummer
Robert Plummer
Lisa Pollina
Lindsay Quella
Jason Ravitz
Robin Reiner
Liz Rood

Tom Rosin
Hank Resnik
Arlette Schlitt-Gerson
Chuck Sefkow
Peggy Sefkow
Adria Popkin Shimada
James Shimada
Mario Sikora
David Silverander
Shannon Small
Phylece Snyder
Hilary Stabb
John Stabb
Kristin Stabb
Tom Stabb
Rob Steiner
Annemarie Sudermann
Vicki Tam
Kirsten Lyu Thelander
Nigel Thomson
Ann Tussing
John Weber
Augie Wagele
Gus Wagele
Nick Wagele
Lynne Wander
Ann Woodward
Gail Wread
Juliana Park Youn

About the Authors

Elizabeth Wagele, known for her humorous cartoons, expertise on personalities, and positive, to-the-point writing style, teams up with Ingrid Stabb (Yale MBA) and her career expertise and multisector experience (in business, nonprofits, and government) to create another first.